STUDY GUIDE

ABEL / BERNANKE

MACROECONOMICS

SECOND EDITION

Charles Johnston

University of Michigan

Flint

Addison-Wesley Publishing Company

Reading, Massachusetts • Menlo Park, California • New York
Don Mills, Ontario • Wokingham, England • Amsterdam • Bonn
Sydney • Singapore • Tokyo • Madrid • San Juan • Milan • Paris

Preface and Acknowledgments

In the 2nd edition of *Macroeconomics*, Abel and Bernanke present contemporary theories, models, and research of intermediate macroeconomics. They use these to identify, describe, explain, analyze, predict, and evaluate macroeconomic events, including changes in government policies. The textbook uses a unified model to teach intermediate macroeconomics; within that model, it presents most of the contemporary beliefs of the major macroeconomic schools of thought. It is an exceptional textbook.

Each chapter of the *Study Guide* includes a fill-in-the-blanks review of chapter highlights, 10 true-false questions, 20 multiple choice questions, 5-10 multiple-part short-answer essay questions, mathematical problem-solving questions, and answers to all questions. The *Study Guide* questions test your understanding of the economic theories, policies, and research presented in the textbook. When you can answer the *Study Guide* questions correctly, you will have a good understanding of the main points taught in the textbook and will be reasonable well prepared for exams. I suggest that you also study the end-of-chapter questions in the textbook and any additional information introduced by your instructor.

While using the *Study Guide*, remember that what you learn by answering one type of question can be used to answer other types of questions. Although many questions are rather narrowly focused and specific, it is thought provoking to step back and consider larger sets of related questions. Some questions are quite general, focusing on the "big picture." For example: What causes recessions? Are Americans saving too little? Are budget deficits bad for the economy? How can we increase the rate of economic growth? Ask yourself what are the principal, useful ideas that I can learn from these questions and answers? It can be fun and educational to make up some questions yourself, try to answer them, and ask some of them in class.

One way to increase your interest in the course is to place yourself into the analysis by viewing yourself as the economic actor being discussed. Picture yourself as a worker and entrepreneur, consumer and saver, borrower and investor, importer and exporter, fiscal policy maker and monetary policy maker. You and people like you are the market participants discussed in the textbook. Your behavior and the behavior of people like you create the economic events in the textbook. While your decisions and actions affect the performance of the macroeconomy, the performance of the macroeconomy affects your decisions and actions. The textbook and *Study Guide* can help you become a better economic decision maker and better understand and appreciate the economic decisions made by others.

Economics teaches us how to analyze, predict, and evaluate business, social, and political events. In many fields of study, economics is used to analyze, predict, and evaluate events that affect how time, production, goods and services, and money and other financial assets are allocated to alternative uses to achieve the goals of households, firms, and governments. This suggests that learning economics will help you in many academic fields of study and in life in general.

I wish you the best in this class and in life. If you have any constructive comments or suggestions concerning the *Study Guide*, I would be happy to hear from you.

The textbook authors, Andrew Abel and Ben Bernanke, reviewed the 1st edition; Ben Bernanke reviewed the 2nd edition. I especially wish to thank them for their careful and complete reviews and for their helpful corrections and suggestions. I wish to thank the anonymous outside reviewers of selected chapters of this text, including reviewers from Cornell University, North Carolina State University, and Claremont McKenna College. I wish to thank Addison-Wesley Publishing Company, especially Lena Buonanno and Bunny Ames, for their excellent guidance, assistance, and patience throughout the preparation of the *Study Guide*. I accept full responsibility for any errors or omissions.

Charles W. Johnston, Assistant Professor
Department of Economics, 350 CROB
University of Michigan-Flint
Flint, MI 48502

Note: All tables mentioned in the *Study Guide* refer to those found in Abel and Bernanke's *Macroeconomics*, 2nd edition.

ISBN 0-201-60252-0
1 2 3 4 5 6 7 8 9 10 VG 97969594

CHAPTER 1: INTRODUCTION TO MACROECONOMICS

A Fill-In-The-Blanks Review of Chapter Highlights: Use the following key terms to fill in the blanks. Each key term is used only once.

aggregation	average labor productivity	closed economy	deflation
economic model	economic theory	empirical analysis	equilibrium
fiscal policy	inflation	invisible hand	macroeconomics
monetary policy	normative analysis	open economy	positive analysis
trade deficit	trade surplus	unemployment	

1. _Macroeconomics_ is the scientific study of the structure and performance of national markets and of government policies that affect market conditions. The principal issues of macroeconomics include: long-run economic growth, business cycles, unemployment, inflation, the international economy, and macroeconomic policies. Macroeconomists use economic theories within economic models to analyze the economic events and economic policies related to these issues.

2. _Avg labor Productivity_, the output produced per unit of labor in the macroeconomy, is a principal determinant of the long-run economic growth rate. Deviations in the national output from the long-run economic growth path are called business cycles. A period of slower than normal growth, known as a contractionary period, is usually followed by a period of faster than normal growth, known as an expansionary period. During a business cycle contraction, the economy is in a recession; national output declines or grows very slowly. Recessions create 3. _Unemployment_, called cyclical unemployment, but some unemployment persists even during sustained periods of economic expansion.

4. _Inflation_ is an increase in the average price of goods. 5. _Deflation_ is a decrease in the average price of goods. Inflation may occur during either phase of the business cycle as well as when the economy is on its long-run economic growth path; the same is true for deflation.

The international economy highlights the interdependence of national economies in global markets. A national economy that participates in international markets is called an 6. _Open Economy_. A national economy that does not participate in international markets is called a 7. _Closed Economy_. A nation that increases its participation in international markets is becoming more open. If the value of a country's exports exceeds the value of its imports in some time period, it has a 8. _Trade Surplus_; if the value of its exports is less than the value of its imports, it has a 9. _Trade Deficit_.

Government policymakers attempt to improve the performance of the macroeconomy by implementing fiscal and monetary policies. 10. _Fiscal Policy_ attempts to improve economic conditions by changing government spending and taxes. 11. _Monetary Policy_ attempts to improve economic conditions by changing the money supply.

To analyze the collective behaviors of all people in a nation, macroeconomists add together the data for each particular kind of economic behavior for the entire economy. This 12. _Aggregation_ provides data on macroeconomic variables, such as aggregate consumption, aggregate investment, and aggregate output.

Macroeconomic researchers employ the scientific method of research investigation to develop economic

theories and economic models that attempt to explain and predict the performance of the national economy. An
13. _Economic Theory_ is a scientifically testable hypothesis or statement of belief about some cause-effect relationship among economic variables that is supported by the empirical evidence. Adam Smith's theory of the
14. _Invisible Hand_ suggests that, under ideal market conditions in a capitalistic economy, people acting in their own rational self-interest will make economic decisions that best promote society's well-being, even when they are not consciously trying to improve the society. An 15. _Economic Model_ is a set of economic theories that are combined to investigate one or more macroeconomic issues.   The classical model is a long-run general
16. _Equilibrium_ model, in which all markets simultaneously clear. Although economic theories and economic models are simplifications of reality (in that they identify only the principal determinants of economic events), it is the ability of these theories and models, confirmed by 17._Empirical Analysis_, to explain and predict repeatedly and accurately real economic events (i.e., their reliability and validity) that determines their widespread acceptance.

All economists agree on the need for the rigorous, scientific investigation of economic events. Economic analysis based solely on the scientific method of research is called 18. _Positive Analysis_; it attempts to explain reality - to tell us "what is."   Positive analysis has provided a high level of agreement among economists on which theories best explain economic events; although it has not provided complete agreement. Positive analysis of macroeconomic policies is strictly scientific analysis of their expected effects. Scientific investigation predicts these effects will occur, regardless of whether we want these to be the effects.

19. _Normative Analysis_ of macroeconomic policies is not strictly scientific even though it may partially rely on positive economic analysis, because the normative analyst imposes personal value judgments about what is good for society to determine which policy "ought to" be adopted or to determine what effects a policy "ought to" have. Normative analysis may lead to disagreements among economists whenever their personal value judgments differ. There is significantly more agreement among economists on positive analysis of economic policy than on normative analysis; the media, nevertheless, tends to highlight the disagreements.

True-False Questions: Circle T for true statements and circle F for false statements.

T (F) 1. The economic growth rates of the various regions in the United States, such as the Northeast or Southwest, are an important topic of study in macroeconomics.

(T) F 2. During each of the recent U.S. recessions of 1973 - 1975, 1981 - 1982, and 1990 - 1991, the unemployment rate increased.

T (F) 3. Since 1970, U.S. monetary policymakers have achieved their goal of maintaining price level stability; so the economy has not suffered from instability in the inflation rate.

(T) F 4. The twin deficits of the 1980s refer to the U.S. federal government budget deficits and the U.S. international trade deficits.

(T) F 5. Average labor productivity in the United States grew at a significantly slower rate in the 1970s and 1980s than in the 1950s and 1960s.

(T) F 6. When it is to their political advantage, government policymakers may often adopt economic policies that are expected to be economically inefficient.

(T)   F   7.   Macroeconomists use economic theories, models, and data to teach, analyze, research, and forecast changes in the national economic conditions, including changes in government policies that affect the national economy.

T   (F)   8.   Good economic theories are often based on unrealistic assumptions, are unnecessarily complex, and are generally inconsistent with even casual empirical evidence.

T   (F)   9.   From an economic perspective, disagreements among economists about normative analysis are more important than disagreement about positive analysis.

(T)   F   10.   Substantial improvements in data development in recent decades have significantly improved the quality of economists' research, analysis, and forecasting.

Multiple Choice Questions: Circle the letter corresponding to the correct answer to each question.

1.   Which of the following is not a principal issue of macroeconomics?
a. business cycles
b. inflation
c. fiscal policies
(d.) competitiveness of firms in the steel industry
e. the international economy

2.   The most direct effect of an increase in the growth rate of average labor productivity would be an increase in
a. the inflation rate.
b. the unemployment rate.
(c) the long-run economic growth rate.
d. imported goods.
e. investment.

3.   Which of the following best describes a typical business cycle?
(a.) Economic expansions are followed by economic contractions.
b. Inflation is followed by unemployment.
c. Trade surpluses are followed by trade deficits.
d. Stagflation is followed by inflationary economic growth.
e. Government budget deficits are followed by government surpluses.

4.   Recessions
a. don't occur in developed countries, like the United States.
(b.) cause the unemployment rate to increase.
c. never last more than two consecutive quarters.
d. are always followed by long periods of high rates of real economic growth.
e. always cause the inflation rate to decline.

5.   Deflation and stagflation
a. always occur at the same time.
b. often but not always occur at the same time.
(c.) cannot occur at the same time.
d. are both causes of economic growth.
e. are both intended effects of macroeconomic policies.

6.   A nation that exports and imports goods has
      a. significantly reduced its national security.
      b. severe trade deficits.
      c. an open economy.
      d. high rates of unemployment.
      e. high interest rates.

7.   Critics of the large government budget deficits of the 1980s contend that these deficits
      a. create recessions.
      b. are disinflationary.
      c. reduce interest rates.
      d. reduce imports.
      e. reduce investment spending.

8.   Which of the following fiscal policies do Keynesians recommend to help the economy recover from a recession?
      a. an increase in government spending
      b. an increase in taxes
      c. an increase in the money supply
      d. an increase in saving
      e. an increase in government regulation

9.   In the United States, monetary policy is directly controlled by
      a. the president of the United States.
      b. the Federal Reserve.
      c. foreign central banks.
      d. the U.S. Congress.
      e. both the U.S. president and the U.S. Congress.

10.   Economic theories
      a. are always correct.
      b. should not be relied on unless they are supported by the empirical evidence.
      c. identify the personal value judgments of economists.
      d. are the only basis for designing economic policies.
      e. are not used in macroeconomic forecasting.

11.   The two most comprehensive, widely accepted macroeconomic models are
      a. the classical model and the supply-side model.
      b. the supply-side model and the real business cycle model.
      c. the classical model and the Keynesian model.
      d. the real business cycle model and the Keynesian model.
      e. the Keynesian model and the monetarist model.

12.   Which of the following best describes empirical analysis?
       a. flipping a coin to decide which of two competing theories will be presented as the accepted economic
          dogma for this year
       b. asking leading economic authorities their opinion on which economic theories they prefer
       c. using advanced, standardized, scientific research techniques to determine whether a theory is consistent
          with the available data
       d. using logical reasoning based on social norms to show that the relationship expressed in the hypothesis is
          morally superior to other theoretical relationships
       e. conducting informal discussions with business leaders to determine which of the competing theories they
          would like to see popularized by academia

13.   The principal distinction between positive analysis and normative analysis is that
       a. positive analysis is useful, and normative analysis is not useful.
       b. positive analysis is optimistic, and normative analysis is neutral.
       c. economists always agree on the conclusions of positive analysis but could disagree on the conclusions of
          normative analysis.
       d. positive analysis tells us "what is," but normative analysis tells us "what ought to be."
       e. positive analysis always supports economic theory regardless of the empirical evidence; normative
          analysis supports economic theory only when it is consistent with the empirical evidence.

14.   Over the 1869 - 1992 period real economic growth in the United States
       a. increased at a stable, average rate of about 10%.
       b. increased the real value of GDP in 1992 to approximately 56 times as large as its value in 1869.
       c. was more unstable after World War II than in the 1920 - 1945 period.
       d. increased at too low a rate to significantly improve the standard of living of the average American.
       e. far exceeded the growth rate of all other nations.

15.   Average labor productivity growth in the United States
       a. increased at a stable, average rate of about 10% over the 1900-1992 period.
       b. increased at too low a rate to significantly improve the standard of living of the average American over the
          1900 - 1992 period.
       c. was higher in the 1950 - 1969 period than in the 1970 - 1992 period.
       d. explains why the average real economic growth rate for the 1980s was unusually high for the United
          States.
       e. is not an important determinant of long-run real economic growth.

16.   During the Great Depression the unemployment rate for the United States peaked at approximately
       a. 10%.
       b. 70%.
       c. 45%.
       d. 25%.
       2. 5%.

17.   The average price of goods in the United States
       a. was relatively constant over the 1800 - 1945 period.
       b. was relatively constant over the decade of the 1980s.
       c. declined over the decade of the 1970s.
       d. is always constant in the long run.
       e. always increases in any five-year period or longer.

18.   Data on exports and imports for the United States over the 1890 - 1992 period show that
    a. the United States had large trade deficits throughout this entire period.
    b. the United States had large trade surpluses throughout this entire period.
    c. the percentage of total output exported by U.S. firms increased dramatically during the First World War and the Second World War.
    d. a much higher percentage of U.S. goods was exported in 1990 than in any previous year of its history.
    e. the value of exports normally equals the value of imports, so that the trade account normally balances each year.

19.   Since the Great Depression the share of national income collected in taxes and spent by the federal government in the United States has
    a. increased from less than 10% to more than 20%.
    b. remained relatively stable at 15%.
    c. remained relatively stable at 35%.
    d. declined from about 40% to less than 15%.
    e. increased until 1945, then declined dramatically.

20.   In most years during the 1970s and 1980s, the U.S. trade balance
    a. was in equilibrium.
    b. was a trade deficit.
    c. was a trade surplus.
    d. was cyclical, fluctuating annually between trade deficits and trade surpluses.
    e. could not be measured.

Short-Answer Essay Questions

1.   **What macroeconomics is about:** Identify and briefly describe five major issues studied by macroeconomists.

2.   **Business cycles and government intervention:** a) Define recession. b) Briefly state the effect, if any, of recessions on the unemployment rate. c) Are recessions always accompanied by deflation? Briefly explain. d) Identify and briefly describe two macroeconomic policies that might be used to help pull the macroeconomy out of a recession. e) In the absence of government intervention, do classical or Keynesian economists believe a macroeconomy would recover from a recession? Briefly explain.

3.   **What macroeconomists do:** Briefly describe the following tasks of macroeconomists: a) forecasting; b) analysis; (c) research; d) data development. e) Briefly evaluate the following comment: "The only useful task macroeconomists perform is forecasting, and they're not even very good at that."

4.   **Classical and Keynesian debate:** Compare and contrast the classical and Keynesian schools of thought for the following economic issues: a) causes of long-run economic growth; b) wage-price flexibility; c) importance of disequilibrium in labor market; d) importance of macroeconomic policies. e) How does the "unified model" of the textbook deal with the debate among classical and Keynesian economists?

5.   **Economic theories and economic history:** a) Why did the Great Depression create dissatisfaction with the classical approach to macroeconomics? b) What explanation of the Great Depression did Keynes give, and what policy solutions did he suggest? c) How did the Keynesian theory influence post-World War II economic policy in the United States? d) Did Keynesian theory accurately predict the occurrence of stagflation in the United States in the 1970s, and how did the experience of the 1970s affect the subsequent development of Keynesian and classical theories? e) Is it important that economic models fit the data? Briefly explain.

Mathematical Problem-Solving Questions

1.   **Economic growth:** Starting from a year in which gross domestic product for the economy is $5 trillion, calculate how much more output the national economy would produce in the next five years if it continued to grow at its potential real growth rate of 3.5%, rather than growing cyclically by -1% the first year, -2% the second year, 1% the third year, 2% the fourth year, and 4% the fifth year.

2.   **Unemployment:** Assuming there are 125 million people in the labor force, calculate how many people are unemployed for each of the following unemployment rates: a) 2.5%; b) 10%; c) 8%, d) 6%; e) 5.5%

3.   **Inflation:** Using the CPI measure of the price level, which was 100 in the base year, calculate the annual inflation rates for: a) the next year, when the index was 110; b) two years later, when the index was 105; for the third year, when the index was 125.

Answers to Fill-In-The-Blanks Questions

1. macroeconomics	2. average labor productivity	3. unemployment	4. inflation
5. deflation	6. open economy	7. closed economy	8. trade surplus
9. trade deficit	10. fiscal policy	11. monetary policy	12. aggregation
13. economic theory	14. invisible hand	15. economic model	16. equilibrium
17. empirical analysis	18. positive analysis	19. normative analysis	

Answers to True-False Questions

1. F   Macroeconomists do not study regional, subnational economic growth rates; they study national economic growth rates, which represent aggregate weighted averages of regional economic growth rates. It is interesting to observe that the various regions of an economy may grow at very dissimilar rates, such that the economic growth rate of a particular region may be very different from the national economic growth rate in some time periods.

2. T   During each of the recent U.S. recessions, the unemployment rate increased, as it typically does. In the 1981 - 1982 recession, the unemployment rate peaked at 10.8%.

3. F   Maintaining price level stability is the long-run goal of the U.S. monetary policymakers at the Federal Reserve, but this goal has not been achieved over the period since 1970. The inflation rate was unstable but had a high average rate for the decade of the 1970s. The inflation rate fell dramatically in the early 1980s and has remained in the 3% - 5% annual rate since that time. While 3% -.5% annual inflation over the last decade is a big improvement over the inflation record of the previous decade,

this creeping inflation is still too high to be called price level stability. The price level rose continuously throughout this period.

4. T   A government budget deficit represents public sector dissaving; this must be financed by domestic private sector saving or by borrowing from foreigners. If a budget deficit is financed by borrowing from foreigners, it creates a trade deficit. The budget deficit and corresponding trade deficit are called the twin deficits.

5. T   The decline in growth of U.S. labor productivity in the 1970s and 1980s compared to the 1950s and 1960s is shown by the data in Fig. 1.2 of the textbook. This slowdown in labor productivity growth has helped to create a slowdown in long-run economic growth.

6. T   Economists believe that people primarily behave in their own rational self-interest. This suggests that policymakers care more about their own future well-being than about the well-being of society. Consequently, policymakers tend to support an economically inefficient policy that promotes their own political and economic future, yet oppose an economically efficient policy that worsens their own political and economic future. Fortunately, when a policy decision does not impose a trade-off between doing what is good for them and doing what is good for society, policymakers tend to support economically efficient policies.

7. T   Macroeconomists study the economic conditions of national economies and changes in those conditions by using economic theories, models, and data in their principal tasks of teaching, analysis, research, and forecasting. Since government policymakers are very important economic decision makers, government policies are an important topic of study for economists.

8. F   Good economic theories are based on realistic assumptions, are not unnecessarily complex, and are consistent with the empirical evidence.

9. F   Disagreements among economists about normative analysis occur because of differences in personal value judgments; these differences are relatively unimportant to economics as a scientific field of study. The preferences or value judgments of economists may be as diverse as the entire range of viewpoints of people in the economy. Economists, as people, are entitled to have and to express their own normative points of view about how things ought to be. The positive analysis of economics as a science does not enable us to rank order preferences or value judgments. Disagreements among economists about positive analysis can be very important and create a need for further economic research. Positive analysis, based on economics as a science, can help to reduce these disagreements.

10. T   Substantial improvements in the quantity and quality of data available to economists in improved formats, such as computerized databases, as well as substantial improvements in data management tools and techniques, have been tremendously important in enabling economists to improve their productivity as teachers, analysts, researchers, and forecasters. Lack of relatively low-cost access to important, high-quality economic data has always been a substantial barrier to progress in economics, but substantial progress in data development in recent decades has greatly relaxed that constraint for most economists.

Answers to Multiple Choice Questions

1.	d	8.	a	15.	c
2.	c	9.	b	16.	d
3.	a	10.	b	17.	a
4.	b	11.	c	18.	c
5.	c	12.	c	19.	a
6.	c	13.	d	20.	b
7.	e	14.	b		

Answers to Short-Answer Essay Questions

1. **What macroeconomics is about**

   Macroeconomists study the causes and effects of the following macroeconomic events to explain and predict these events.

   1) Long-run economic growth: increases in real GDP over extended periods of time. Real GDP is a measure of national output.

   2) Business cycles: Periods of economic contraction, when real GDP grows more slowly than its potential rate, are usually followed by periods of economic expansion, when real GDP grows faster than its potential rate.

   3) Unemployment and inflation: Unemployment is the inability of some people to find jobs, even though they are willing to work at market wages. Inflation is the rate of growth in the macroeconomic price level (i.e., the average price of goods).

   4) The international economy: the values and patterns of international trade, international aid, direct foreign investment, and borrowing among nations.

   5) Macroeconomic policy: includes both fiscal policies and monetary policies. Fiscal policies attempt to improve the performance of the macroeconomy by changing government spending and taxation. Monetary policies attempt to improve the performance of the macroeconomy by changing the money supply.

2. **Business cycles and government intervention**

   a) A recession is a contraction in the business cycle. The contraction phase of the business cycle is sometimes called the recession phase. A recession is characterized as a slowdown in the growth rate of aggregate output, which may become negative.

   b) The unemployment rate increases during recessions. For example, Fig. 1.3 in the textbook shows that the unemployment rate increased during the 1973 - 1975, 1981 - 1982, and 1990 - 1991 recessions.

c)   No, recessions are not always accompanied by deflation. For example, Fig. 1.4 in the textbook shows that the recent recessions of 1973 - 1975, 1981 - 1982, and 1990 - 1991 were accompanied by inflation (i.e., increases in the CPI measure of the price level).

d)   The two macroeconomic policies that might be used to help pull the macroeconomy out of a recession are fiscal policy increases in government spending and/or reductions in taxes, and monetary policy increases in the money supply.

e)   Yes, both classical and Keynesian economists believe the economy will recover from a recession in the absence of government intervention. However, classical economists believe the recovery will occur quickly; Keynesians believe the recovery will occur slowly.

3.   **What macroeconomists do**

a)   Forecasting: Macroeconomists develop macroeconomic models to predict the future values of macroeconomic variables in one or more markets. These models are usually mathematical in form, use macroeconomic data, and are based on economic theory.

b)   Analysis: Macroeconomists analyze changes in macroeconomic policies as well as other changes in macroeconomic market conditions. This analysis is based on economic theory, uses analytic reasoning techniques, and may rely on forecasting models.

c)   Research: Macroeconomic research is the scientific testing of hypotheses to develop, improve, and test economic theories and economic models that employ these theories.

d)   Data development: Macroeconomic data development provides the data needed in macroeconomic research, analysis, and forecasting. Macroeconomic data is developed by adding together the local market data for the entire national economy for each specific variable, using standardized aggregation techniques. Governments and international development organizations provide economists with the majority of their data; although some large private research organizations, such as the National Bureau of Economic Research and the Brookings Institution, are important data developers.

e)   Evaluation of the statement: "The only useful task macroeconomists perform is forecasting and they're not even very good at that."

This is a statement by someone who has a narrow view of what macroeconomists do and is not impressed with the forecasting performance of economists. Macroeconomic forecasters are, themselves, somewhat discontented with their inability to forecast the future path of the macroeconomy accurately. Yet, such high expectations set an unreasonable standard. Forecasting is a relatively new aspect of economics; since its early development in the 1950s, the predictive validity of macroeconomic forecasts has significantly improved. However, forecasting is only a small part of what macroeconomists do; macroeconomic data development, research, and analysis are their other principal, useful tasks. Only a small share of macroeconomists are forecasters. Economists like to employ a "market test" of the social value of any task. Given the high and increasing market demand by both the private sector and public sector for what economists do, it appears that the market highly values macroeconomists.

4.   **Classical and Keynesian debate**

    a)   Causes of long-run economic growth: There is no substantial disagreement between classical economists and Keynesians over the principal causes of long-run economic growth. Both schools of macroeconomists would agree that increases in the supplies of the factors of production, such as labor and capital, as well as increases in their productivities, such as those provided by technological progress and human capital investments, increase the rate of long-run economic growth.

    b)   Wage-price flexibility is a principal point of disagreement between classical economists and Keynesians. Classical economists believe that wages and prices are perfectly flexible; in response to some change in market conditions, wages and prices adjust quickly to their new market-clearing levels. Keynesians believe that wages and prices are rigid or, at least, sticky in a downward direction; in response to deflationary pressures, wages and prices adjust slowly to their new market-clearing levels.

    c)   Importance of disequilibrium in labor markets is another principal point of disagreement between classical economists and Keynesians. Classical economists believe flexible wage-price adjustments will quickly return the labor market to full-employment equilibrium; in the classical model, business cycle contractions do not usually create any substantial period (e.g., a year or longer) of disequilibrium in the labor market, characterized by a high rate of cyclical unemployment. Keynesians believe wages and prices adjust slowly in a downward direction; in the Keynesian model, business cycle contractions often produce a substantial period of disequilibrium in the labor market, characterized by a high rate of cyclical unemployment.

    d)   Importance of macroeconomic policies: Classical and Keynesians also disagree about the use of macroeconomic policies. Given wage-price flexibility, classical economists believe that the market economy normally provides for full employment. They believe that government intervention in the form of macroeconomic fiscal and monetary policies is not needed to prevent recessions and cyclical unemployment. Given slow adjustments in wages and prices, Keynesians believe that economic recessions and substantial cyclical unemployment could plague the economy for several years. They believe that efficient use of macroeconomic policies could return the economy to the full-employment level of output more quickly.

    e)   Debate within a unified model: The textbook provides a model that highlights both the agreement of classical economists and Keynesians on the macroeconomic issues for the long run and disagreement on these issues for the short run. The debate between classical economists and Keynesians on the length of economic recessions and the effectiveness of macroeconomic policies stems from their disagreement about whether wages and prices adjust quickly or slowly. The unified model enables us to analyze macroeconomic events, assuming rapid wage-price adjustment, then assuming slow wage-price adjustment.

Economic theories and economic history

    a)   The classical model and the Great Depression: The classical model predicts that the economy will normally provide for full employment, even during business cycle fluctuations in macroeconomic activity. According to the classical model, any increase in unemployment during a business cycle contraction will be small and short-lived. The Great Depression was an economic contraction that was too severe and too long-lived to fit the classical model of economic contractions. Classical economists opposed macroeconomic policy intervention to help the economy recover, because they believed that the macroeconomy would recover more efficiently on its own. Given an unemployment rate that had been increasing for several years and approached 25% by 1933, policymakers wanted a policy solution that would help the economy recover more quickly. By 1933, the classical view that the market economy is self-regulating and quickly, efficiently adjusts to economic shocks to maintain full-employment, was a view that did not seem to fit the macroeconomic data of the 1930s.

b)   A Keynesian explanation of the Great Depression: Keynes provided a plausible explanation of the Great Depression that seemed to fit the macroeconomic data. He contended that the Great Depression was caused by a decline in the aggregate demand for the output produced in the national economy. Profit-maximizing businesses responded to the decline in demand for their output by reducing the amount they produced and laid off workers as they cut production levels. Consequently, the equilibrium level of national output demanded and supplied declined and the rate of unemployment increased. Keynes contended that there was no market mechanism that would quickly return the economy to full-employment output. Businesses would not supply more output unless the demand for that output increased, and there is no market mechanism that would automatically cause demand to quickly increase. The economy could continue producing a low level of output, with a substantial amount of excess productive capacity and a high rate of unemployment, for a long period of time. Keynes contended that the government could use expansionary fiscal and monetary policies to increase the level of aggregate demand, which would help to quickly return the economy to the level of national output needed to provide for full-employment.

c)   The use of stabilization policies: In the post-World War II period, U.S. government policymakers have largely relied on Keynesian theory to explain business cycle fluctuations in macroeconomic activity and to justify their use of fiscal and monetary policies to help reduce the severity and duration of business cycle fluctuations.

d)   Keynesians' failure to predict stagflation: Keynesians did not accurately predict the occurrence of stagflation in the U.S. in the 1970s. Keynesian theory highlighted the importance of fluctuations in the national demand for output (i.e., shifts in aggregate demand); it assumes that the national supply of goods and services is stable over the business cycle (i.e., the aggregate supply curve is fixed). Contrary to the Keynesian view that recessions are caused by a decline in aggregate demand along a fixed aggregate supply curve, the stagflation of the 1970s was caused by a decline in aggregate supply along a fixed aggregate demand curve. Keynesian theory suggests that recessions are deflationary, but inflation increased in the recessions of the 1970s. Keynesian theory suggests that expansionary fiscal and monetary policies can increase the level of national output by increasing the aggregate demand for that output, but increasing aggregate demand in response to a decline in aggregate supply caused inflation to increase substantially. The experience of the 1970s, led economists to revise the Keynesian and classical models to better predict and explain the macroeconomic effects of both supply shocks and demand shocks. These recent developments in macroeconomic theories and policies have brought these models closer together; thereby, moving economists from different schools of thought towards a unified model of the macroeconomy.

e)   Models that fit the data: The ultimate test of macroeconomic models is whether they can explain macroeconomic events, predict their occurrence, and offer policy solutions, if needed, to help reduce these problems. To achieve all this, the models must fit the data (i.e., be consistent with the data and be supported by the data). The classical model dominated economic thought until the Great Depression because it best fit the data. After the Great Depression, the Keynesian model dominated economic thought until around 1970, because it best fit the data. After 1970, economists recognized the need for a model that would highlight the importance of changes in both aggregate supply and aggregate demand. In each period, economists and market actors, relying on economic research, analysis, and forecasting, have demanded a model that fits the data. Whenever a widely-accepted model fails to fit current macroeconomic data, the model will be revised so that it can explain both the current and historical data.

Answers to Mathematical Problem-Solving Questions

1. **Economic growth**:   The economy would produce $.741 trillion or $741 billion, which is approximately 3/4 of a trillion dollars more if it grew each year at its potential economic growth rate over the five-year period. Explanation: If an economy with a $5 trillion GDP grew at 3.5% per year, its GDP would be $5.175 trillion after one year, $5.175 x 1.035 = $5.356 trillion after two years, $5.544 trillion after three years, $5.738 trillion after four years, and $5.938 trillion after five years.   If the $5 trillion GDP grew at -1% the first year, its GDP would be $4.950 trillion after one year. Growing at -2% in the second year, its GDP would be $4.95 trillion x .98 = $4.851 trillion after two years. With 1% growth in the third year, its GDP would be $4.895 trillion after three years. With 2% growth in the fourth year, its GDP would be $4.998 trillion. With 4% growth in the fifth year, its GDP would be $5.197 after five years. $5.938 trillion - $5.197 trillion = $.741 trillion.

2. **Unemployment:** a) 31.25 million people unemployed; b) 12.5 million people unemployed; c) 10.0 million people unemployed; d) 7.5 million people unemployed; and e) 6.875 million people unemployed. Explanation: To get each number, multiply 125 million by the unemployment rate.

3. **Inflation**: The annual inflation rate = $\dfrac{\text{price level in the current year - price level in the previous year}}{\text{price level in the previous year}}$

    a) inflation the first year = (110 - 100)/100 = 10/100 = 10%.

    b) inflation the second year = (105 - 110)/110 = - 5/110 = -4.5%.

    c) inflation the third year = (125 - 105)/105 = 20/105 = 19%.

CHAPTER 2: THE MEASUREMENT AND STRUCTURE OF THE NATIONAL ECONOMY

A Fill-In-The-Blanks Review of Chapter Highlights: Use the following key terms to fill in the blanks. Each key term is used only once.

budget deficit
capital good
consumption
depreciation
expenditure approach
fixed-weight price index
fundamental identity of national income accounting
government outlays
government receipts
gross domestic product
income approach
interest rate
inventories
national income
national saving
net exports
net foreign assets
nominal GDP
nominal variables
private disposable income
product approach
real interest rate
saving
transfers
uses-of-saving identity
variable-weight price index

budget surplus
consumer price index
current account balance
expected real interest rate
final goods and services
flow variable
GDP deflator
government purchases
government saving
gross national product
income-expenditure identity
intermediate goods and services
investment
national income accounts
national wealth
net factor payments from abroad
net national product
nominal interest rate
price index
private saving
real GDP
real variable
stock variable
underground economy
value added
wealth

During the first half of this century, economists gathered and organized macroeconomic data into 1. _National Income Accts,_ .

These accounts include three approaches to measuring the value of national output - a product approach, an expenditure approach, and an income approach. The 2. _Product Approach_ adds together the 3. _Value Added_ by all producers of goods and services in the entire country by the domestic and foreign factors of production during a specified time period (e.g., a year). For the same time period, the 4. _Income Approach_ adds together the before-tax income, including profits, earned by all the resource suppliers who produced the output. The 5. _Expenditure Approach_ to calculating national output adds together the domestic and foreign consumption, investment, government, and net export spending on new, final goods and services produced in the national economy that particular time period. The 6._Income-Expenditure identity_ highlights that the value of national output is always equal to the value of spending on that output. The

7. _fundamental_ ——————— tells us that all three approaches, once adjusted for statistical errors, provide the same calculated value of national output.

8. _Gross Domestic Product_ is the most widely used measure of national output; it equals 9. _Gross National Product_ minus 10. _Net factor Payments from Abroad_. Since net factor payments from abroad are small, GNP and GDP have approximately the same value for the United States. Although the value of GDP excludes the value of nonmarketed outputs, it does include an estimated value for goods and services produced in the 11. _Underground Economy_. To avoid double counting, GDP figures exclude the value of 12. _Intermediate Goods & Services_, because their value is already included in the value of 13. _final Goods & Services_ that they helped to produce. A 14. _Capital Good_ is a final good that is purchased by investors to be used as a factor of production in a later time period. Those products that are produced but not sold in the same time period are added to the inventory of the firms that produced them; the net addition to the 15. _Inventories_ of all firms is the nation's inventory investment.

Household spending on final goods and services, called 16. _Consumption_, makes up approximately two-thirds of all expenditures. Business 17. _Investment_ is the purchase of new fixed capital equipment and structures, residential structures, and inventories. 18. _Govt. Purchases_ of final goods and services include the purchases made by all levels of government - federal, state, and local. Social Security payments and welfare payments are examples of government 19. _transfers_. Government transfers and interest payments are not added as government expenditures in the expenditure approach to calculating GDP, because they are already included in the private disposable income used to finance private sector expenditures. 20. _Net Exports_ measures the difference between exports and imports; if foreign expenditures on the nation's exports exceeds domestic expenditures on goods and services imported from abroad, then the value of net exports is positive.

GDP + NFP = GNP. GNP minus 21. _Depreciation_ (i.e., the value of capital consumed in production of final outputs) equals 22. _Net National Product_. By subtracting the value of indirect business taxes, such as sales taxes and excise taxes, from NNP, we obtain the value of 23. _National Income_. National income is the portion of GDP + NFP that can be distributed to the owners of the factors of production as compensation to employees, proprietors' income, rental income, net interest, and corporate profits.

For analytic purposes, the economy can be divided into four sectors - the household sector, the business sector, the government sector, and the foreign sector. The household and business sectors combined represent the private sector of the domestic economy; the government sector is sometimes called the public sector. 24. _Private Disposable Income_ is the after-tax income received by the private sector.

The government receives its income in the form of tax revenue, called 25. _Govt. Receipts_. 26. _Govt. Outlays_ or expenditures include government purchases, transfers, and interest payments. A government 27. _Budget Surplus_ exists when taxes exceed government outlays. A government 28. _Budget Deficit_ exists when taxes are less than government outlays.

All after-tax income received by the various market participants is either spent or saved. 29. _Saving_ is the income received but not spent on current needs during the period. 30. _Private Saving_ is the private disposable income spent on consumption. 31. _Govt. Saving_ is tax revenue left over after paying for government outlays. 32. _National " "_ is the sum of private saving and government saving. The 33. _Uses of Saving Identity_ shows that national saving equals the sum of investment and the 34. _Current Acct. Balance_.

Saving is a 35. <u>flow Valiable</u> because it is measured per unit of time. Because saving finances the purchase of assets and the reduction of liabilities, saving creates 36. <u>Wealth</u>. Wealth is a 37. <u>Stock Valiable</u> because it is measured at a point in time. The 38. <u>National Wealth</u> of the United States is the total value of domestic physical assets and net foreign assets owned by U.S. residents. The total value of 39. <u>Net foreign Assets</u> is positive if the value of foreign assets, both physical and financial, exceeds the value of foreign liabilities of domestic residents.

All macroeconomic variables have both nominal values and real values. The values of 40. <u>Nominal Valiables</u> are measured at current market prices and change with changes in the macroeconomic price level. The value of a 41. <u>Real Variable</u> is measured at some fixed price level and does not change with changes in the price level. Because nominal values do not distinguish between changes in physical quantities and changes in price, 42. <u>Nominal GDP</u> could increase at the same time that 43. <u>Real GDP</u> decreased, remained unchanged, or increased, given appropriate changes in the average level of product prices.

Calculation of the average level of product prices in some year relative to the price level in some base year provides a 44. <u>Price Index</u> for these products. A 45. <u>Variable-Weight Price Index</u> compares the average price of products in the current period with what they would have cost in the base year. One complexity, however, is that some of the goods and services may not have been produced in the base year. A 46. <u>Fixed-Weight Price Index</u> compares the current price level to the base-year price level of some fixed set of goods and services that were produced in the base year. One complexity, however, is that these products may no longer be produced in the current year. The 47. <u>GDP Deflator</u> is a variable-weight price index that is used to measure changes in the average price of all goods and services. Real GDP is calculated by dividing nominal GDP by the GDP deflator. The 48. <u>Consumer Price Index</u> is a fixed-weight price index used to measure changes in the average price of a fixed basket of consumer goods and services. The rate of inflation in consumer products for some year is the percent increase in the CPI.

The 49. <u>Interest Rate</u> is the rate of return paid by borrowers to lenders. The 50. <u>Real Interest Rate</u> is the current market rate of return at which people can borrow. To know how much they are paying to borrow in real terms, market participants must know the 51. <u>Nominal Interest Rate</u>, which is calculated by subtracting the rate of inflation from the nominal interest rate. Most lending and borrowing decisions, however, are based on the 52. <u>Expected Real Interest Rate</u>, because the rate of inflation is not known with certainty at the time most lending/borrowing decisions are made. To calculate the expected real interest rate from the nominal interest rate, analysts must use one of several techniques to estimate the expected rate of inflation.

True-False Questions: Circle T for true statements and circle F for false statements.

(T) F 1.   The U. S. government collects and publishes quarterly data on the major macroeconomic variables.

T (F) 2.   If net factor payments from abroad are positive, the GDP measure of national output will exceed GNP.

T (F) 3.   The fundamental identity of national income accounting is Y = C + I + G + NX.

T (F) 4.   All of the goods and services included in GDP are produced by businesses employing domestically owned factors of production.

T (F) 5.   In the expenditure approach to calculating national output, the purchase of a car would always be classified as a consumer good.

(T) F 6.   In the United States, consumers spend more of their income buying consumer services than they do buying consumer goods.

(T) F 7.   With other things held constant, a tax increase would increase government saving but would reduce private saving.

(T) F 8.   The uses-of-saving identity shows that if national saving exceeds national investment spending, the country has a current account surplus.

T (F) 9.   The nation's money supply and government debt are important sources of national wealth.

T (F) 10.   The expected real interest rate is always equal to the real interest rate.

Multiple Choice Questions: Circle the letter corresponding to the correct answer to each question.

1.   National income accounts
   a. can be understood only by accountants.
   b. clearly identify who owes how much to whom.
   (c.) provide macroeconomists with much of the data needed for macroeconomic analysis, research, and forecasting.
   d. avoid the technical problems of aggregating data.
   e. exist for only the most developed countries.

2.   The product approach to calculating GDP
   (a.) adds together the market values of final goods and services produced by domestic and foreign-owned factors of production within the nation in some time period.
   b. multiplies the values of inputs by the values of outputs to achieve a product value.
   c. is superior to the income approach because, unlike the income approach, it gives us the real value of output.
   d. adds together the market values of final goods, intermediate goods, and goods added to inventories.
   e. includes the market value of goods and services produced by households for their own consumption but excludes the value of the underground economy.

3.   Gross national product
      a. is identical to gross domestic product in the United States and Canada.
      b. will exceed gross domestic product if a substantial value of domestic factors of production are employed in foreign countries and only a small value of foreign-owned resources are employed in the domestic economy.
      c. will always exceed gross domestic product for a closed economy.
      d. will be higher in a private sector economy than in an economy where there is also a public sector that taxes the private sector.
      e. is equal to net national product in a closed economy.

4.   Unlike final goods and services, intermediate goods and services
      a. are purchased by businesses.
      b. are purchased by government.
      c. are not exported.
      d. are completely used up in the current time period.
      e. become part of inventory investment.

5.   Fixed business investments include purchases of
      a. capital equipment and structures.
      b. land and energy.
      c. long-term bonds.
      d. inventory investments.
      e. residential housing.

6.   Government purchases
      a. are recorded as either consumption or investment in the national income accounts, since those are the only two types of goods produced.
      b. are larger than private sector purchases in the post - World War II U.S. economy.
      c. do not include purchases of foreign goods.
      d. are less than government outlays.
      e. are the value of goods and services bought by the federal government.

7.   Which of the following is not a government transfer?
      a. a transfer of money from the defense budget to the space exploration budget
      b. Social Security payments
      c. Medicaid
      d. Medicare
      e. unemployment insurance

8.   For a given value of GDP, the measure of income that would not be affected by changes in the amount of depreciation or indirect business taxes is
      a. private disposable income.
      b. personal income.
      c. national income.
      d. net national product.
      e. gross national product.

9.   The principal actors in the private sector national economy are domestic
      a.   households.
      b.   households and businesses.
      c.   businesses.
      d.   businesses and government.
      e.   domestic and foreign households.

10.   Other things held constant, private disposable income would increase if
      a.   taxes increase.
      b.   government purchases increase.
      c.   consumption increases.
      d.   government transfers increase.
      e.   interest payments on government debt decrease.

11.   Which of the following equations describes a government budget deficit?
      a.   T < (G + TR + INT)
      b.   (T - G) > (TR + INT)
      c.   T > G
      d.   (T + TR + INT) > G
      e.   (T - TR - INT) > G

12.   For a given level of private disposable income, an increase in private saving would
      a.   reduce exports.
      b.   reduce the government budget deficit.
      c.   reduce investment.
      d.   reduce wealth.
      e.   increase the private saving rate.

13.   Which of the following equals national saving (S)?
      a.   (Y + NFP - T + TR + TR) - C
      b.   Y + NFP - (C + G)
      c.   T - (G + TR + INT)
      d.   Y - (C + I + G + NX)
      e.   Y + NFP - (I + CA)

14.   Wealth
      a.   is a flow variable, measured per unit of time.
      b.   is a flow variable, measured at a point in time.
      c.   is a stock variable, measured at a point in time.
      d.   is a stock variable, measured per unit of time.
      e.   and saving are flow variables.

15.   National wealth is the value of
      a.   domestic and foreign physical and financial assets.
      b.   domestic physical and financial assets.
      c.   domestic physical assets plus net foreign physical and financial assets.
      d.   net foreign assets.
      e.   domestic financial wealth.

16.   An increase in real GDP
       a. requires that nominal GDP increase.
       b. could be achieved while nominal GDP declined.
       c. is inflationary.
       d. requires that nominal GDP decrease.
       e. is always smaller than an increase in nominal GDP.

17.   The consumer price index is a
       a. fixed-weight price index that measures the current price level of a base-year basket of consumer goods
           and services.
       b. fixed-weight price index that measures the current price level of a current basket of consumer goods and
           services.
       c. a variable-weight price index that measures the current price level of a current basket of consumer goods
           and services.
       d. a variable-weight price index that measures the current price level of a base-year basket of consumer
           goods and services.
       e. a price index, but neither a fixed-weight nor variable-weight index.

18.   The nominal interest rate equals the
       a. real interest rate minus the expected rate of inflation.
       b. real interest rate minus the rate of inflation.
       c. expected real interest rate plus the rate of inflation.
       d. expected real interest rate minus the rate of inflation.
       e. expected real interest rate plus the expected rate of inflation.

19.   According to the fundamental identity of national income accounting,
       a. GDP = GNP - NFP.
       b. Y = C + I + G + NX.
       c. S = (Y + NFP - T + TR + INT) - C.
       d. total production = total income = total expenditure.
       e. S = I + CA.

20.   The uses-of-saving identity shows that net foreign investment is financed by
       a. a budget deficit.
       b. a trade deficit.
       c. domestic investment.
       d. an excess of national saving over investment.
       e. a budget deficit in excess of the current account deficit.

Short-Answer Essay Questions

1.   **National output, income, and expenditure:** a) State the fundamental identity of national income
      accounting. b) How does an "identity" relationship differ from an "equality" relationship? c) Define GDP.
      d) Identify and briefly describe three approaches to measuring GDP. e) If you were given the value of GDP,
      how would you calculate the value of NNP, NI, and private disposable income?

2.   **Consumption**: a) Briefly define consumption. b) Give an example of each of the following: consumer durables, nondurable goods, and services. c) Approximately what share of GDP does personal consumption expenditures represent? d) Approximately what share of personal consumption expenditures do services represent? e) How are consumption and the private saving rate related?

3.   **Investment**: a) What does investment have to do with capital goods? b) Give an example of each of the following types of business fixed investment: equipment and structures. c) Why is spending on new houses and apartments a part of fixed investment? d) Why are household purchases of human capital not a part of investment? e) Briefly describe the role that inventory investment plays in the income-expenditure identity.

4.   **Government output, purchases, and outlays**: a) In the product approach to calculating GDP, how is the market value of government output determined? b) Do government outlays represent approximately 20% of GDP? Briefly explain. c) Are combined state and local government purchases small compared to federal government purchases? Briefly explain. d) How does the government obtain income to spend? e) How could the government achieve a budget surplus?

5.   **Net exports**: a) Would an increase in goods imported from a foreign subsidiary of a U.S. multinational firm, produced mostly with U.S.-owned capital and labor, increase GDP for the United States? Briefly explain. b) Could GDP increase while GNP declined? Briefly explain. c) Why are net exports added into the expenditure calculation of GDP? d) How are net exports, net factor payments from abroad, and the current account balance related? e) If net exports represent only plus or minus 1% of a nation's GNP, is it fair to say that international trade is unimportant for that nation? Briefly explain.

6.   **Saving and wealth**: a) Briefly state one way that each of the following could be increased: private saving, government saving, and national saving. b) State the "uses-of-saving identity." c) For given levels of private saving and the current account, use the "uses-of-saving identity" to show the effect of an increase in the government budget deficit on investment. d) Does saving create wealth? Briefly explain. e) Is the saving rate in the United States high compared to other major OECD countries, and did this saving rate increase in the 1980s?

7.   **Price indexes, inflation, and real variables**: a) Identify three macroeconomic real variables that are calculated from nominal variables using price indexes. b) Briefly state the difference between a fixed-weight and variable-weight price index. c) If the CPI is 3.50 for the current year, how much inflation has there been since the base year? d) If the CPI increased to 3.75 over the next year, what would be the inflation rate for that year? e) Why do lenders add the expected rate of inflation into the interest rate they charge borrowers?

Mathematical Problem-Solving Questions

1. **National output:** Use the following data to calculate national output using the expenditure approach and the income approach for some economy, and show that GDP has the same value when calculated by either approach.

consumption	$4480 billion	compensation to employees	$4200 billion
investment	980	proprietors' income	420
government purchases	1400	rental income of persons	70
net exports	140	corporate profits	490
		net interest	420
		indirect business taxes	700
		consumption of fixed capital	770
		factor income received from rest of world	140
		payments of factor income to rest of world	70

2. **Saving, private saving, and government saving:** Use the following data to calculate private saving, government saving, and national saving for some economy.

national income	$7000 billion	taxes	$2450 billion
net factor payments from abroad	- 70	transfers	1050
consumption	4480		
government purchases	1400		
interest payments on government debt	210		

3. **Inflation, real GDP, and the real interest rate:** Calculate real GDP and the real interest rate for an economy where nominal GDP is $7350 billion, the nominal interest rate is 8%, and the inflation rate is 5%. In calculating real GDP, assume that the base year is the year immediately prior to the current year.

4. **Real rate of return:** Imagine that you have certificates of deposit worth $500,000 in the bank as part of your savings for retirement. The bank is paying you a fixed interest rate of 5% per year for the CDs which mature in three years. Calculate your real return on these CDs, when inflation is 5% the first year, 15% the second year, and 15% the third year.

Answers to Fill-In-The-Blanks Questions

1. national income accounts
2. product approach
3. value added
4. income approach
5. expenditure approach
6. income-expenditure identity
7. fundamental identity of national income accounting
8. gross domestic product
9. gross national product
10. net factor payments from abroad
11. underground economy
12. intermediate goods and services
13. final goods and services
14. capital good
15. inventories
16. consumption
17. investment
18. government purchases
19. transfers
20. net exports
21. depreciation
22. net national product

23. national income
24. private disposable income
25. government receipts
26. government outlays
27. budget surplus
28. budget deficit
29. saving
30. private saving
31. government saving
32. national saving
33. uses-of-saving identity
34. current account balance
35. flow variable
36. wealth
37. stock variable
38. national wealth
39. net foreign assets
40. nominal variables
41. real variable
42. nominal GDP
43. real GDP
44. price index
45. variable-weight price index
46. fixed-weight price index
47. GDP deflator
48. consumer price index
49. interest rate
50. real interest rate
51. nominal interest rate
52. expected real interest rate

Answers to True-False Questions

1. T The Bureau of Economic analysis is part of the U.S. Department of Commerce; it prepares the quarterly data reports on the macroeconomic variables for the National Income and Product Accounts. The Census Bureau, the Internal Revenue Service, the Federal Reserve, and the Bureau of Labor Statistics within the U.S. Department of Labor are some other U.S. government agencies that collect and publish substantial amounts of data on U.S. macroeconomic variables.

2. F GDP = GNP - NFP; so GDP is less than GNP when NFP is positive.

3. F [Y = C + I + G + NX] is the income-expenditure identity. The fundamental national income identity is [total production = total income = total expenditure].

4. F GDP includes services outputs produced by the government, called government services, in addition to goods and services produced by businesses. GDP includes outputs produced within the nation's territory by foreign-owned resources in addition to outputs produced with domestically owned resources.

5. F In the expenditure approach to calculating national output, goods are classified according to the type of market participant that buys them. Cars purchased by households are classified as consumer goods. Cars purchased by businesses are called investment goods. Cars purchased by government are called government purchases. Cars purchased by foreigners are called exports.

6. T In 1993, for example, expenditures on consumer services accounted for approximately 57% of total consumption spending, while expenditures on consumer goods accounted for approximately 43% of total consumption spending.

7. T Government saving is $[S_{govt} = (T - TR - INT) - G]$; it increases with taxes (T). Private saving is $[S_{pvt} = (Y + NFP - T + TR + INT) - C]$; it declines with increases in taxes.

8. T The uses-of-saving identity is $[S_{pvt} = I + (-S_{govt}) + CA]$, where CA is the current account balance. National saving is $[S = S_{pvt} + S_{govt}]$. Therefore, $[S - I = CA]$, which shows that if national saving exceeds investment spending, then CA > 0, which is a current account surplus.

9. F The nation's money supply and government debt are financial assets to those who hold them but liabilities of the government, so they have no net asset value for the nation and, consequently, do not contribute to a nation's wealth.

10. F The expected real interest rate equals the real interest rate when the expected rate of inflation equals the rate of inflation; when inflationary expectations overestimate or underestimate the actual rate of inflation in some time period, the expected real interest rate will differ from the real interest rate.

Answers to Multiple Choice Questions

1. c	7. a	13. b	19. d
2. a	8. e	14. c	20. d
3. b	9. b	15. c	
4. d	10. d	16. b	
5. a	11. a	17. a	
6. d	12. e	18. e	

Answers to Short-Answer Essay Questions

1.   **National output, income, and expenditure**

   a)   The fundamental identity of national income accounting is total production = total income = total expenditure.

   b)   An equation that expresses an identity is always true by definition, regardless of the particular values of the variables. For an identity, any change in the total value of variables on the right-hand side of the equality will be accompanied by an equal change in the total value of the variables on the left-hand side. For an equation that expresses an equality that is not an identity, a change in the total value of variables on one side of the equality will create an inequality.

   c)   GDP = gross domestic product = the market value of final goods and services produced by all domestic and foreign-owned factors of production within a nation's territory during a specified time period.

   d)   The three approaches to measuring GDP are called the product approach, income approach, and expenditure approach. The product approach adds together the market values of the goods and services produced within the borders of the nation's domestic economy during a specified time period (e.g., one-quarter of a year or one year). The income approach adds together the compensation to employees, interest income, rental income of persons, proprietors' income, and corporate profits earned from domestic production before taxes and depreciation, less net factor payments from abroad. The expenditure approach adds together consumption, investment, government, and net exports to measure spending on all domestically produced goods and services.

   e)   Calculation of NNP, national income, and private disposable income from GDP:
   1)   NNP = net national product = GNP + NFP - depreciation.
   2)   national income = NNP - indirect business taxes.
   3)   Given that GDP = Y, private disposable income = Y + NFP - T + TR + INT.

2.   **Consumption**

    a)   Definition: Consumption is the domestic household purchases of domestic and foreign new final goods and services during some specified time period.

    b)   Examples:
        1) Consumer durables: long-lived consumer goods, such as family automobiles, refrigerators, lawn mowers, home computer, household furniture.
        2) Nondurable goods: short-lived consumer goods, such as household purchases of food, clothing, fuel, cosmetics, prescription drugs.
        3) Services: consumer products that cannot be dropped on your foot, such as education services, medical services, legal services, accounting services, travel agency services, restaurant and hotel services.

    c)   Personal consumption expenditures currently represent approximately two-thirds of GDP for the United States.

    d)   Services represent approximately 57% (i.e., 39/69 x 100) of personal consumption expenditures for the United States, per Table 2.1.

    e)   Private saving = S_{pvt} = (Y + NFP - T + TR + INT) - C = private disposable income - consumption. For a given level of private disposable income, a reduction in consumption will increase the saving rate. Likewise, an increase in the private saving rate will reduce consumption for a given level of private disposable income.

3.   **Investment**

    a)   There are two major types of investment: fixed investment and inventory investment. Fixed investment is the purchase of capital goods for business fixed investment in equipment and structures, and for residential investment. In brief, fixed investment is the purchase of capital goods.

    b)   Examples:
        1) Business equipment includes tools and machines, such as harvesters for farms, printing presses for newspaper businesses, tractors for construction companies, cash registers for retail stores, office equipment, furniture, company-owned vehicles, and so on.
        2) Business structures include construction of plant facilities that house the businesses, such as factory buildings, warehouses, retail store buildings, and so on.

    c)   Construction of residential houses and apartments is treated as investment in capital because the dwellings provide a service over such a long period. The investment is done by the business that constructs the residential dwellings, rather than the individuals who buy them. A great deal of economic output is directly or indirectly dependent on the health of the residential construction industry.

    d)   In brief, households do not invest, they consume. Household spending such as university tuition payments to acquire human skills and training is consumption spending, even though such spending may increase the productivity of labor and promote technological progress. Attempts to include part of these expenditures as investment spending would confront severe measurement problems.

e)   The income-expenditure identity states that $Y = C + I + G + NX$. This equation suggests that all the goods and services produced are sold. If all the goods and services produced are not sold in the recorded time period, inventory investment increases by the amount of the unsold goods to satisfy the identity condition. From an accounting viewpoint the unsold goods are recorded as being sold to the firms that produced them.

4.   **Government output, purchases, and outlays**

a)   In national income accounting the cost of producing government output is the recorded market value of that output.

b)   No. Government purchases currently represent approximately 20% of GDP for the United States, but government outlays exceed purchases by the value of transfers and interest payments on government debt.

c)   No. Combined state government and local government purchases exceed federal government purchases. State and local government purchases represented 58% (i.e., 11/19 x 100) of total government purchases for 1992, per Table 2.1.

d)   The income of the government is its tax revenue. If it spends more than its tax revenue, it must borrow the income needed to finance the budget deficit from the private sector and foreign sector. Taxes and borrowings finance government spending.

e)   The government has a budget surplus when its tax revenue (T) exceed its outlays (G + TR + INT). Starting from a balanced budget, it could achieve a budget surplus by increasing taxes and reducing outlays.

5.   **Net exports**

a)   No. Goods produced abroad, including goods produced with U.S.-owned factors of production are not part of the GDP of the United States. If the increase in output of foreign goods by U.S.-owned capital and labor resulted from the migration of these resources from the United States, total production in the United States would decline, causing GDP to decline. The expenditure approach to calculating GDP shows that an increase in United States imports would reduce GDP by reducing the net exports.

b)   Yes. GDP = GNP - NFP, so GDP would increase if a decline in NFP exceeded the decline in GNP.

c)   Net exports = exports - imports. Exports are added to the expenditure calculation of GDP because they represent foreign spending on goods and services produced in the domestic economy. Imports are subtracted because they were included in the figures for consumption, investment, and government purchases.

d)   NX + NFP = CA.

e)   No. Table 2.1 shows, for example, that net exports for the United States in 1992 represented less than 1% of GDP, but 10.7% of United States' outputs were exported and 11.2% of foreign outputs were imported. Even if 50% were exported and 51% were imported, the net figure would still be 1%. Even 1% of a $6 trillion economy is $60 billion. Even if only 5% of U.S. goods were traded, a small reduction in that trade could significantly affect the health of the U. S. economy, if critical imports suddenly became unavailable to U. S. businesses (e.g., certain capital goods).

6.   **Saving and wealth**

a)   How to increase saving:
1) Private saving could be increased by increasing private disposable income for a given saving rate or by reducing consumption for a given level of private disposable income.
2) Government saving could be increased by increasing taxes for a given amount of government outlays or by reducing outlays for a given level of taxes.
3) National saving could be increased by increasing private saving or government saving.

b)   The following equation is the "uses-of-saving identity": $S_{pvt} = I + (-S_{govt}) + CA$

c)   An increase in the government budget deficit is an increase in the value of $(G + TR + INT - T)$, which causes investment to decline by the amount of the increase in the budget deficit, to maintain the equality of private saving and its uses.

d)   Yes. National saving finances increases in domestic physical assets (I) and increases in net foreign assets (CA); saving creates wealth in the sense of financing it. For example, saving could finance the purchase of business computers; this increase in capital would be an increase in wealth.

e)   The data presented in Fig. 2.2 in the textbook shows that the United States has a low national saving rate compared to the other major OECD countries, and that the U.S. saving rate declined during the 1980s. Over the entire period, we observe a decline in the national saving rate for OECD countries.

7.   **Price indexes, inflation, and real variables**

a)   All macroeconomic variables have both real and nominal values. GDP, C, and I provide three examples of real variables calculated from data on their nominal values.

b)   Price indexes measure the current average price of goods and services compared to the average price in some base year. A fixed-weight index measures the prices of a fixed set of goods and services produced in the base year; a variable-weight index measures the prices of a current set of goods and services.

c)   If the CPI = 3.50, there has been 250% inflation since the base year. On average, goods that cost $1.00 in the base year now cost $3.50, which is $2.50 more than in the base year.

d)   If the CPI increased from 3.50 to 3.75 in the next year, the inflation rate for that year would be $[(3.75 - 3.50)/3.50] = .07 = 7\%$.

e)   Inflation decreases the purchasing power of each dollar borrowed. Lenders have to charge an inflation premium equal to the inflation rate during the loan period to have the loan value returned by the borrower. However, lenders and borrowers may not know with certainty the inflation rate at the time the loan is made, so the loan is based on the expected rate of inflation. The nominal interest rate equals the expected real interest rate plus the expected rate of inflation.

Answers to Mathematical Problem-Solving Questions

1. **National output**: In the expenditure approach, national output is $Y = C + I + G + NX$, which totals $7000 billion. The income approach is calculated by adding all the payments received by domestic resources suppliers, then subtracting the $70 billion of net factor payments from abroad, which also totals $7000 billion.

2. **Saving, private saving, and government saving**: The values of these variables can be calculated by plugging the appropriate data values into the following equations.

    $S_{pvt} = (Y + NFP - T + TR + INT) - C = \$1260$ billion.

    $S_{govt} = (T - TR - INT) - G = -\$210$ billion.

    $S = S_{pvt} + S_{govt} = Y + NFP - C - G = \$1050$.

3. **Inflation, real GDP, and the real interest rate**: Real GDP = (nominal GDP/GDP deflator) = ($7350 billion/1.05) = $7000 billion. The real interest rate = the nominal interest rate - the inflation rate = 8% - 5% = 3%.

4. **Real rate of return**: The total real return after three years is a loss of $95,000, which is a 19% loss. Explanation: The real return for a year is the amount of the real savings at the beginning of the year multiplied by (the nominal interest rate minus the inflation rate). The 5% inflation just offset the 5% interest rate of return in the first year, so you still have $500,000 after one year. The 15% inflation exceeded the 5% nominal interest rate by 10%, so you experienced a 10% loss in each of the second and third years. $500,000 x .90 = $450,000 balance after two years. $450,000 x .90 = $405,000 balance after three years. $500,000 - $405,000 = $95,000 loss over the three-year period. [($405,000 - $500,000)/$500,000] = -.19 or -19% rate of return.

CHAPTER 3: PRODUCTIVITY, OUTPUT, AND EMPLOYMENT

A Fill-In-The-Blanks Review of Chapter Highlights: Use the following key terms to fill in the blanks. Each key term is used only once.

aggregate demand for labor
cyclical unemployment
duration
frictional unemployment
labor force
marginal product of labor
Okun's law
productivity
supply shock

aggregate supply of labor
diminishing marginal productivity
employment ratio
full-employment level of employment
leisure
marginal revenue product of labor
participation rate
real wage
unemployment rate

chronically unemployed
discouraged workers
factors of production
full-employment output
marginal product of capital
natural rate of unemployment
production function
structural unemployment
unemployment spell

In the classical model of the labor market, labor demand and labor supply jointly determine the equilibrium level of employment. The labor demand curve is also the marginal product of labor curve. A 1. _Productivity_ shock or a change in the capital stock will shift the labor demand curve. The labor supply curve identifies the number of units of labor supplied at each possible real wage. A change in labor's preference for work, relative to leisure, or a change in the size of the labor force will shift the labor supply curve. At the equilibrium 2. _Real Wage_, the amount of labor supplied equals the amount of labor demanded.

Given full employment, the 3. _Production Function_ determines the equilibrium level of output, called 4. _Full-Employment Output_. The production function specifies how changes in the 5. _factors of Production_ create changes in the level of output. Adding labor to a given amount of capital (or adding capital to a given amount of labor) causes output to increase at a declining rate. The production functions let us calculate the 6. _Marginal Product of Labor_ and the 7. _Marginal Product of Capital_ at various levels of factor employment. The marginal product of labor is the increase in output produced by adding one unit of labor (e.g., one worker) to production, holding capital constant. The marginal product of capital is the increase in output produced by adding one unit of capital to production, holding labor constant. The tendency for the marginal product of a factor to fall as more of that factor is added to production is called 8. _Diminishing Marginal Productivity_

A productivity shock is also known as a 9. _Supply Shock_. An adverse productivity shock will shift the production function down to a lower level of output at each possible level of employment and capital stock. A beneficial productivity shock will shift the production function up to a higher level of output at each possible level of employment and capital stock.

The 10. _Aggregate Demand for Labor_ is the number of workers (N) that all firms and governments in the national economy are willing to employ at various real wage rates (w = W/P) in some time period. In real terms each purely competitive firm will demand the number of workers needed to equate the real wage and the marginal product of labor. In nominal terms each firm will demand the number of workers needed to equate the nominal wage and the 11. _Marginal Revenue Product of Labor_ which is the revenue produced by the last worker hired. The aggregate labor demand curve is negatively sloped so that more labor is demanded at a lower real wage.

The 12. <u>Aggregate Supply of Labor</u> is the number of workers who are willing to work at various real wage rates in some time period. At each possible real wage, individuals will supply the amount of labor that maximizes their utility from income and leisure. 13. <u>Leisure</u> is the time not allocated to working in the market economy. The aggregate supply of labor curve is positively sloped so that more labor is supplied at a higher real wage.

Economists have several measures of employment and unemployment. The 14. <u>labor force</u> is the number of adults in the national economy who are working or actively looking for work in the market economy. The 15. <u>Unemployment Rate</u> is the percentage of people in the labor force who are unable to secure employment. The 16. <u>Participation Rate</u> is the percentage of the adult population that is in the labor force. The 17. <u>Employment Ratio</u> is the percentage of the adult population that is working. 18. <u>Discouraged Workers</u> have stopped participating in the labor force because they have lost hope of finding a job; if job opportunities increased for them, they would enter the labor force. Discouraged workers are not counted as unemployed because they are not part of the labor force. However, the existence of discouraged workers causes the unemployment rate to understate the percentage of adults who would be willing to work if market opportunities for employment were better.

Continuous unemployment for an individual over some time period is called an 19. <u>Unemployment Spell</u>. The 20. <u>duration</u> of an unemployment spell is its length in weeks or months. Frictional unemployment has a short duration for most people, because it is the unemployment of readily employable people who are temporarily unemployed upon entering the labor force or after quitting one job to search for another. Some people, however, are 21. <u>Chronically Unemployed</u>, which means that they tend to suffer long or frequent spells of unemployment. 22. <u>Structural Unemployment</u> has a long duration for most people. Structurally unemployed people tend to be chronically unemployed because they lack the job skills, education, or personal attributes demanded by employers. Structural changes in the economy, such as those created by technological progress and by changes in competition, create structural unemployment.

Even at the 23. <u>full-Employment level of Employment</u>, the unemployment rate is not zero, because some 24. <u>frictional Unemployment</u> and structural unemployment always exist.

The 25. <u>Natural Rate of Unemployment</u> is the rate of unemployment when the economy is at full employment, after complete wage and price adjustment. Any policy attempt to reduce unemployment below the natural rate of unemployment will cause the price level to rise and inflation to rise. The natural rate of unemployment is some positive percentage rate (e.g., 6%) because there is some frictional unemployment and structural unemployment at the full-employment level of output, but there is no 26. <u>Cyclical Unemployment</u> at the natural rate of unemployment. At the natural rate of unemployment, there is no need for countercyclical stabilization policies, because there is no cyclical unemployment.

27. <u>Okun's Law</u> specifies the relationship between cyclical unemployment and output. According to the levels form of Okun's law, each 1% decline in unemployment below the natural rate causes output to rise by 2.5% above the full-employment level of output. According to the growth rate form of Okun's law, each 1% increase in cyclical unemployment causes the growth rate of output to fall by 2.5% below the growth rate of full-employment output. If the growth rate of full-employment output is 3%, for example, then a two percentage point increase in cyclical unemployment would cause the growth rate of output to be -2%.

True-False Questions: Circle T for true statements and circle F for false statements.

T   (F)   1.   A decline in the size of the working-age population and an increase in the participation rate will reduce the aggregate labor supply.

(T)   F   2.   Because of diminishing marginal productivity, the aggregate labor demand curve is negatively sloped.

T   (F)   3.   A beneficial productivity shock will cause the production function to shift down, except at the origin, so that output will decline for any given level of labor employment.

(T)   F   4.   An increase in the aggregate demand for labor will cause both the full-employment level of output and the real wage to increase.

T   (F)   5.   An increase in the aggregate supply of labor will cause both the real wage and full-employment output to fall.

(T)   F   6.   Workers whose labor productivity is relatively high typically receive a relatively high real wage.

(T)   F   7.   Dramatic increases in oil prices in the 1970s caused employment, the real wage, and output to fall.

T   (F)   8.   The unemployment rate is the percentage of the labor force that is collecting unemployment compensation.

T   (F)   9.   Workers experiencing cyclical unemployment typically have the longest duration of unemployment spells.

(T)   F   10.   According to Okun's law, if the unemployment rate is 3% higher than the natural rate of unemployment, output will be 7.5% lower than full-employment output.

Multiple Choice Questions: Circle the letter corresponding to the correct answer to each question.

1.   The factors of production include
       a.   capital, labor, energy, and materials.
       b.   households, firms, and government.
       c.   supply factors and demand factors.
       d.   wages, interest, rents, and profits.
       e.   human capital, real capital, and financial capital.

2.   The production function shows the effect on
       a.   labor employment when output is increased.
       b.   labor employment when capital is increased.
       c.   goods production when production of services declines.
       d.   consumer goods when production of intermediate goods is increased.
       e.   output when labor is increased.

3.   An increase in the productivity of capital will always
      a.   increase the unemployment rate.
      (b.) increase the full-employment level of output.
      c.   lower the rate of return to capital.
      d.   shift the production function down to the right.
      e.   move us up along a given production function to a lower level of output.

4.   Because of diminishing marginal productivity
      a.   the labor supply curve is not vertical.
      b.   nominal wages are sticky in a downward direction.
      (c) the labor demand curve is negatively sloped.
      d.   households save only a small share of their income.
      e.   the average productivity of labor is always below the marginal productivity of labor.

5.   The marginal product of labor
      a.   exceeds the average product of labor at high levels of employment.
      b.   decreases as more capital is added to the production process.
      c.   depends on the product price.
      (d) declines as more labor is added to the production process.
      e.   equals the output produced per unit of labor employed.

6.   The real wage
      (a.) is the nominal wage divided by the price level.
      b.   automatically increases with the cost of living.
      c.   is determined by labor-management negotiations within each firm in an industry when labor markets are
           purely competitive.
      d.   is set by explicit contract in the classical model.
      e.   is the nominal wage multiplied by the price level.

7.   In the production function equation, an increase in the productivity of labor is represented by
      a.   a decrease in F.
      (b) an increase in N.
      c.   an increase in K.
      d.   an increase in A.
      e.   a reduction in K.

8.   The symbol N is fixed in the full-employment output equation. N represents
      a.   only labor supply.
      b.   labor supplied = labor demanded.
      c.   only labor demand.
      (d) only output supplied.
      e.   output supplied = output demanded.

9.   In the production function diagram, a beneficial supply shock is shown by
      (a.) an upward shift in the production function, except at the origin.
      b.   a movement up along the production function.
      c.   a downward shift in the production function, except at the origin.
      d.   an increase in the convexity of the curve.
      e.   a movement down along the production function.

10. Which of the following does not illustrate leisure?
    a. repairing your home
    b. a night out for dinner and dancing
    c. studying for an upcoming economics exam
    d. enjoying a productive day at the office
    e. figuring out how to pay your household bills on your limited income

11. The labor force participation rate is the percentage of the
    a. population that is employed.
    b. population that is willing to work but unable to find jobs.
    c. adult population that is unemployed.
    d. adult population that is working or actively looking for work.
    e. adult population that is employed.

12. Discouraged workers are discouraged because
    a. their employers continue to underpay them.
    b. they are working part-time, but they want full-time work.
    c. they don't have jobs and are pessimistic about their chances of finding a suitable job.
    d. their employers are too demanding.
    e. their bosses won't listen to their ideas about how to cut costs and improve product quality.

13. In the United States the duration of most unemployment spells is
    a. less than two weeks.
    b. about two months or less.
    c. approximately one year.
    d. two or three years.
    e. four or more years.

14. The type of unemployment for which the net economic costs are most likely to be small is
    a. structural unemployment.
    b. frictional unemployment.
    c. seasonal unemployment.
    d. cyclical unemployment.
    e. chronic unemployment.

15. Most of the chronically unemployed workers in the U.S. economy are unemployed because
    a. they are too old or too young to work.
    b. they are too sick or too disabled to work.
    c. they do not want to work; they would rather live on welfare.
    d. of frictional unemployment.
    e. they do not have the job skills and personal attributes their employers demand of labor.

16. The kind of unemployment created by technological progress and by changes in competition is called
    a. progressive unemployment.
    b. competitive unemployment.
    c. frictional unemployment.
    d. structural unemployment.
    e. capitalist unemployment.

17.   In a labor market diagram
   a. labor demand is a positively sloped curve.
   b. labor supply is a negatively sloped curve.
   c. the quantity of labor demanded equals the quantity of labor supplied at the equilibrium real wage.
   d. a change in labor supply creates a change in labor demand.
   e. a temporary adverse productivity shock causes the labor supply curve to shift to the left.

18.   Over the 1955 - 1990 period in the United States the natural rate of unemployment
   a. declined dramatically.
   b. declined gradually.
   c. increased gradually until the early 1970s, then declined gradually.
   d. increased dramatically.
   e. increased gradually.

19.   Cyclical unemployment is caused by
   a. people entering the labor force to search for jobs.
   b. technological progress, which causes some industries to expand employment and others to reduce employment.
   c. reducing international trade barriers, which causes some industries to expand employment and others to reduce employment.
   d. the deindustrialization of America.
   e. business cycle fluctuations.

20.   Assuming that the natural rate of unemployment is 6%, that the full-employment growth rate is 3%, and that the actual unemployment rate is 8%, Okun's law predicts that the actual output growth rate is
   a.   3%.
   b.   -3%.
   c.   0%.
   d.   -2%.
   e.   2%.

Short-Answer Essay Questions

1.   **Labor demand**: a) Draw an aggregate labor demand curve. Label the axes and curve. b) Identify and briefly explain the slope of the curve. c) Identify two shift variables for the labor demand curve and state whether labor demand is positively related or negatively related to each of these variables. d) Can the quantity of labor demanded change without a change in labor demand? Briefly explain. e) State the employment rule that an individual firm uses to determine how much labor to employ, and use the rule to show when a firm is employing too much labor.

2.   **Labor supply**: a) Draw an aggregate labor supply curve. Label the axes and curve. b) Identify and briefly explain the slope of the curve. c) Identify four shift variables and state whether labor supply is positively related or negatively related to each of these variables.   d) State the decision rule that an individual worker uses to determine how much labor to supply, and use the rule to show when an individual is supplying too much labor.

3.   **Aggregate labor demand and supply**: a) Briefly explain how to use labor demand curves for individual firms and labor supply curves for individual workers to develop aggregate labor demand and supply curves. b) Draw a labor market diagram. Label the axes, curves, and equilibrium values. c) Draw a corresponding aggregate production function diagram. Label the axes, curves, and equilibrium values. d) Use the diagrams to show the real effects of a temporary beneficial supply shock. e) Would an increase in the capital stock create an increase in the level of employment? Briefly explain.

4.   **Unemployment**: a) Briefly describe the method by which the Bureau of Labor Statistics determines the unemployment rate. b) Identify two types of unemployment and briefly explain the cause of each type. c) Are job skills a determinant of unemployment? Briefly explain. d) Does the duration of a typical unemployment spell depend on the type of unemployment? Briefly explain. e) Identify two government policies or programs that attempt to reduce unemployment.

5.   **Okun's Law and the natural rate of unemployment**: a) State the growth rate form of Okun's Law and define the variables. b) Briefly explain Okun's Law in terms of changes in labor market conditions during a recession. c) Assuming that the growth rate of full-employment output is 3%, the natural rate of unemployment is 6%, and the unemployment rate is 5%, use Okun's Law to calculate the growth rate of output. d) Why is the natural rate of unemployment not equal to zero?

Mathematical Problem-Solving Questions

1.   **Production function**: Using $(Y = AK^{0.5}N^{0.5})$ as the production function for the national economy, calculate total factor productivity (A), where: a) $Y = \$4878$ billion, $K = \$4773$ billion, $N = 117.9$ million workers; b) $Y = \$4821$ billion, $K = \$4824$ billion, $N = 116.9$ million workers.

2.   **Okun's Law**: For an economy that operated last year at the natural rate of unemployment of 6%, with full-employment output of $7000 billion, and where full-employment output growth rate is 3%, use Okun's Law to calculate the level of national output and the economic growth rate when the unemployment rate is: a) 11%; b) 4%.

Answers to Fill-In-The-Blanks Questions

1.	productivity	2.	real wage
3.	production function	4.	full-employment output
5.	factors of production	6.	marginal product of labor
7.	marginal product of capital	8.	diminishing marginal productivity
9.	supply shock	10.	aggregate demand for labor
11.	marginal revenue product of labor	12.	aggregate supply of labor
13.	leisure	14.	labor force
15.	unemployment rate	16.	participation rate
17.	employment ratio	18.	discouraged workers
19.	unemployment spell	20.	duration
21.	chronically unemployed	22.	structural unemployment
23.	full-employment level of employment	24.	frictional unemployment
25.	natural rate of unemployment	26.	cyclical unemployment
27.	Okun's Law		

Answers to True-False Questions

1. F   A decline in the size of the working-age population will reduce labor supply, but an increase in the participation rate will increase labor supply. The net effect on the aggregate supply curve depends on the sizes of the changes in these variables and the relative importance of these changes in determining the position of the aggregate supply curve.

2. T   The aggregate labor demand curve is the marginal productivity of labor schedule for various possible levels of labor employment. As more labor is added to production, the marginal product of labor declines. The negative slope of the aggregate demand curve depicts this negative relationship between the marginal productivity of labor and the level of employment. At any given level of employment, firms in the economy are willing to pay labor a real wage equal to the marginal productivity of labor. Along a given marginal productivity schedule (i.e., labor demand schedule), they will be willing to employ more labor only when the real wage falls enough to match the decline in the marginal productivity of labor that accompanies increased employment.

3. F   A beneficial productivity shock will increase the marginal productivity of labor at every possible level of employment, thereby causing the production function to shift up, not down.

4. T   The equilibrium real wage and the full-employment level of output is determined by the aggregate demand for labor and the aggregate supply of labor. An increase in the aggregate demand for labor will shift the labor demand curve to the right along a fixed labor supply curve, causing both the real wage and full-employment output to increase.

5. F   An increase in the aggregate supply of labor will shift the labor supply curve to the right along a fixed labor demand curve, causing the real wage to fall enough to restore equilibrium at a higher level of full-employment output.

6. T   In an efficient market economy, firms are constrained by competitive market forces to pay labor the value of its marginal product, so workers whose productivity is relatively high earn a relatively high real wage. We can think of the real wage in a macroeconomic model as the aggregate weighted average of the various real wages paid to all the different kinds of labor employed in a country.

7. T   The OPEC oil price increases of the 1970s created an adverse supply shock in the U.S. economy, which caused the production function to shift down and the labor demand curve to shift to the left. The decline in labor demand caused the real wage to fall and employment to fall. The decline in employment moved the economy down the new, lower production function to a lower level of national output.

8. F   The unemployment rate is calculated by the Bureau of Labor Statistics of the U.S. Department of labor from the data they gather in a nationwide survey of 60,000 households. Many workers who are unemployed according to the economic definition of unemployment used by the BLS may not apply for unemployment compensation or may not be eligible to receive it; therefore, the unemployment rate will usually exceed the percentage of the labor force collecting unemployment compensation.

9. F   Of the various types of unemployment, structural unemployment is the type that usually creates unemployment spells of the longest duration. Unlike structurally unemployed workers, cyclically unemployed are readily employable in a healthy economy. Most recessions are not severe enough and persistent enough to keep the typical cyclically unemployed worker unemployed for as long as the typical structurally unemployed worker.

10. T   According to Okun's Law each percentage point increase in unemployment above the natural rate of unemployment will reduce the level of national output by 2.5% below full-employment output. Since the natural rate of unemployment includes both structural unemployment and frictional unemployment, any increase in the unemployment rate is an increase in cyclical unemployment. Output falls below the full-employment level of output by 7.5% (i.e., 3 x 2.5%) when unemployment exceeds the natural rate of unemployment by 3%.

Answers to Multiple Choice Questions

1. a	7. d	13. b	19. e
2. e	8. b	14. b	20. d
3. b	9. a	15. e	
4. c	10. d	16. d	
5. d	11. d	17. c	
6. a	12 c	18. e	

Answers to Short-Answer Essay Questions

1.   **Labor demand**

    a)   An aggregate labor demand curve diagram.

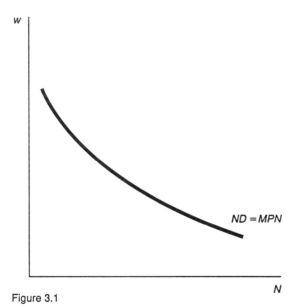

Figure 3.1

       w = W/P = real wage per unit of labor time (e.g., per hour per worker)
       N = units of labor time (e.g., number of workers)

b)   The labor demand curve has a negative slope, which means that at a lower real wage, more labor will be demanded. The labor demand curve is the same as the marginal product of labor (MPN) schedule. MPN declines as N increases, because of diminishing marginal returns to labor. At each possible real wage, firms are willing to employ the amount of labor needed to equate the real wage and the marginal product of labor (w = MPN). Because adding labor reduces MPN, firms will add labor only at a lower real wage for each worker employed.

c)   Two shift variables for labor demand are productivity (A) and capital stock (K).

   1)   Labor demand is positively related to productivity. A beneficial productivity shock will increase labor demand, shifting the curve to the right. An adverse productivity shock will decrease labor demand, shifting the curve to the left.

   2)   Labor demand is positively related to capital stock. Adding capital to production will increase the demand for labor, shifting the labor demand curve to the right. A decline in the level of capital stock employed will decrease labor demand, shifting the labor demand curve to the left. Capital principally complements labor in production, but an increase in capital may reduce the labor/capital ratio (N/K), since capital is, to some extent, a substitute for labor in production.

d)   Yes. Moving along a given labor demand curve to another real wage changes the quantity of labor demanded without changing labor demand. Labor demand is the entire set of (N, w) points, depicting various quantities of labor demanded at each possible real wage.

e)   Industry supply and demand for each type of labor will determine the real wage that each competitive firm will pay for a given type of labor. Each firm in the industry can buy as much labor as it wants to buy at the industry-determined market wage; the market real wage is given to the firm. At the market real wage, the firm will maximize profits by hiring enough labor to minimize the amount by which the marginal product of labor exceeds the real wage - minimize (MPN > w). When MPN = w, the last worker hired earns the value that he or she contributes to production. This profit-maximizing employment rule shows that the firm is employing too much labor when MPN < w.

2.   **Labor supply**

a)   An aggregate labor supply curve diagram.

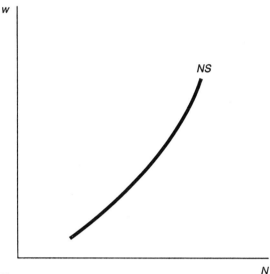

Figure 3.2

w = W/P = real wage per unit of labor time (e.g., per hour per worker)
N = quantity of labor supplied (e.g., number of workers)

b)   The labor supply curve is positively sloped, indicating that more labor time will be supplied at a higher real wage. The change in the real wage along a given labor supply curve is a change in the current real wage, holding the expected future real wage constant (i.e., a temporary change in the real wage). A permanent change in the real wage is a change in the current real wage and a change in the expected future real wage. Along a given labor supply curve, a temporary increase in the real wage increases the reward to working, which causes workers to increase the amount of labor time they are willing to work; as the real wage increases, workers substitute away from leisure and toward work.

c)   Shift variables for labor supply include wealth, expected future real wage, working-age population, and participation rate.:

1) Labor supply is negatively related to wealth. An increase in workers' wealth will reduce labor supply, shifting the labor supply curve to the left.

2) Labor supply is negatively related to workers' expected future real wage. An increase in the expected future real wage will reduce labor supply, shifting the labor supply curve to the left.

3) Labor supply is positively related to the working-age population. An increase in the number of working-age people in the economy will increase labor supply, shifting the labor supply curve to the right.

4) Labor supply is positively related to the participation rate. An increase in the participation rate will increase labor supply, shifting the labor supply curve to the right.

d)   Each worker attempts to maximize his or her utility from labor income and leisure by working the number of hours needed to equate the marginal utility of income to the marginal disutility of working. The marginal utility of income is the expected benefit of the last hour worked. The marginal disutility of working is the expected cost, in terms of foregone happiness, of the last hour of leisure traded for work.

3.   **Aggregate labor demand and supply**

a)   If the labor demand curves by all individual firms and government are summed horizontally, the resulting curve is the aggregate labor demand curve. Horizontal summation requires that the amounts of labor demanded at each possible real wage are added together. If the labor supply curves of all individual workers are summed horizontally, the resulting curve is the aggregate labor supply curve.

b)   An aggregate labor demand-labor supply diagram.

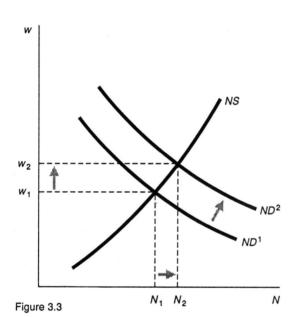

Figure 3.3

Equilibrium = (N_1, w_1) $ND^2 > ND^1$

c)   An aggregate production function diagram.

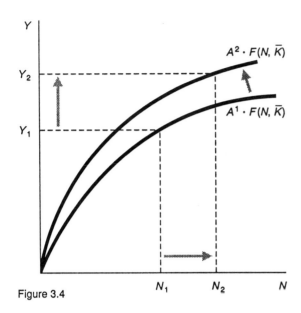

Figure 3.4

N – labor employed   Y = aggregate output
Equilibrium = (N_1, Y_1) $A^2 > A^1$

d)   A temporary beneficial supply (i.e., productivity) shock causes the slope of the production function (MPN) to increase at every level of employment. Since the labor demand curve is the schedule of MPN values, the labor demand curve also shifts upward. In the diagrams, A_1 increases to A_2 and ND^1 increases to ND^2.

e)   Yes. Assuming that the additional capital stock does not simply substitute for labor, the expected effects are similar to a beneficial supply shock. An increase in K increases the slope of the production function at every level of N and causes ND to shift to the right along a given labor supply curve. The equilibrium level of employment (N) increases.

4.   **Unemployment**

a)   The Bureau of Labor Statistics (BLS) undertakes a survey of about 60,000 households each month to estimate the unemployment rate. The BLS categorizes people into three categories: employed, unemployed, and not in the labor force. The employed have jobs. The unemployed are actively looking for work and would accept a position at the market wage if they could find one. About half the population of the United States is "not in the labor force"; these people are neither working nor unemployed. Among the people who are "not in the labor force" are those who are too young to work, too old to work, or too sick to work; some are students, some are homemakers, some are rich and prefer not to work.

b) Two types of unemployment are structural unemployment and frictional unemployment.

1) Structural unemployment is caused by changes in market structures creating a mismatch in the job skills of unemployed workers and those skills required by firms looking for workers to fill vacancies. Examples of structural changes that create structural unemployment include technological advances and changes in foreign competition. Structurally unemployed labor must often relocate or acquire further education or technical training to gain employment.

2) Frictional unemployment is created by people entering the labor force to search for a job and by people quitting one job to search for a better one. Unemployment spells for the frictionally unemployed are usually of short duration, since these people have the job skills and personal attributes needed to fill available vacancies.

c) Yes. Workers who don't have the job skills that employers demand may be structurally unemployed. Workers with low-level job skills are more likely to be unemployed than workers with higher-level job skills.

d) Yes. The duration of a typical unemployment spell for frictional unemployment is relatively short; the duration of a typical unemployment spell for structural unemployment is relatively long.

e) Education policies and worker retraining policies attempt to reduce structural unemployment. Fiscal stabilization policies and monetary stabilization policies attempt to reduce cyclical unemployment.

5. **Okun's Law and the natural rate of unemployment**

a) Okun's Law is $\frac{\Delta Y}{Y} = \frac{\Delta \overline{Y}}{\overline{Y}} - 2.5U$, where

$\frac{\Delta Y}{Y}$ = growth rate of output, $\frac{\Delta \overline{Y}}{\overline{Y}}$ = growth rate of full-employment output, and

ΔU = the change in the unemployment rate.

b) An explanation of Okun's Law: Since 100% of employed labor produces 100% of output, we might expect that a 1% increase in cyclical employment would lower output by only 1%. In a recession, however, an increase in cyclical unemployment is highly correlated with a decline in the size of the labor force, a decline in the average number of hours worked per week by workers, and a decline in labor productivity. The 2.5% decline in the growth rate of output for each 1% increase in unemployment is the combined effect of all these changes.

c) Per Okun's law, the calculated growth rate of output is 5.5%.

5.5% = 3.0% - 2.5 x (5% - 6%) = 3.0% + 2.5%

d) The natural rate of unemployment exceeds zero because there is always some frictional and structural unemployment at the full-employment level of output.

Answers to Mathematical Problem-Solving Questions

1. **Production function:** Given that $(Y = AK^{0.5}N^{0.5})$, then $[A = Y/(K^{0.5}N^{0.5})]$, where $K^{0.5}$ is the square root of K, and $N^{0.5}$ is the square root of N.   Total factor productivity $= A$

    a) $A = 6.50 = 4878/[(4773)^{0.5}(117.9)^{0.5}] = 4878/[(69.09)(10.86)] = 4878/750.32$

    b) $A = 6.42 = 4821/[(4824)^{0.5}(116.9)^{0.5}] = 4821/[69.46)(10.81)] = 4821/750.86$

2. **Okun's Law:**   The output level form of Okun's Law tells us that national output = full-employment output - 2.5 x (the difference between the unemployment rate and the natural rate of unemployment) x full-employment output. The growth rate form of Okun's Law tells us that the output growth rate = the full-employment growth rate - 2.5 x (the change in the unemployment rate above or below the natural rate of unemployment). By plugging in the given values into these equations, we can calculate the national output level and economic growth rate as follows:

    a) $Y = \$7000$ billion - 2.5 x (11% - 6%)($7,000 billion).
             $- \$7000$ billion - .125($7000 billion) = $6125 billion.

         Economic growth rate = 3% - 2.5 x (11% - 6%) ▪ 3% - 12.5% – - 9.5%.

    b) $Y = \$7000$ billion - 2.5 x (4% - 6%)($7000 billion).
             $= \$7000$ billion + .05($7000) = $7350 billion.

         Economic growth rate = 3% - 2.5 x (4% - 6%) = 3% + 5% = 8%.

CHAPTER 4: CONSUMPTION, SAVING, AND INVESTMENT

A Fill-In-The-Blanks Review of Chapter Highlights: Use the following key terms to fill in the blanks. Each key term is used only once.

desired capital stock
gross investment
net investment
user cost of capital

effective tax rate
Keynesian consumption function
Ricardian equivalence proposition

expected after-tax real interest rate
marginal propensity to consume
tax-adjusted user cost of capital

The macroeconomic model presented in this chapter assumes that output is at its full-employment level and that the economy is closed. In assuming full employment, we are ignoring for now the possibility that the economy can be away from its full-employment level in the short run.

In a closed economy, the demand for goods is the total value of all consumption, investment, and government spending on the goods and services that make up national output. Households spend most of their after-tax income on consumer goods and services. Private saving is the part of private disposable income not spent on consumer products. National saving is the sum of private saving and government saving. The government saves by having a budget surplus and dissaves by having a budget deficit. National saving is the part of national income that is not spent in the current period by consumers and government.

The 1. _Keynesian Consumption Function_ focuses on national income (equivalently, output) as the principal determinant of aggregate consumption and saving. Consumption and saving are both positively related to income. The 2. _Expected, after tax real Interest Rate_ is the change in consumption spending created by a change in income. Since households save a portion of their income, MPC is some number greater than zero but less than one. The Keynesian consumption function allows for the possibility that income is not the only determinant of consumption, but the other determinants of consumption are not explicitly identified in the Keynesian consumption function equation. In the consumption equation, $C = c_o + c_y Y$; changes in the values of these other determinants of consumption would change C by changing c_o.

In addition to output, the principal determinants of consumption and saving are expected future output, wealth, the expected real interest rate, and two fiscal policy variables - government purchases and taxes. An increase in expected future income or wealth will increase desired consumption and reduce desired saving. Most economists agree that an increase in the 3. _Expected After-Tax real Interest Rate_ will reduce desired consumption and increase desired saving, although the reverse of this is possible in theory and the empirical evidence is mixed. The interest rate effect on consumption and saving is small. An increase in government purchases reduces desired consumption but also reduces desired national saving, since $S^d = Y - C^d - G$.

The 4. _Ricardian Equivalence Proposition_ contends that tax changes alone do not affect desired consumption, because people should realize that for given levels of government spending, a tax cut today will be balanced by higher taxes in the future. If desired consumption does not change, desired national saving does not change either. However, if people do not realize that a tax cut today means higher future taxes (so that Ricardian equivalence is wrong), then a tax cut today may cause people to consume more, leading to a decline in national saving.

Investment is the purchase of capital goods to add to firms' existing capital stocks. For each firm, the 5. _desired Capital stock_ is the amount of spending on capital goods that maximizes the firm's profits. Three principal determinants of desired capital stock are the user cost of capital, the effective tax rate, and the expected future marginal product of capital.

The 6. user cost of Capital ____ is the sum of the interest cost and the depreciation cost of the real capital investment. Desired capital stock is negatively related to the user cost of capital. An increase in the user cost will reduce the equilibrium level of desired capital stock.

To maximize profits, when firms' revenues are taxed, each firm will purchase just enough capital to equate the expected future marginal product of capital to the 7. tax-adjusted user cost of Capital on the last unit of capital purchased. Although several taxes exist that affect after-tax profits (e.g., corporate profits tax, depreciation schedules, and investment tax credits), the 8. Effective tax rate ____ is the revenue-tax equivalent of all these taxes.

9. Gross Investment ____ is the total purchases of new capital goods, including replacements of worn-out capital. 10. Net Investment ____ is gross investment minus depreciation, which equals the increase in capital stock. Net investment by a firm in some year is the increase in capital stock needed to achieve the desired capital stock - the level needed to maximize profits.

The goods market is in equilibrium when all the national output produced is purchased, so that income equals $Y = C^d + I^d + G$. Alternatively stated, the goods market is in equilibrium when $S^d = I^d$; since $S^d = Y - C^d - G$. In the saving-investment diagram, the saving curve shows that desired saving is positively related to the real interest rate, desired investment is negatively related to the real interest rate, and the real interest rate flexibly adjusts to maintain goods market equilibrium where desired saving = desired investment. Any change that increases desired national saving at a given real interest rate, such as a decrease in government purchases, will shift the saving curve to the right, thereby causing the real interest rate to fall and the equilibrium level of desired saving and desired investment to increase. Any change that increases desired investment at a given real interest rate, such as a decline in the effective tax rate, would cause the investment curve to shift to the right, thereby causing the real interest rate to rise and the equilibrium level of desired saving and desired investment to increase.

True-False Questions: Circle T for true statements and circle F for false statements.

T (F) 1. Small changes in the expected after-tax real interest rate create relatively large changes in the share of output purchased by consumers.

T (F) 2. A decline in output would reduce both MPC and consumption spending.

(T) F 3. The most important determinants of interest rate differences are risk, length of time for which the funds are borrowed, and tax status.

T (F) 4. A country with a high nominal interest rate will also have a high user cost of capital.

T (F) 5. The tax-adjusted user cost of capital increases with the level of capital stock.

T (F) 6. Desired capital stock will fall if the user cost of capital and MPK^f both fall.

(T) F 7. In 1990 the effective tax rate for the United States was substantially higher than in Japan, Germany, and France.

T F 8.   After the tax rate on investments in equipment declined in 1962, investment in equipment in the United States increased relative investments in structures.

T F 9.   When $S^d = C^d$, the goods market is in equilibrium.

T F 10.   A temporary reduction in government purchases will cause the equilibrium level of desired investment to increase.

Multiple Choice Questions: Circle the letter corresponding to the correct answer to each question.

1.   In a closed economy model
    a.   NX = 0.
    b.   NX < CA.
    c.   NFP > 0.
    d.   GNP > GDP.
    e.   exports < imports.

2.   In an economic model with output fixed at full-employment output, a decline in
    a.   desired consumption will increase both the real interest rate and output.
    b.   desired investment will increase both the real interest rate and output.
    c.   government spending will increase both the real interest rate and output.
    d.   desired saving will increase the real interest rate and output.
    e.   desired saving will increase the real interest without changing output.

3.   According to the Keynesian consumption function, a decline in current income will
    a.   reduce both consumption and the marginal propensity to consume.
    b.   reduce consumption while increasing the marginal propensity to consume.
    c.   reduce consumption without changing the marginal propensity to consume.
    d.   increase both consumption and the marginal propensity to consume.
    e.   not change consumption but will increase the marginal propensity to consume.

4.   At full-employment output, desired consumption spending will increase if
    a.   income falls.
    b.   wealth falls.
    c.   expected future income falls.
    d.   the expected real interest rate falls.
    e.   government purchases increase.

5.   Historically, national surveys of consumer confidence show that consumers' expectations
    a.   are very stable over the business cycle.
    b.   are very sensitive indicators of recessions and other macroeconomic shocks.
    c.   are unaffected by foreign shocks to the national economy.
    d.   are insensitive to important changes in labor market conditions.
    e.   do not affect their consumption and saving decisions.

6.   A small increase in the real interest rate will most likely
    a.   increase desired saving, but the effect will be relatively small.
    b.   increase desired saving substantially.
    c.   decrease desired saving substantially.
    d.   decrease desired saving, but the effect will be relatively small.
    e.   have no effect on desired saving.

7.   An increase in the personal income tax rate on interest income will
    a.   unambiguously increase desired saving.
    b.   unambiguously decrease desired saving.
    c.   decrease desired saving, if desired saving is positively related to the interest rate.
    d.   decrease desired saving, if desired saving is negatively related to the interest rate.
    e.   not affect the expected after-tax real interest rate.

8.   The expected real after-tax rate of return on saving is the after-tax nominal rate of return minus expected
    a.   future income.
    b.   future wealth.
    c.   future capital gains.
    d.   rate of interest.
    e.   rate of inflation.

9.   The desired level of capital stock will increase if the
    a.   user cost of capital increases.
    b.   expected future marginal product of capital increases.
    c.   effective tax rate increases.
    d.   price of capital increases.
    e.   investment tax credit decreases.

10.   An increase in the price of capital goods will
    a.   increase the expected future marginal product of capital.
    b.   reduce the expected future marginal product of capital.
    c.   increase the interest cost and the depreciation cost of capital.
    d.   increase the interest cost but not affect the depreciation cost of capital.
    e.   not affect the interest cost of capital.

11.   In calculating the tax-adjusted user cost of capital, the user cost of capital is
    a.   multiplied by the tax rate.
    b.   multiplied by (1 - tax rate).
    c.   divided by (1 - tax rate).
    d.   divided by the tax rate.
    e.   added to the tax rate.

12.   The effective tax rate
    a.   is another name for the corporate profits tax rate.
    b.   is the inflation-adjusted corporate profits tax rate.
    c.   is the risk-adjusted corporate profits tax rate.
    d.   increases with investment tax credits.
    e.   is the revenue-tax rate equivalent of the actual tax rates.

13.   The level of capital stock increases
        a. in every year.
        b. if gross investment exceeds depreciation.
        c. if net investment plus depreciation exceeds zero.
        d. if a majority of firms make investments.
        e. if gross investment exceeds net investment.

14.   The principal effect of an increased capital stock on the economy is to
        a. increase the unemployment rate.
        b. increase real national output and income.
        c. increase inflation.
        d. decrease consumption.
        e. increase the user cost of capital.

15.   If the expected marginal product of capital exceeds the tax-adjusted user cost of capital at some level of
        capital stock purchases, the profit-maximizing business will
        a. increase its investment spending on capital goods.
        b. reduce its investment spending on capital goods.
        c. not change its investment spending on capital goods.
        d. increase the tax-adjusted user cost of capital.
        e. reduce the expected marginal product of capital.

16.   According to the Ricardian equivalence proposition, a temporary government budget deficit created by
        cutting taxes
        a. will cause desired consumption to increase.
        b. will cause future taxes to increase but will have no real economic effects.
        c. will have the same real economic effects as a budget deficit created by raising government spending.
        d. would have the same real effects whether or not consumers expect future taxes to change.
        e. will cause desired national saving to increase.

17.   In the goods market equilibrium equation for a closed economy, the total demand for goods equals
        a. $C^d + I^d$.   d. $C + I + G^d$.
        b. $C^d + I^d + G$.   e. $C + I + T$.
        c. $C + I + G$.

18.   One way of writing the goods market equilibrium equation for a closed economy is
        a. $Y + C + G = S$.
        b. $Y + C^d + G^d = S$.
        c. $Y - C^d - G = S^d = I^d$.
        d. $Y - C^d - G - S^d = I^d$.
        e. $Y - C^d + S^d = I^d$.

19.   In the saving-investment diagram, an increase in national income would
        a. shift both the saving and investment demand curves to the right.
        b. shift the saving curve to the left.
        c. shift the investment demand curve to the right.
        d. not shift the curves.
        e. shift the saving curve to the right.

20.   A reduction in government spending will shift the
    a.   investment curve to the left, thereby reducing the real interest rate.
    b.   investment curve to the left, thereby increasing the real interest rate.
    c.   saving curve to the right, thereby reducing the real interest rate.
    d.   saving curve to the right, thereby increasing the real interest rate.
    e.   saving curve to the left, thereby increasing the real interest rate.

Short-Answer Essay Questions

1.   **Consumption and saving**: a) State the Keynesian consumption function. b) Define MPC and explain why its value is always less than one. c) At a given output level, how are desired saving and desired consumption related? Briefly explain. d) How do the determinants of desired consumption show that consumers take the future into consideration when deciding how much to consume? e) What role do expectations have in determining desired consumption and saving? Briefly explain.

2.   **Tax incentives for saving**: a) Identify two types of taxes on interest earnings. b) Does an increase in the tax rate on interest earnings reduce desired saving? Briefly explain. c) According to most empirical research studies, how strong is the overall effect of a change in the expected real interest rate on desired saving? d) State the expected real after-tax rate of return equation. e) How would the expected real after-tax rate of return be affected by each of the following events? 1) taxes increase; and 2) expected inflation declines.

3.   **The real interest rate, the user cost of capital, and the investment decision**: a) Draw an MPK^f curve and user cost of capital curve. Label the axes, curves, and equilibrium values. b) Briefly explain why MPK^f curve has a negative slope. c) How would desired investment be affected by a decline in the user cost of capital? d) State one reason why investment is a volatile component of total spending, and explain how this volatility could be shown in your diagram. e) Use your diagram to show the effects of a technological advance.

4.   **Taxes and the desired capital stock**: a) State the user cost of capital equation. b) How would each of the following changes affect the user cost of capital? 1) an increase in the price of capital goods; and 2) an increase in the real interest rate. c) State the desired capital stock equation. d) How would each of the following changes affect the level of desired capital stock? 1) an increase in the capital gains tax; and 2) an increase in the depreciation rate of capital goods. e) Briefly define the "effective tax rate."

5.   **The saving-investment diagram**: a) Draw a saving-investment diagram. Label the axes, curves, and equilibrium values. b) Define the investment curve and explain its slope. c) Define the saving curve and explain its slope. d) Use the diagram to show the effect of a government budget deficit created by a temporary increase in government purchases. e) What does the Ricardian equivalence proposition tell us about the expected real economic effects of a temporary government budget deficit? Briefly explain.

6.   **Goods market determination of investment**: a) Draw a saving-investment diagram of goods market equilibrium. Label the axes and curves. b) Identify two shift variables (i.e., nonprice determinants) for the desired saving curve (S) and state whether desired saving is negatively related or positively related to each of these variables. c) Identify two shift variables for the desired investment demand curve and state whether desired investment is negatively related or positively related to each of these variables. d) Briefly explain how the diagram depicts goods market equilibrium, given that it explicitly shows a demand for only one type of good. e) Would an increase in desired saving prevent some capital goods suppliers from being able to sell some of their output? Briefly explain.

Mathematical Problem-Solving Questions

1. **Consumption and saving**: Use the Keynesian consumption function, to calculate changes in household consumption and saving when MPC = .80, c_o = $100 billion, and income increases by 10% from $4000 billion to $4400 billion.

2. **Expected after-tax real interest rate**: Let i = 3%, t = 15%, and expected inflation = 4%. Calculate the initial expected after-tax real interest rate and changes in the rate created by each of the following changes: a) the nominal interest rate rises to 6%; b) the tax rate increases to 30%; c) expected inflation increases to 8%.

3. **Gross investment and net investment**: Calculate the value of net investment for each of the following values for gross investment (I_t) and depreciation (d), assuming that K_t = $5000 billion: a) I_t = $1000 billion and depreciation is 10%; b) I_t = $500 billion and depreciation is 5%.

Answers to Fill-In-The-Blanks Review Questions

1. Keynesian consumption function
2. marginal propensity to consume
3. expected after-tax real interest rate
4. Ricardian equivalence proposition
5. desired capital stock
6. user cost of capital
7. tax-adjusted user cost of capital
8. effective tax rate
9. gross investment
10. net investment

Answers to True-False Questions

1. F In theory, a change in the expected after-tax real interest rate has two opposing effects on desired consumption, so the net effect on desired consumption is expected to be small. Similarly, saving is relatively insensitive to small changes in the expected after-tax real interest rate.

2. F A decline in output would reduce consumption, but it would not reduce MPC. MPC is a constant number, like .90, greater than zero but less than one.

3. T Differences in risk, length of time for which the funds are borrowed, and tax status largely explain differences in interest rates. Higher-risk assets, assets with a longer term to maturity, and assets with higher tax rate liabilities each earn higher interest rates.

4. F If the rate of inflation is high, the real interest rate and the user cost of capital may be low, despite a high nominal interest rate.

5. F The tax-adjusted user cost of capital is independent of the level of capital stock, as illustrated by the horizontal tax-adjusted user cost of capital curve. None of the values of the variables that determine the tax-adjusted user cost of capital are affected by changes in the amount of capital goods that a firm chooses to purchase.

6. F A decline in the user cost of capital will increase the desired capital stock. A decline in the expected marginal product of capital will increase the desired capital stock. Consequently, desired capital stock may rise or fall, depending on which effect is greater.

7. T   The data presented in Table 4.2 of the textbook show that the effective tax rate in 1990 was substantially higher in the United States than in Japan, Germany, and France; the effective tax rates on capital were 24.0%, 6.1%, 4.6%, and -33.4%, respectively.

8. T   The data presented in Figs. 4.5(a) and 4.5(b) of the textbook show that U.S. investments in equipment increased relative to investments in structures after the 1962 decline in the tax rate on investments in equipment.

9. F $S^d = I^d$, is the goods market equilibrium equation.

10. T   A temporary decrease in government purchases, for a given tax revenue, will increase government saving and national saving, causing the saving curve to shift to the right, which causes the real interest rate to decline and increases the equilibrium level of desired saving and investment.

Answers to Multiple Choice Questions

1.	a	8.	e	15.	a
2.	e	9.	b	16.	b
3.	c	10.	c	17.	b
4.	d	11.	c	18.	c
5.	b	12.	e	19.	e
6.	a	13.	b	20.	c
7.	c	14.	b		

Answers to Short-Answer Essay Questions

1. **Consumption and saving**

    a) The Keynesian consumption function is $C = c_o + c_y Y$. C = consumption spending. c_o = the part of consumption spending that does not depend on national income. c_y = MPC. Y = national income.

    b) Marginal propensity to consume (MPC) is the change in consumption spending created by a one-unit change in income. MPC > 0, because a part of any increase in income is consumed. MPC < 1, because a part of any increase in national income is saved.

    c) At a given output level, desired consumption is negatively related to desired saving. Any increase in desired consumption is a decrease in desired saving. Any decrease in desired consumption is an increase in desired saving.

    d) Among the determinants of desired consumption and desired saving are expected future income, wealth, the expected real interest rate, government purchases, and taxes; all of these determinants highlight that households consider the future in making consumption and saving decisions. Households save to increase consumption in the future. The value of wealth is the current value of the future income payments that the wealth will provide. The expected real interest rate depends on some expected inflation rate - the actual inflation rate will not be known until the future. The effects of changes in government purchases and/or taxes on desired consumption and desired saving depend on expectations of changes in the values of these fiscal policy variables in the future.

e)   Expectations play a major role in determining desired consumption and desired saving. Expected future income and expected inflation are two examples of expectations variables that partly determine desired consumption and desired saving.

2.   **Tax incentives for saving**

a)   The personal income tax and the estate tax both tax interest earnings. Interest earned on saving is taxed at the personal income tax rate of each household. The estate tax is a tax on the value of accumulated saving (i.e., wealth) when it is left to the next generation.

b)   An increase in the tax rate on interest earnings has the same effect on desired saving as a decline in the interest rate, since both reduce the after-tax real interest rate. Given the usual assumptions that most people are savers, and that the tendency for people to save more at a higher after-tax real interest rate exceeds their tendency to save less, a tax increase would cause national saving to decline. However, individual savers could choose to either increase or decrease saving, since the strength of these opposing effects on desired saving may vary across market participants. Borrowers would decrease saving. Individuals who neither borrow nor lend would decrease saving.

c)   Empirical researchers have not been able to agree on the strength of the effect of a change in the real interest rate on desired saving. Most researchers believe that desired saving is positively related to the interest rate, but that the interest rate is a relatively weak determinant of saving. This is because the incentive to save more at a higher rate of return on saving relative to consumption is at least partially offset by the incentive to save less for target savers who do not need to save as much at a higher interest rate to achieve their target level of accumulated wealth.

d)   The expected real after-tax rate of return equation is $r_{a-t} = i(1 - t) - \pi^e$

e)   The expected real after-tax rate of return would decline if taxes increased. However, r_{a-t} would increase if expected inflation declined.

3.   **The real interest rate, the user cost of capital, and the investment decision**

a)   An MPK^f curve and user cost curve diagram.

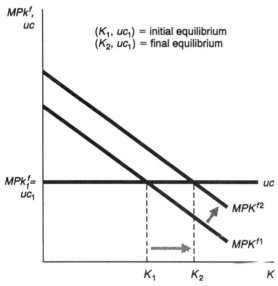

Figure 4.1

b)   The MPK^f curve shows quantity of capital goods demanded at each possible user cost. The MPK^f curve is negatively sloped because the marginal productivity of capital declines as capital is added to a fixed set of other factors of production. Desired capital stock is the level of capital stock where MPK^f equals the user cost. Because the MPK^f curve is negatively sloped, a decline in user cost increases the level of desired capital stock. Desired capital stock minus existing capital stock equals desired investment.

c)   Desired capital stock is the equilibrium level of capital stock purchases, where MPK^f = user cost. A decline in the user cost requires that MPK^f increase to achieve a new equality. MPK^f measures the marginal benefit of employing capital, and user cost measures the marginal cost of employing capital. The desired capital stock equation illustrates the general economic efficiency rule of buying something up to the level where its marginal benefit equals its marginal cost. An increase in desired capital stock translates to an increase in desired investment as well.

d)   One reason why investment is a volatile component of total spending is that the desired level of investment will change whenever the expected marginal product of capital changes, and such expectations are volatile. For example, good news about the macroeconomy tends to increase the expected marginal product of capital because investors become more optimistic, whereas bad news tends to decrease the expected marginal product of capital because investors become more pessimistic. Volatility in the investment demand for capital goods, caused by changes in the expected marginal product of capital at each possible level of capital stock, would be shown by rightward and leftward shifts in the MPK^f curve.

e)   As shown in part (a), a technological advance causes the MPK^f schedule to shift to the right. This increases the equilibrium level of capital stock purchases from K_1 to K_2. Because the user cost curve is horizontal the equilibrium user cost (uc_1) does not change. The horizontal user cost curve illustrates that the individual firm can buy all it wants at one user cost.

4.   **Taxes and the desired capital stock**

a)   The user cost of capital equation is [$uc = rp_k + dp_k = (r + d)p_k$], where r = the expected real interest rate, d = the depreciation rate for capital, and p_k = the real price of capital goods.

b)   The user cost of capital would increase if the price of capital goods increased or the real interest rate increased.

c)   The desired capital stock equation is $MPK^f = uc/(1 - \tau) = (r + d)p_k/(1 - \tau)$

d)   An increase in the capital gains tax or an increase in the depreciation rate of capital goods would reduce desired capital stock, since either would increase tax-adjusted user cost of capital.

e)   The effective tax rate is a theoretical construct that measures the revenue-tax equivalent of the actual taxes on the marginal product of capital.

5.   **The saving-investment diagram**

a)   A saving-investment diagram. The equilibrium quantity is where $S^d_1 = I^d_1$. The equilibrium interest rate is r_1. The diagram depicts desired national saving and investment.

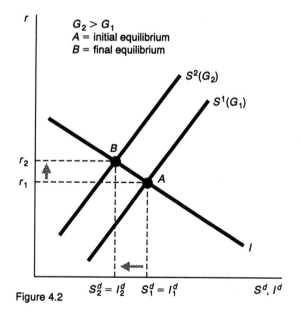

Figure 4.2

b)   By definition, the investment curve is the set of (I^d, r) points, which depict the various aggregate levels of desired capital stock purchases that all firms in the macroeconomy are willing and able to buy at various real interest rates. The slope of the investment demand curve is negative, because a decline in the real interest is needed to induce firms to purchase more capital goods at lower MPK^f

values. MPK^f declines as capital stock purchases increase, per the law of diminishing marginal returns.

c)   By definition, the saving curve is the set of (S^d, r) points, which depict the various aggregate levels of saving that all households, firms, and levels of government are willing and able to supply (i.e., make available for investment) at various real interest rates. Consistent with the law of supply, the saving curve is positively sloped. The interest rate is the rate of return on funds saved. An increase in the interest rate raises the rate of return to saving, which causes desired saving to increase.

d)   As shown in part (a), a government budget deficit created by a temporary increase in government purchases causes the saving curve to shift to the left. The equilibrium level of desired saving and desired investment declines from $S^d_1 = I^d_1$ to $S^d_2 = I^d_2$. The equilibrium interest rate increases from r_1 to r_2.

e)   According to the Ricardian equivalence proposition, a temporary government budget deficit created by a tax cut will not have any real economic effect, because it will not change national saving; so it will not shift the saving curve. The proposition assumes that households realize they will have to save all the income received from the tax cut in order to pay off the future tax increase needed to pay off the government debt created by the temporary tax cut. Even if the Ricardian equivalence proposition is correct, however, a temporary budget deficit created by an increase in government purchases would be expected to reduce national saving and thus have real economic effects.

6.   **Goods market determination of investment**

a)

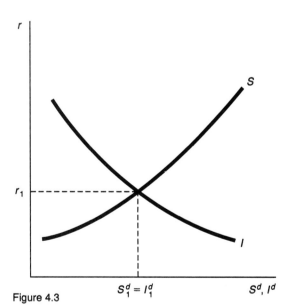

Figure 4.3

b)   Two shift variables for the desired saving schedule (S) are current income and expected future income. Saving is positively related to current income but negatively related to expected future income. An increase in current income will cause the saving to increase; the S curve will shift to the right. An increase in expected future income will cause the saving to decline; the S curve will shift to the left.

  c) Two shift variables for the desired investment schedule (I) are the expected future marginal product of capital (MPK^f) and corporate taxes. Desired investment demand is positively related to MPK^f but negatively related to corporate taxes. An increase in MPK^f would increase I; the curve would shift to the right. An increase in corporate taxes could decrease I; the curve would shift to the left.

  d) Goods market equilibrium is achieved when: $Y = C^d + I^d + G$. Desired saving, $S^d = Y - C^d - G$. By substitution, goods market equilibrium is also achieved when: $S^d = I^d$ Goods market equilibrium exists when $S^d = I^d$, because all the goods supplied are demanded (i.e., purchased and sold).

  e) No. An increase in desired saving would shift the saving curve to the right. At the initial interest rate, $S^d > I^d$, but the flexible interest rate will decline enough to return the market to equilibrium at a higher equilibrium level of saving and investment. In equilibrium, all goods supplied are sold.

Answers to Mathematical Problem-Solving Questions

1. **Consumption and saving**: The Keynesian consumption function is $C = c_o + c_y Y$, where c_y = MPC. Since all household income is either consumed or saved, $S = Y - C$. By plugging in the values for these variables given in the problem, we can calculate the increase in C and S.

When Y = $4000 billion, C = $100 billion + .80 x $4000 billion = $3300 billion.
When Y = $4400 billion, C = $100 billion + .80 x $4400 billion = $3620 billion.
Consumption has increased by $3620 billion - $3300 billion = $320 billion.
Saving has increased by $400 billion - $320 billion = $80 billion.

2. **Expected after-tax real interest rate**: The expected after-tax real interest rate equation is: $r_{a-t} = i(1-t) - \pi^e$.

Given the initial values, $i_{a-t} = .03(1 - .15) - .04 = -0.0145 = -1.45\%$.

a) When i = 6%, $i_{a-t} = .06(1 - .15) - .04 = 0.011 = 1.1\%$.
  i_{a-t} has increased by 1.1 - (-1.45) = 2.55 percentage points.

b) When t = 30%, $i_{a-t} = .03(1 - .30) - .04 = -0.019 = -1.9\%$.
  i_{a-t} has declined by 1.9 - (1.45) = .45 percentage points.

c) When π^e = 8%, $i_{a-t} = .03(1 - .15) - .08 = -0.0545 = -5.45\%$.
  i_{a-t} has declined by 5.45 - 1.45 = 4.00 percentage points.

3. **Gross investment and net investment**: Net investment = $I_t - dK_t$.

a) Net investment = $1000 billion - .10 x $5000 billion = $500 billion.

b) Net investment = $500 billion - .05 x $5000 billion = $250 billion.

CHAPTER 5: SAVING AND INVESTMENT IN THE OPEN ECONOMY

A Fill-In-The-Blanks Review Of Chapter Highlights: Use the following key terms to fill in the blanks. Each key term is used only once.

absorption

capital account

capital outflow

large open economy

official settlements balance

unilateral transfers

balance of payments

capital account balance

current account

merchandise trade balance

small open economy

world real interest rate

balance of payments accounts

capital inflow

current account balance

official reserve assets

statistical discrepancy

The two principal 1. _Balance of Payments Accounts_ are the current account and the capital account. The 2. _Current Account_ measures the values of currently produced net exports of goods and services, net income from foreign assets, and net unilateral transfers into the domestic national economy. The value of net exports of goods is called the 3. _Merchandise Trade Balance_. 4. _Unilateral Transfers_ are the international flow of funds, such as foreign aid transfers, that do not represent payments for goods, services, or assets. If the 5. _Current Acct. Balance_ has a negative value, the country has a current account deficit.

The 6. _Capital Acct._ measures the net value of international trade in existing real and financial assets, including net changes in official reserves assets. The sale of domestic assets to foreigners creates a 7. _Capital Inflow_; foreign income flows into the domestic economy. The purchase of foreign assets by domestic residents creates a 8. _Capital Outflow_; domestic income flows out of the domestic economy. If the value of the 9. _Capital Acct. Balance_ is positive, the country has a capital account surplus.

The central banks of different countries also buy and sell 10. _Official Reserve Assets_ internationally. The Federal Reserve's purchase of foreign official reserve assets increases U.S. reserves and creates a U.S. capital outflow. Foreign central banks' purchases of dollar-denominated reserve assets increases foreign official reserves and creates a U.S. capital inflow. If a country experiences a net increase in the value of its official reserves (i.e., a net capital outflow) it has an 11. _Official Settlements Balance_ surplus, also called a 12. _Balance of Payments_ surplus. Changes in the official settlements balance are included in the capital account balance.

If there were no statistical measurement errors in the balance of payments accounts data, the sum of the current account balance and the capital account balance would always equal zero. The 13. _Statistical discrepancy_ is the net value of measurement errors in the balance of payments account. The statistical discrepancy has a positive value if the current account deficit is larger than the capital account surplus.

Total domestic spending, C + I + G, is called 14. _absorption_. In goods market equilibrium, output equals absorption plus net exports. If output exceeds absorption, the country has a current account surplus; since foreigners purchase the excess output that domestic residents do not purchase, all of the output is sold in the current period in which it is produced.

A country that engages in international transactions has an open economy. It lends the value of its current account surplus to other countries, which enables foreigners to buy more output than they produce in the current period; the outflow of funds gives the country a capital account deficit. Alternatively, a country borrows the value of its current account deficit; the inflow of funds gives it a capital account surplus. An economy that is too small to affect the world real interest rate by its lending and borrowing is called a 15._Small Open Economy_. The 16._World Real IR_ is the lending rate and borrowing rate in a perfect international capital market equilibrium. A 17._Large Open Economy_ lends or borrows enough to affect the equilibrium world real interest rate by its behavior. For example, an increase in international lending by a large open economy increases the supply of savings in the international capital market, which causes the world real interest rate to decline.

The goods market equilibrium equation for an open economy, $S^d = I^d + NX$, tells us that $NX = S^d - I^d$. Desired saving is the sum of private saving and government saving, $S^d = S_{pvt} + S_{govt}$. Government saving is the budget surplus; a budget deficit is government dissaving. An increase in the budget deficit reduces government saving. A decline in government saving reduces national saving if private saving does not increase as much as government saving declines. An increase in a budget deficit created by a temporary increase in government purchases will reduce national saving. According to the Ricardian equivalence proposition, an increase in a budget deficit created by a temporary tax cut will not reduce national saving, because private saving will increase just enough to offset the effect of the decline in government saving on national saving. Contrary to the Ricardian equivalence proposition, however, a temporary tax cut would reduce national saving if households fail to save all of the increase in after-tax income created by a temporary tax cut. If an increase in a budget deficit causes desired saving to decline, it will cause the equilibrium level(s) of desired investment and/or net exports to decline. The sum of the reductions in investment and net exports will just equal the amount of the increase in the budget deficit. Net exports refer to the country's trade balance. If investment declines by less than the increase in the budget deficit, then country's trade balance will also decline. Thus, a budget deficit may create a trade deficit; this is called the twin deficits problem.

True-False Questions: Circle T for true statements and circle F for false statements.

T F   1.   If we assume that both net factor payments and net unilateral transfers have a value of zero, then NX = CA.

T F   2.   The balance of payments, also called the official settlements balance, equals CA + KA = 0.

T F   3.   If an American business purchases a business in Mexico, this purchase will create a capital outflow that reduces the U.S. capital account balance.

T F   4.   According to the absorption equation version of goods market equilibrium, an increase in a country's desired consumption will increase its net exports.

T F   5.   A country with a $100 billion current account deficit also has a capital account surplus of $100 billion when there is no statistical discrepancy.

T F   6.   If a small country's desired saving exceeds its desired investment, the world interest rate must fall to achieve goods market equilibrium.

T F   7.   If technological innovations in a large country raise MPK^f, its desired investment will increase, causing the world real interest rate to increase.

T F   8.   To service their foreign debts in the 1980s, the LDC countries had to reduce their imports of capital goods and intermediate goods, causing their real economic growth to fall.

T F   9.   German reunification increased desired saving and lowered desired investment in Germany, causing its net lending in the international capital market to increase.

T (F) 10.   According to the Ricardian equivalence proposition, a temporary increase in government purchases by a large country will not shift the desired saving curve to the left, so it will not increase the world interest rate.

Multiple Choice Questions: Circle the letter corresponding to the correct answer to each question.

1.   The two principal accounts in the balance of payments accounts are the
   a.   merchandise trade account and the current account.
   b.   merchandise trade account and the services trade account.
   c.   net exports account and income payments account.
   (d) current account and capital account.
   e.   capital account and the official settlements account.

2.   Which of the following transactions would not be included in the current account of the home country?
   a.   A consumer good is imported into the home country.
   b.   A capital good is imported into the home country.
   c.   A foreign student pays tuition to a university in the home country.
   d.   A home country resident receives income on his or her foreign assets.
   (e.) A home country resident makes a deposit in a foreign bank.

3.   The principal reason why the merchandise trade balance gets so much attention in the news media is that
   a.   the news media love bad news.
   b.   news reporters prefer to report international data much more than domestic data.
   c.   the balance is reported quarterly, whereas most of the other data is reported only semiannually.
   (d.) the balance is reported monthly, whereas most of the other data is reported only quarterly.
   e.   it tells us how well domestic suppliers of goods and services can compete in international markets.

4.   If foreigners working in the United States send 50% of their income to their families in their home countries, each transaction will show up in the U.S. balance of payment accounts as
   a.   an income payment outflow.
   b.   a capital account outflow.
   (c.) a unilateral transfer outflow.
   d.   a current account deficit.
   e.   a capital account surplus.

5.   A country has a current account surplus if
   (a.) the value of its exports exceeds the value of its imports, assuming net income from foreign assets and net unilateral transfers have a value of zero.
   b.   the value of its net exports of services exceeds the value of its net exports of goods.
   c.   it receives more income from foreign assets than it pays to foreigners for foreign-owned domestic assets.
   d.   its financial inflows exceed its financial outflows.
   e.   it sells more currently produced goods than existing assets to foreigners.

6.   The two principal accounts in the capital account are the
   a.   net capital inflows and net capital outflows.
   (b.) net capital inflows and the net change in official reserves.
   c.   short-term capital and long-term capital accounts.
   d.   debt capital and equity capital accounts.
   e.   new capital and existing capital accounts.

7. To achieve a net reduction in its foreign indebtedness, an LDC must
   a. reduce its GNP growth rate.
   b. stop importing.
   c. export a higher value of goods and services than it imports.
   d. not accept any capital inflows.
   e. form a debtor cartel with other LDC debtors.

8. An economic benefit of capital outflows is that they
   a. reduce domestic unemployment.
   b. reduce domestic saving.
   c. increase domestic investment.
   d. create future income payment inflows.
   e. increase domestic output.

9. A country's capital account surplus decreases if
   a. its current account deficit decreases.
   b. its income payment inflows on foreign assets decrease.
   c. its domestic residents working abroad reduce the income they send home to their families.
   d. foreigners increase their purchases of its existing assets.
   e. its residents reduce their purchases of existing foreign assets.

10. A negative value for the U.S. official reserve assets line in the balance of payments accounts means that
    a. U.S. residents have sold more gold to foreigners than they bought.
    b. U.S. residents bought more gold from foreigners than they sold.
    c. the U.S. central bank has increased its holdings of foreign reserve assets.
    d. the U.S. central bank has decreased its holdings of foreign reserve assets.
    e. the U.S. has a balance of payments deficit.

11. The official settlements balance
    a. is always negative when there is a current account deficit.
    b. always equals zero.
    c. declines when U.S. official reserves increase.
    d. is always positive when the capital account is positive.
    e. is also called the balance of payments.

12. If a country has a balance of payments deficit, then
    a. its capital outflows exceeded its capital inflows.
    b. it cannot compete in international markets.
    c. it reduced its holdings of official reserve assets.
    d. it has a current account deficit.
    e. it must increase its exports.

13. In the balance of payments accounts for the United States, the statistical discrepancy figure
    a. would never exceed plus or minus $5 billion.
    b. is the measurement error in the current account.
    c. is the measurement error in the capital account.
    d. used to exceed plus or minus $5 billion, but recent improvements in the quality of data reduced the error to under plus or minus $1 billion by 1992.
    e. exceeded plus or minus $10 billion in 1992.

14.   Which of the following represents absorption?

a. $C^d + I^d$

b. $C^d + I^d + G$

c. $C^d + I^d + G + NX$

d. $Y + NX$

e. $I^d + NX$

15.   In a saving-investment diagram for a small open economy

a.   the saving curve is vertical at some fixed level of output.

b.   the saving curve is horizontal at some fixed interest rate.

c.   the I + NX curve is negatively sloped.

d.   the interest rate is fixed at the world real interest rate.

e.   equilibrium requires that $S^d = I^d$.

16.   In a model of two open economies the real interest rate will increase in one economy

a.   if saving declines in the other small economy.

b.   if saving declines in the other large economy.

c.   if investment declines in the other small economy.

d.   if investment declines in the other large economy.

e.   if investment increases in its small economy.

17.   A large open economy

a.   dominates world trade in one or more products.

b.   is physically larger than all small open economies.

c.   has a larger population than all small open economies.

d.   is a lender in international markets.

e.   lends or borrows enough in the international capital market to influence the world real interest rate.

18.   The goods market equilibrium equation in an open economy shows that

a. $NX = S^d - I^d$

b. $S^d + NX = I^d$

c. $S^d + I^d = NX$

d. $S^d = I^d$

e. $NX = Y - S^d$

19.   Which of the following does not publish the data on the U.S. balance of payments accounts?

a.   The Bureau of Economic Analysis in the U.S. Department of Commerce

b.   The Survey of Current Business

c.   The Federal Reserve Bulletin

d.   The Economic Report of the President

e.   Business magazines such as Business Week and Fortune

20.   In a two-economy model of the United States and another large economy made up of the rest of the world, if net lending by the rest of the world declined,

a.   net lending by the world would increase.

b.   net lending by the United States would decline.

c.   net borrowing by the United States would increase.

d.   net borrowing by the United States would remain unchanged.

e.   the world real interest rate would increase.

Short-Answer Essay Questions

1.   **Balance of payments accounting**: a) Identify and briefly define the two principal accounts in the balance of payments accounts. b) Briefly explain why the sum of the two principal accounts is zero. c) Identify two types of transactions that would create capital inflows. d) Why do central banks buy and sell official reserve assets? e) Briefly evaluate the economic significance of a merchandise trade deficit compared to a current account deficit.

2.   **Goods market equilibrium in an open economy**: a) State the goods market equilibrium equation for an open economy. b) How would a current account surplus be affected by a decline in investment? Briefly explain. c) How would a current account surplus be affected by a decline in saving? Briefly explain. d) State the absorption equation for goods market equilibrium in an open economy. e) Use the absorption equation to identify two possible causes of a decline in the current account balance.

3.   **Saving and investment in a small open economy**: a) Define the term "small open economy." b) What determines the interest rate in a small open economy? c) Draw a saving-investment diagram for a small open economy that lends internationally. Label the axes, curves, and equilibrium values. d) Can it be determined whether or not the country has a current account surplus? Briefly explain. e) Could this country become a net borrower internationally without changing its willingness to save or invest at various interest rates? Briefly explain.

4.   **LDC debt crisis**: a) Briefly explain why LDCs are typically net borrowers in international capital market. b) Why is the LDC debt problem called a "crisis"? c) Identify and briefly explain two causes of the LDC debt crisis. d) Why do debtor countries have to be net exporters to service their debt; why don't they pay off the debt with domestic income? e) If the debt burden on LDCs has become severe, should they default on their foreign loans? Briefly discuss.

5.   **Saving and investment in a large open economy**: a) Is the United States a large open economy? Briefly explain. b) When there are so many countries involved in international transactions, is a two-economy model too simplistic? c) Draw a goods market equilibrium diagram for the home country and foreign country in a two-economy model, making the home country a net borrower. Label the axes, curves, and equilibrium values. d) Identify the line segments on your graphs that show the current account deficit or surplus of each country, and state how these line segments are related. e) Identify one event in the home country that would cause the world real interest rate to increase, and identify one event in the foreign country that could offset this effect.

6.   **Twin deficits of the 1980s**: a) What was the principal cause of the U.S. government budget deficits of the 1980s? b) Use the goods market equilibrium equation to explain the expected effect, if any exists, of the government budget deficit on U.S. net exports. c) Use the absorption version of the goods market equilibrium equation to explain the expected effect, if any exists, on U.S. net exports. d) According to the Ricardian equivalence proposition, what is the expected effect on U.S. net exports of the government budget deficit, and why might the proposition fail to predict the actual effect? e) What is the expected effect of the government budget deficit on the U.S. capital account balance? Briefly explain.

Mathematical Problem-Solving Questions

1. **Balance of payments accounts:** Use the following data to calculate net exports (NX), the current account balance (CA), the capital account balance (KA), and the sum of CA + KA: exports = $800 billion, imports = $900 billion, net income from foreign assets = $25 billion, net unilateral transfers = - $25 billion, net increase in U.S.-owned assets abroad other than official reserve assets = $90 billion, official settlements balance = - $10 billion, and statistical discrepancy = 0.

2. **Goods market equilibrium:** Use the following data to calculate desired saving, absorption, net exports, and net borrowing from foreigners for an open economy with goods market equilibrium, assuming NX = CA: $Y = \$6000$ billion, $C^d = \$4000$ billion, $G = \$1500$ billion, and $I^d = \$1000$ billion.

3. **Twin deficits:** Assume that the trade deficit equals the current account deficit (NX = CA), and that the trade deficit = $50 billion initially. Use the goods market equilibrium equations for an open economy to calculate the effect of a temporary tax cut of $200 billion on the trade deficit under each of the following conditions: a) S^d and I^d remain unchanged; b) S^d declines by $50 billion and I^d declines by $50 billion; c) S^d declines by $200 billion and I^d remains unchanged.

Answers to Fill-In-The-Blank Questions

1. balance of payments accounts	2. current account	3. merchandise trade balance
4. unilateral transfers	5. current account balance	6. capital account
7. capital inflow	8. capital outflow	9. capital account balance
10. official reserve assets	11. official settlements balance	12. balance of payments
13. statistical discrepancy	14. absorption	15. small open economy
16. world real interest rate	17. large open economy	

Answers to True-False Questions

1. T   The current account balance, CA = NX + net income from foreign assets + net unilateral assets; so CA = NX when the value of these other two accounts is zero.

2. F   The balance of payments, or official settlements balance, is included in the capital account balance (KA); it is the change in official reserve assets needed to increase or decrease the capital account balance to the value at which CA = KA. For example, if the U.S. current account deficit exceeds the net capital inflows from nonofficial trading of existing assets by $40 billion, then the official settlements balance will equal -$40 billion, which results from the U.S. central bank selling official reserve assets for dollar-denominated assets and the foreign central banks buying enough dollar-denominated reserve assets to create an additional $40 billion capital inflow into the United States.

3. T   When an American business purchases a business in Mexico, U.S. dollars are flowing out of the United States and into Mexico; this outflow of dollars is a financial capital outflow. A financial capital outflow reduces the capital account balance by reducing a surplus or increasing a deficit.

4. F   The absorption equation version of goods market equilibrium is [NX = Y - C^d - I^d - G]. An increase in desired consumption will reduce net exports.

5.   T   If the statistical discrepancy = 0, then CA + KA = 0.

6.   F   If a small country's desired saving exceeds its desired investment, it will have a net export surplus and will be a net lender in the international capital market. A small country can achieve goods market equilibrium at any world real interest rate. Changes in a small country's desired saving and desired investment decisions do not affect the world real interest rate.

7.   T   An increase in the expected future marginal product of capital in a large country will cause its desired investment curve to shift to the right, causing the world real interest rate to rise.

8.   T   With the onset of the LDC crisis, commercial banks in developed countries reduced their lending to the LDCs, which caused net capital inflows into the LDCs to decline. When net capital inflows declined, the LDCs were forced to improve their current account balances, by increasing net exports. LDCs had to increase net exports by more than the decline in net capital inflows, because increased payments on their foreign debt reduced their net income from foreign investments. LDCs also experienced a decline in exports, because world recession in the early 1980s followed by a slowdown in the economic growth of developed countries reduced the demand for these exports. To substantially increase net exports LDCs had to dramatically reduce imports, including imports of capital goods and intermediate goods. However, production in many LDCs is heavily dependent on imported capital goods and intermediate goods. This substantial decline in the supply of factors of production caused real economic growth in the LDCs to decline.

9.   F   German reunification caused government purchases to increase, which reduced desired saving; it also raised the expected future marginal product of capital in Germany, which increased desired investment. The leftward shift in the saving curve and the rightward shift in the investment curve reduced net exports, which is a reduction in net lending in the international capital market. Since Germany is a large country, these changes also raised the world real interest rate.

10.   F   The Ricardian equivalence proposition predicts that a temporary tax cut will not reduce national saving; it tells us nothing about the effects of temporary changes in government purchases. A temporary increase in government purchases will reduce national saving. A decline in national saving by a large country will cause the world real interest rate to rise.

Answers to Multiple Choice Questions

1. d	8. d	15. d
2. e	9. a	16 b
3. d	10. c	17 e
4. c	11. e	18. a
5. a	12. c	19. e
6. b	13. e	20. e
7. c	14. b	

Answers to Short-Answer Essay Questions

1.   **Balance of payments accounting:**

   a)   The two principal accounts in the balance of payments accounts are the current account and the capital account.
   1) The current account measures the value of net exports of currently produced goods and services, plus net factor payments from abroad, and net unilateral transfers into a country.
   2) The capital account measures the value of net capital inflows into a country from trade in existing real and financial assets.

   b)   (CA + KA = 0), because every international transaction is a swap of goods, services, or assets, and the two sides to any transaction always have offsetting effects on the current account and the capital account. Capital account surpluses (i.e., net borrowing from foreigners) finance (i.e., pay for) current account deficits. Current account surpluses finance capital account deficits (i.e., net lending to foreigners).

   c)   Two types of transactions that create capital inflows are: 1) foreigners' purchases of existing domestic assets; and 2) foreign central banks' purchases of domestic reserve assets.

   d)   Central banks buy and sell official reserves to officially settle their international balance of payments account surpluses and deficits. Changes in the official settlements balances cause the capital account balance to be equal but opposite in value to the current account balance.

   e)   A current account deficit is more important because it represents the amount that must be borrowed from abroad, whereas a merchandise trade deficit may be offset by a surplus in services trade, net factor payments income, and net transfers.

2.   **Goods market equilibrium in an open economy**

   a)   The goods market equilibrium equation for an open economy is $S^d = I^d + NX$.

   b)   The goods market equilibrium equation shows that for a given level of saving, a decline in investment would increase a current account surplus, where NX equals the current account surplus. A decline in the domestic investment use of available saving would increase the amount of saving available for foreign investment. NX is the value of net foreign investment, also called net lending.

   c)   The goods market equilibrium equation shows that, for a given level of investment, a decline in saving would create a decline in a current account surplus, where NX equals the current account surplus. Less saving would be available to finance foreign investments, so fewer foreign investments would be made.

   d)   The absorption equation for goods market equilibrium in an open economy is
   $NX = Y - (C^d + I^d + G)$.

   e)   The absorption equation shows that a decline in the right-hand-side value of the equation would cause the current account balance (NX) to decline, to restore equilibrium. A decline in national income (Y) or an increase in any form of desired domestic spending - desired consumption, desired investment, or government purchases - would cause NX to decline.

3.   **Saving and investment in a small open economy:**

a)   A small open economy is the national economy of a country that engages in (i.e., is open to) international transactions, but whose lending and borrowing in the international capital market is too small to affect the world real interest rate. Many developing countries are small open economies.

b)   Changes in domestic saving or investment in a small open economy do not affect the interest rate at which funds are borrowed and lent in that country; they can borrow or lend all they want at the world real interest rate. The world real interest rate is determined by the aggregate supply of saving and demand for investment in the international capital market.

c)   A saving-investment diagram for a small country that lends internationally:

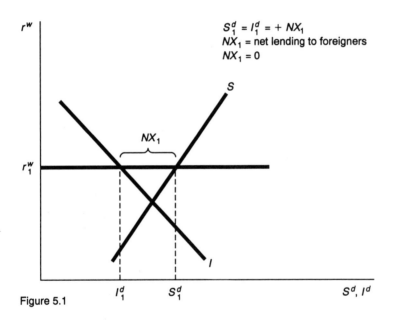

Figure 5.1

d)   In equilibrium a country that lends internationally must have a current account surplus, because it can lend only the surplus foreign exchange that it earns from selling more exports than it imports. The country's capital account deficit is the value that it lends internationally, which is equal to its current account surplus (NX): $S^d - I^d$ = net capital outflows = NX > 0.

e)   Yes. For given domestic saving and investment curves, a sufficient decline in the world real interest rate would cause $S^d < I^d$, at which point the country would have become a net borrower internationally.

4.   **LDC debt crisis:**

a)   Less developed countries (LDCs) are typically net borrowers in the international capital markets because their supply of saving is low relative to their investment demand. Consequently, $S^d < I^d$ in these countries at the world real interest rate. In LDCs the supply of saving is low because their national income is relatively low compared to the income of developed countries; saving is positively related to income. In LDCs investment demand is high because the expected future marginal product of capital (MPK^f) is high compared to MPK^f schedules in developed countries.

b)   The LDC debt problem is called a crisis because developed country lenders incurred extraordinarily large losses on these loans in the 1980s. Some debtor countries threatened to default on the remainder of their huge foreign debts, but such large defaults could have threatened the health of some large bank lenders. Furthermore, attempts of LDCs to repay their debt create a major burden on their economies, as highlighted by the consequent slowdown in their economic growth rates.

c)   Two causes of the LDC debt crisis were

1)   unexpected global macroeconomic events, including the OPEC oil crisis in the 1970s followed by worldwide recessions in the 1979 - 1982 period, both of which reduced nonoil-exporting LDCs' net exports; and

2)   careless lending and poor investment decisions. Banks loaned these countries too much, partly because they were lending recycled petrodollars, and the LDC borrowers did not efficiently invest all the funds in projects that would produce enough investment income to repay the loans.

d)   Debtor countries have to service their foreign debt with the foreign exchange income they receive as net exporters of goods and services. Debt service payments reduce the current account balance by reducing net income from foreign assets. For a given capital account balance, balance of payments equilibrium requires that a decline in net income from foreign assets must be offset by an increase in net exports, assuming net unilateral transfers remain unchanged.

e)   No. The long-term, high economic costs and political costs of defaulting on the debt made that option unattractive. The IMF, the World Bank, the national governments, banks, and industry leaders of concerned countries all worked to resolve the LDC crisis. In 1989 the Brady Plan provided a reduction in the immediate debt burden of the LDC countries that was acceptable to debtor and creditor countries.

5.   **Saving and investment in a large open economy**

a)   Yes. The United States is an *open economy* because it engages in international transactions; it is a *large economy* because it lends and borrows enough in international capital markets to affect the world real interest rate. Consequently, the United States is a large open economy.

b)   No. A two-economy model could include all the open economies in the world. For example, the U.S. economy could be one economy in the model; all the other national economies in the world together could represent the other economy. Although the two-economy model is a simplification, it is suitable for most economic analysis of international transactions.

c)   A two-economy diagram of goods market equilibrium, with the home country a net borrower:

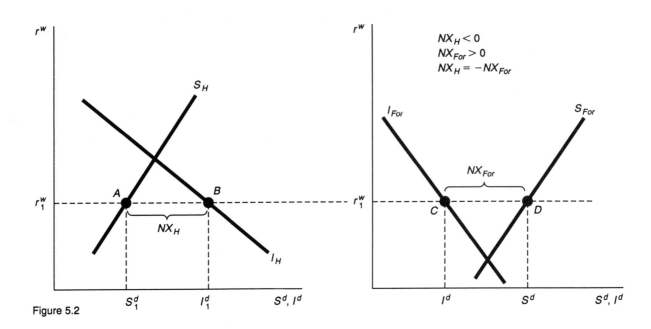

Figure 5.2

d)   The line segment AB represents the current account deficit of the home country; this line segment equals the length of the line segment CD, which represents the equivalent current account surplus in the foreign country.

e)   A decline in home country saving would cause the world real interest rate to increase, as the home country saving curve shifted to the left. An increase in saving in the foreign large open economy could offset this effect.

6.   **Twin deficits of the 1980s:**

a)   The principal cause of the U.S. federal government budget deficits of the 1980s was the Economic Recovery Act of 1981, which cut tax revenue without cutting government spending.

b)   The goods market equilibrium equation for an open economy is $S^d = I^d + NX$. If the government budget deficit reduces saving for a given investment demand, then net exports (NX) must decline. If $S^d = I^d$, so that $NX = 0$ initially, then the decline in saving creates a current account deficit. This is the *twin deficits* hypothesis; a budget deficit creates a trade deficit. However, we cannot say with certainty that the tax cut reduced saving.

c)   The absorption version of the goods market equilibrium equation for an open economy is $NX = Y - (C^d + I^d + G)$. This equation shows that an increase in any type of domestic absorption (i.e., $C^d + I^d + G$) for a given level of national income (Y) causes net exports to decline. For a given level of G, the tax cut is expected to increase C^d, which would cause NX to decline. However, we cannot say with certainty that the tax cut did increase absorption.

d)   According to the Ricardian equivalence proposition, a government budget deficit, created by a tax cut, will have no real economic effects because it will not affect saving. According to this theory the government budget deficit and the trade deficit are independent events; they are unrelated occurrences. The Ricardian equivalence proposition may fail to predict the actual effects of the tax cut when a significant share of U.S. households fail to predict that the future taxes will increase enough to finance the current tax cut.

e)   If the government budget deficit had no effect on the current account balance (NX), then it had no effect on the capital account balance, since these balances are equal but opposite in value in equilibrium. If the budget deficit caused the current account deficit, then it caused the capital account surplus. For balance of payments equilibrium the capital account surplus is needed to finance the current account deficit (i.e., the excess domestic spending in foreign markets).

Answers to Mathematical Problem-Solving Questions

1.   **Balance of payments accounts**:

NX = exports - imports
    = $800 billion - $900 billion − - $100 billion.

CA = NX + net income from foreign assets + net unilateral transfers
    = - $100 billion + $25 billion - $25 billion = - $100 billion.

KA = net increase in U.S.-owned assets abroad - official settlements balance
    = $90 billion + $10 billion = $100 billion.

CA + KA = 0.

2.   **Goods market equilibrium**:

S^d = Y - C^d - G = $6000 billion - $4000 billion - $1500 billion = $500 billion.

Absorption = C^d + I^d + G = $4000 billion + $1000 billion + $1500 billion = $6500 billion.

NX = Y - absorption = $6000 billion - $6500 billion = - $500 billion.

NX = S^d - I^d = $500 billion - $1000 billion = - $500 billion.

NX = net borrowing from foreigners in the international capital market = - $500 billion.

3.   **Twin deficits**: A budget deficit created by a tax cut directly increases the trade deficit only if it reduces desired saving, but desired investment may change independent of the tax cut. $NX = S^d - I^d$.

a) With no change in S^d and I^d, the trade deficit (NX = - $50 billion) remains unchanged.

b) When S^d declines by $50 billion and I^d declines by $50 billion, then ($NX = S^d - I^d$ = - $50 billion) remains unchanged.

c) When S^d declines by $200 billion and I^d remain unchanged, NX declines by $200 billion to - $250 billion.

CHAPTER 6: LONG-RUN ECONOMIC GROWTH

A Fill-In-The-Blanks Review of Chapter Highlights: Use the following key terms to fill in the blanks. Each key term is used only once.

capital-labor ratio   conditional convergence   growth accounting
growth accounting equation   human capital   industrial policy
new growth theory   steady state   unconditional convergence

1. _Growth Accounting_ identifies the relative importance of productivity growth, labor growth, and capital growth in determining the average yearly rate of real output (i.e., economic or national income) growth in the long run. The 2._Growth Acct. Equation_ is derived by converting the production function into its growth rate form. In the long run both capital and labor can be added to production simultaneously; all the factors of production are variable.

We use real per capita (i.e., per person) income as a measure of a country's standard of living. An increase in real per capita income is the same as an increase in output per worker if a fixed share of the population work in each year. The Solow model of economic growth studies the behavior of real output per worker in the long run. In the Solow model, output is a positive function of the 3._Capital - Labor Ratio_, which is the amount of real capital (e.g., equipment and structures) employed on average with each worker in the national economy.

The Solow model shows that an economy would reach a steady state in the long run if there were no productivity growth. The long run is a period of time in which all markets continuously clear; it is a sustained period of general equilibrium growth. In a 4._Steady State_, output, investment, and consumption increase each year at the same rate of growth as population growth but output per worker, capital per worker (i.e., the capital-labor ratio), and consumption per worker do not change. Thus there is no increase in a country's standard of living in a steady state. If there is productivity growth, output per worker can continue to grow indefinitely.

The Solow model explains how productivity growth contributes to long-run economic growth, but it does not explain what causes productivity growth. 5._New Growth Theory_ explains how human capital and technological innovations create productivity growth. Increases in 6._human Capital_ include improvements in the education, skills, health, and mobility of labor and entrepreneurs.

Although a wide gap currently exists in the living standards of people in rich and poor countries, the Solow model predicts that their living standards will eventually converge (i.e., become similar) if both rich and poor countries have the same production function, saving rate, and population growth; convergence under these conditions is called 7._Conditional Convergence_. If both rich and poor countries have open economies, free international trade is expected to cause their standards of living to converge despite initial differences in their production techniques and saving rates; this type of convergence is called 8._Unconditional Convergence_. Differences in human capital and population growth rates as well as inefficiencies in the international capital market help to explain the weak empirical support for unconditional convergence.

Some government policies attempt to increase their nation's long-run growth rate by raising the saving rate and the rate of productivity growth. 9._Industrial Policy_ attempts to promote economic growth by subsidizing firms in certain targeted industries, with the expectation that growth in these selected industries will create growth in other industries linked to them. Given certain types of market failure, including borrowing constraints and spillovers, industrial policies could possibly be economically beneficial. However, most economic research suggests that industrial policies do not usually improve countries' standards of living.

True-False Questions: Circle T for true statements and circle F for false statements.

T F 1.   Although real GDP per capita was lower in the United States than in the United Kingdom in 1870, it was relatively higher in the United States in 1989, because long-run economic growth over the 1870-1989 period was higher in the United States.

T F 2.   Over the 1870 - 1989 period long-run economic growth was higher in Japan and Germany than in the United States, so the standards of living in these three countries are converging.

T F 3.   In the growth accounting equation, increases in human capital increase a_N, while technological innovations increases a_K.

T F 4.   Any economic event that reduces the amount of output produced for any given amounts of labor and capital is an adverse productivity shock.

T F 5.   Given the U.S. historical estimates of the output elasticities of labor and capital, $a_N = 0.7$ and $a_K = 0.3$, increasing employment by 5% would increase economic growth by more than if the capital stock increased by 5%.

T F 6.   The slowdown in productivity growth is the principal cause of the post-1973 slowdown in long-run economic growth in the United States.

T F 7.   Given the high capital-labor ratios in the United States and Japan, further increases in the saving rate would lower steady-state consumption per worker.

T F 8.   Without productivity growth a national economy will eventually reach a steady state in which there is no growth in output per worker and consumption per worker.

T F 9.   Government policies that effectively reduce the population growth rates in developing countries are always economically efficient because they raise the steady-state consumption standard of living.

T F 10.   Empirical research suggests that the international capital market is efficient in causing the capital-labor ratios in high-saving countries and low-saving countries to converge.

Multiple Choice Questions: Circle the letter corresponding to the correct answer to each question.

1.   Which of the following is not an important variable in growth accounting calculations?
   a. Productivity growth
   b. Money supply growth
   c. Labor growth
   d. Capital growth
   e. Output growth

2. The steady state capital-labor ratio will decline if
    a. the saving rate per worker increases.
    b. the consumption rate per worker declines.
    c. population growth increases.
    d. investment per worker increases.
    e. productivity increases.

3. Which of the following best describes a steady state?
    a. Political stability is maintained by the state.
    b. People's standard of living is increasing at a stable rate.
    c. Each firm in the economy receives a steady stream of income.
    d. An economy has no output growth.
    e. An economy is experiencing no change in saving per worker or investment per worker over time.

4. The rapid recovery of the Japanese and West German economies after World War II is best explained by their
    a. expansionary monetary policies.
    b. expansionary fiscal policies.
    c. protectionist trade policies.
    d. high level of human capital.
    e. high level of real capital.

5. According to Solow's model of output growth, the standards of living of people in rich and poor countries
    a. will conditionally converge.
    b. will converge in the short run but will diverge in the long run.
    c. are the same today and will continue to be the same in the future.
    d. will converge for closed economies but not for open economies.
    e. will become increasingly unequal in the near future.

6. Which of the following is not proposed by advocates of an industrial policy for U.S. high-technology industries?
    a. Increased trade protection from high-technology imports
    b. Reduced regulation of high-technology firms
    c. Research and development funding assistance by government to high-technology firms
    d. Reduced business taxes
    e. Elimination of all subsidies to high-technology firms

7. To the extent that saving, investment, and educational achievements are higher in a democracy than in countries with nondemocratic forms of government, democratic nations will achieve
    a. lower consumption per worker standards of living than nondemocratic nations.
    b. lower output per worker than nondemocratic nations.
    c. higher output per worker than nondemocratic nations.
    d. higher population growth rates than nondemocratic nations.
    e. higher depreciation rates for capital stock than nondemocratic nations.

8.   In the growth accounting equation, productivity growth is
      a. the difference between output growth and labor growth.
      b. the difference between output per worker growth and labor per worker growth.
      c. the difference between labor growth and capital growth.
      d. the sum of labor growth and capital growth.
      e. output growth minus the sum of labor growth and capital growth, weighted by the elasticities of output
          with respect to labor and capital.

9.   The per-worker production function relates
      a. output per worker to capital per worker.
      b. output per worker to production per worker.
      c. output per worker to factors of production per worker.
      d. production per worker to the size of the work force.
      e. production per worker to the size of the capital stock.

10.   Steady state consumption per worker is
      a. larger in the short run than in the long run.
      b. less than steady state investment per worker.
      c. less than steady state saving per worker.
      d. steady state production per worker minus steady state investment per worker.
      e. larger in large economies than in small economies.

11.   According to the Solow model
      a. there are constant returns to capital in the long run.
      b. there are increasing returns to labor in the long run.
      c. an increase in saving per worker will produce continuing increases in a country's standard of living in the
          long run.
      d. the steady state capital-labor ratio will be such that steady state saving per worker and investment per
          worker per year are equal in the long run.
      e. for any given rate of saving per worker, there are many possible rates of investment per worker that are
          consistent with the steady state condition.

12.   In analyzing the sources of economic growth in the United States, Denison and Shigehara found that
      a. economic growth in the 1980s was much higher than in other decades since World War II.
      b. productivity growth declined significantly after 1973.
      c. capital growth is usually a more important source of economic growth than labor growth.
      d. labor growth is more variable than capital growth.
      e. the U.S. economy achieved steady state growth for the 1948 - 1990 period.

13.   According to the Solow model, a decline in the rate of population growth in the United States would
      a. increase steady state output per worker.
      b. not affect steady state consumption per worker.
      c. reduce steady state consumption per worker.
      d. reduce the capital labor ratio.
      e. reduce steady state saving per worker in the long run.

14.   In a steady state diagram, if saving per worker initially exceeds investment per worker
       a.   the economy will enter a recession.
       b.   the economy will experience inflation.
       c.   the capital-labor ratio will increase.
       d.   investment per worker will decline.
       e.   saving per worker will decline.

15.   According to economic theory, an increase in the capital-labor ratio will
       a.   always reduce steady state consumption per worker.
       b.   always increase steady state consumption per worker.
       c.   reduce steady state consumption per worker if starting from a low capital-labor ratio.
       d.   increase steady state consumption per worker if starting from low capital-labor ratio.
       e.   reduce steady state consumption per worker if starting from a high capital-labor ratio, and empirical
            studies show that most countries already invest too much.

16.   In a steady state diagram, an increase in saving per worker is shown by
       a.   shifting the saving-per-worker curve down to the right.
       b.   shifting the saving-per-worker curve up along a given investment-per-worker curve to a higher steady
            state capital-labor ratio.
       c.   moving to the right along a given saving-per-worker curve to a higher steady state investment per worker.
       d.   shifting the production function down along an investment-per-worker curve.
       e.   a pivot of the investment-per-worker curve to the left at the origin.

17.   In a steady state diagram, a decline in productivity
       a.   is shown by shifting the saving-per-worker curve down to the right to a lower steady state capital-labor
            ratio.
       b.   is shown by a pivot of the investment-per-worker curve to the left at the origin.
       c.   is shown by shifting the saving-per-worker curve up along a given investment-per-worker curve to a
            higher steady state capital-labor ratio.
       d.   is shown by a movement to the left along a given saving-per-worker curve.
       e.   reduces saving and investment but does not change the steady state capital-labor ratio.

18.   If the gap in the standards of living declines for those rich and poor nations that have the same
       saving per worker and investment per worker, this is evidence
       a.   that rich nations inevitably decay and poor nations inevitably prosper.
       b.   that rich nations inevitably prosper and poor nations inevitably decay.
       c.   that economic growth is inevitably higher in poor nations than in rich nations.
       d.   of unconditional convergence.
       e.   of conditional convergence.

19.   Which of the following is not an example of human capital formation?
       a.   Increases in the educational achievements of the population
       b.   Increases in job skills of the labor force
       c.   Improvements in the nutrition and health of the labor force
       d.   Increases in the birth rate of the population
       e.   Increases in the entrepreneurial capabilities of the population

20.   Which of the following government policies is the least likely to be used to increase a nation's long-run economic growth?
a.   Industrial policies
b.   Infrastructure investment policies
c.   Human capital formation policies
d.   Research and development policies
e.   Pollution control, labor market, and product quality regulation policies

Short-Answer Essay Questions

1.   **Sources of economic growth**: a) Identify and briefly describe the three principal sources of economic growth. b) Identify and briefly describe one cause of a change in each of these three variables that would increase economic growth. c) State the growth accounting equation. d) Define the variable a_N. e) How do we know that the growth accounting equation is an identity?

2.   **Causes of post-1973 growth slowdown**: Identify and briefly explain five causes of the post-1973 growth slowdown in the United States.

3.   **The Solow model of growth**: a) Draw an investment-per-worker/production-per-worker-diagram. Label the axes and curves and identify the capital-labor ratio where long-run consumption is maximized. b) Briefly explain the shape of the per-worker production curve. c) Draw a steady state diagram, which shows how the steady state capital-labor ratio is determined. Label the axes and curves. d) Identify and briefly explain the slopes of the two curves. e) If investment per worker initially exceeds saving per worker, how is the steady state capital-labor ratio achieved?

4.   **Fundamental determinants of long-run living standards**: Draw steady state diagrams showing the effect of the following changes on the capital-labor ratio: a) a decline in saving-per-worker; b) a decline in population; and c) a decline in productivity. d) In the Solow growth model, is investment-per-worker a fundamental determinant of long-run living standards? Briefly explain. e) Why does the Solow growth model predict convergence in the standards of living of people in rich and poor countries, and why does the empirical evidence appear to reject the theory?

5.   **Government policies to raise long-run living standards**: Briefly discuss whether or not the government should adopt the following policies to raise long-run living standards: a) Introduce a 5% national sales tax. b) Provide a tax credit to firms proportional to their research and development expenses. c) Require high school students to pass some standardized achievement tests at some minimum performance level before they can graduate. d) Adopt a less democratic form of government. e) Adopt an industrial policy to subsidize production by high-tech firms.

Mathematical Problem-Solving Questions

1.   **Productivity growth**: Use the growth accounting equation to calculate productivity growth, given economic growth of 3.5%, capital stock growth of 5%, labor employment growth of 2%, the output elasticity of capital of 0.3, and the output elasticity of labor of 0.7.

2.   **Convergence of standards of living**: Calculate the real GDP per capita after four years of 10% annual economic growth for a country starting with a real GDP per capita of $15,000. Compare this to the real GDP per capita after four years of 1% annual economic growth for a country starting with a real GDP per capita of $20,000. Assume there is no population growth in either country.

3.   **Steady state**: Use the steady state equation, which says that saving equals investment in the steady state, to calculate steady state saving per worker, investment-per-worker, capital-labor ratio, and consumption per worker for a nation whose saving rate of 15%, output-per-worker = $20,000, population growth = 2%, and depreciation rate = 10%.

Answers to Fill-In-The-Blank Questions

1. growth accounting
2. growth accounting equation
3. capital-labor ratio
4. steady state
5. new growth theory
6. human capital
7. conditional convergence
8. unconditional convergence
9. industrial policy

Answers to True-False Questions

1.   T   As shown by Table 6.1 in the textbook, real GDP per capita was higher in the United Kingdom than in the United States in 1870. In the 1870 - 1989 period, long-run economic growth of 1.3% in the United Kingdom was lower than the 1.6% long-run economic growth in the United States. Consequently, real GDP per capita was higher in the United States than in the United Kingdom in 1989, even though population growth was higher in the United States than in the United Kingdom during this period.

2.   T   As shown by Table 6.1 in the textbook, real GDP per capita was substantially higher in the United States than in Germany and Japan in 1870. In the 1870 - 1989 period, long-run economic growth of 2.5% in Japan and 1.9% in Germany exceeded the 1.6% long-run growth rate of the United States. Consequently, the percent difference in their real GDP per capita levels is declining, so their standards of living are converging.

3.   F   Both a_N and a_k are constants in the growth accounting equation. Human capital increases that improve labor skills increase N, which is the amount of labor employed, adjusted for changes in the quality of labor. Technological innovations that increase the quality of capital increase K, which is the amount of capital employed, adjusted for the quality of capital. Any errors in adjusting N and K to measure human capital improvements in labor and technological improvements in capital would increase A, which measures improvements in the overall productivity of the factors of production. Technological innovations in outputs other than capital goods are measured as increases in output, Y.

4.   T   Output is a function of labor and capital inputs and their productivities. Holding constant the amounts of labor and capital used in production, any decline in output is caused by a decline in productivity, called an adverse productivity shock.

5.   T   With a_N = 0.7, a 5% increase in N will increase output by 3.5% = .05 x 0.7. With a_K = 0.3, a 5% increase in the capital stock would increase output by 1.5% = .05 x 0.3. With its higher output-elasticity coefficient, adding 5% more labor to a fixed amount of capital in production is more effective in increasing output than adding 5% more capital to a fixed amount of labor in production.

6. T   As shown in Table 6.3 of the textbook, Denison estimated that U.S. productivity growth was negative in the 1973 - 1982 period. As shown in Table 6.4 of the textbook, Shigehara estimated that U.S. productivity growth was zero in the 1973 - 1990 period. Compared to the 1948 - 1973 period, U.S. productivity growth declined by 1.8 percentage points and output growth declined by 2.15 percentage points. The decline in productivity growth largely explains the decline in output growth in the post-1973 period.

7. F   Increases in saving per worker increase the capital-labor ratio, which increases output per worker at a diminishing rate. At a high capital-labor ratio, it is possible that the marginal productivity of capital is so low that increasing saving per worker to increase the capital-labor ratio would increase output per worker less than the increase in saving, so that consumption per worker would decline. Recent research by Abel, Mankiw, Summers, and Zeckhauser concluded that increases in saving per worker would increase steady state consumption per worker in any country in the world today, even for the United States and Japan, which already have high capital-labor ratios compared to most countries.

8. T   A steady state exists in a nation when there is no change in output per worker, consumption per worker, and the capital-labor ratio. Although an increase in the saving rate or a decline in the population growth rate produce a one-time increase in output per worker, consumption per worker, and the capital-labor ratio, only productivity growth can continue to increase steady state output per worker and consumption per worker. Without ongoing increases in productivity, the consumption standard of living of a nation cannot continue to increase in the long run.

9. F   According to the Solow model, government policies of developing countries that effectively reduce the population growth rate will increase the steady state consumption standard of living in a country; this is shown in Figure 6.5 of the textbook. However, these policies are not necessarily economically efficient. To be efficient they would not only have to achieve their policy objective of reducing population growth to some desired population growth rate; they would have to do so at a lower economic cost than could be achieved by any alternative policy. There are many different population control policies used by the different governments of developing countries. Some are more efficient than others.

10. F   Most empirical evidence suggests that there is little tendency for the standards of living in poor and rich countries to unconditionally converge, even for countries with open economies. With open economies, an efficient capital market should cause savings to flow out of the rich countries, where the marginal productivity of capital is relatively low at their high capital-labor ratios; savings should flow into poor countries, where the marginal productivity of capital is relatively high at their low capital-labor ratios. Efficiency requires that saving flows to the highest valued uses in the world economy, which in theory is into investments in the poor countries, where capital is relatively scarce. The outflow of savings from rich countries would reduce their capital-labor ratio; while the inflow of foreign savings into the poor countries would increase their capital-labor ratios, causing the capital-labor ratios in rich and poor countries to converge. Contrary to theoretical expectations, poor countries have frequently had large net capital outflows; while rich countries have frequently had large net capital inflows. Substantial barriers to international trade and capital flows by many countries provide one explanation for this market inefficiency. Another possible explanation is political instability in poor countries, which leads potential foreign investors to fear that they will not be able to recoup their investments.

Answers to Multiple Choice Questions

1. b	8. e	15. d
2. c	9. a	16. b
3. e	10. d	17. a
4. d	11. d	18. e
5. a	12. b	19. d
6. e	13. a	20. e
7. c	14. c	

Answers to Short-Answer Essay Questions

1.   **Sources of economic growth:**

   a)   The three principal sources of economic growth are

      1) labor growth - increases in the work force;
      2) capital growth - increases in the amount of capital employed in the economy;
      3) productivity growth - increases in output for given amounts of labor and capital.

   b)   Causes of positive changes in the sources of economic growth:

      1) Labor growth. An increase in the size of the population through immigration or birth and an increase in the share of the population that works (e.g., more women) will increase labor growth.
      2) Capital growth. An increase in the rate of saving will increase capital growth.
      3) Productivity growth. An increase in human capital and a technological advance will increase productivity.

   c)   The growth accounting equation is $\dfrac{\Delta Y}{Y} = \dfrac{\Delta A}{A} + a_k \cdot \dfrac{\Delta k}{k} + a_N \cdot \dfrac{\Delta N}{N}$.

   d)   The variable a_N = the output-elasticity of labor = percent increase in output when labor increases by 1%.

   e)   An identity is an equation that is always true. The growth accounting equation is an identity because the value of productivity growth is always whatever it needs to be to achieve the equality. Productivity growth is a residual term in the equation. Because the equality always holds, the equation is an identity.

2.   **Causes of post-1973 growth slowdown:**

   Five of the significant causes of the post-1973 growth slowdown in the United States are as follows:

   1) Measurement problems. Actual growth may have exceeded measured economic growth during this period; the slowdown may be, at least in part, an illusion. Production of services now dominates production of goods, but increases in the quality and quantity of services (e.g., haircuts and financial consultant services) are harder to measure than increases in the quality and quantity of goods.

2) Legal and human environment. New legislated regulations to reduce pollution and improve worker safety and health caused some workers and capital to be allocated to meeting these new regulatory requirements, which reduced the amount of labor and capital available to produce goods and services. Increased use of labor and capital to fight crimes and a decline in educational quality (e.g., human capital) also reduced overall productivity.

3) Technological depletion. Per the technological depletion hypothesis, there were relatively few valuable technological innovations in this period and the earlier innovations are no longer producing significant productivity gains. Although significant breakthroughs in electronics (e.g., computers) and in biogenetic engineering (e.g., gene-splicing) have been achieved, they have not as yet produced significant productivity increases.

4) Commercial adaptation. American firms have been slow during this period to make commercially profitable use of recent scientific and technological breakthroughs, whereas some foreign firms, including Japanese firms, have benefited greatly from these breakthroughs.

5) Oil price increases. The substantial oil price increases in the post-1973 period lowered the amount of output that could be produced from a given amount of capital and labor, thus lowering productivity. Oil price increases caused the prices of all sources of energy and the prices of all intermediate products to increase, thereby significantly increasing final production costs.

3.   **The Solow model of growth:**

a)   An investment-per-worker and production-per-worker diagram follows. Consumption per worker, which is the difference between output per worker and investment per worker, is maximized at k_1.

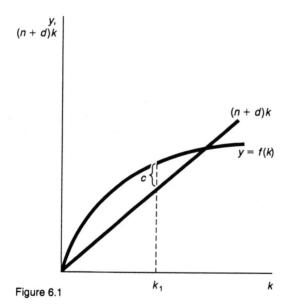

Figure 6.1

b)   The per-worker production curve is positively sloped because adding capital to each unit of labor increases output per worker. The curve is concave (i.e., increasing at a decreasing rate) because of diminishing marginal productivity of capital; output increases at a slower rate than capital when capital is added to production.

c)   A steady state diagram follows. At k*, steady state saving per worker = steady state investment per worker.

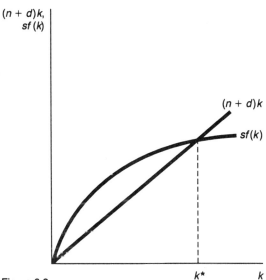

Figure 6.2

d)   The slopes of the two curves are as follows:

1)   The saving-per-worker curve is positively sloped, since saving is proportional to output per worker, which increases with the capital-labor ratio.

2)   The investment-per-worker curve is positively sloped, since investment per worker equals net investment per worker (nk) plus depreciation of capital per worker (dk), which both increase with the capital-labor ratio. The positive slope of the investment-per-worker curve is (n + d), with n and d both having positive values.

e)   If investment per worker initially exceeds saving per worker, then the initial capital-labor ratio exceeds the steady state capital-labor ratio. However, the capital-labor ratio will decline, because saving is insufficient to provide enough capital to maintain the initial capital-labor ratio. The capital-labor ratio will continue to decline until it reaches the steady state capital-labor ratio.

4. Fundamental determinants of long-run living standards:

a)   The following steady state diagram shows the effect of a decline in saving per worker, which causes the steady state capital-labor ratio to decline from k_1 to k_2.

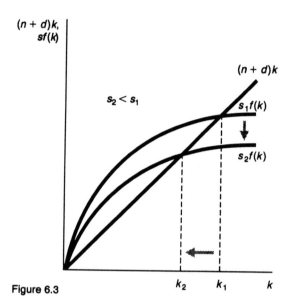

Figure 6.3

b)   The following steady state diagram shows the effect of a decline in population, which causes the steady state capital-labor ratio to increase from k_1 to k_2.

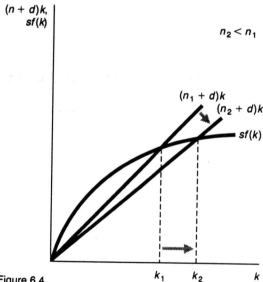

Figure 6.4

c)   The following steady state diagram shows the effect of a decline in productivity, which causes the steady state capital-labor ratio to decline from k_1 to k_2.

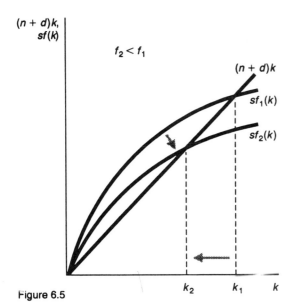

Figure 6.5

d)   No. In the Solow growth model, steady state investment per worker does not change over time in the long run, so investment per worker is proportional to labor growth plus depreciation (n + d). Steady state investment per worker is not an independent variable but a dependent variable; it is determined by population growth, the depreciation rate of capital, and saving per worker.

e)   The Solow model predicts that the standards of living of two closed-economy countries with different capital-labor ratios will eventually converge if they have the same production function, saving rate, and population growth rate. This is because they will have the same steady state capital-labor ratio toward which both economies move, and the steady state capital-labor ratio determines their long-run standard of living. If the two countries have open economies, convergence will be faster and will occur even if the two countries have different saving-per-worker functions; in this case, saving will flow out of the rich, high-saving-rate country into the poor country until the investment per worker is the same in each country. The lack of strong empirical support for unconditional convergence may be explained by inefficiencies in the international capital market and by variables that are missing from the model, including differences in human capital, political stability, and the availability of natural resources.

5.   **Government policies to raise long-run living standards:**

Economic theory alone cannot fully answer "should" questions, since those questions require us to say what we "want" or "prefer." Although science cannot tell us what we want, it can help us make policy decisions by identifying the economic costs and benefits of alternative choices. Among economists, there are those who favor and those who oppose each of the following policies: I offer one argument for and one argument against each policy proposal.

a)   A national sales tax

PRO: An increase in tax revenue that lowered private consumption and was not spent by the government would represent an increase in national saving. The Solow model shows that this increase in saving would produce a one-time jump in the country's standard of living.

CON: Although the tax increase may increase saving per worker, the government should not be using its taxation power to manage the aggregate saving rate. Households and firms can better decide how much they want to save without this kind of government intervention.

b)   A tax credit for research and development

PRO: A tax credit would raise the after-tax rate of return to firms investing in research and development, which would increase the rate of technological advances in the economy, thus increasing productivity. The Solow model shows that continuing productivity increases will produce continuing improvements in a country's standard of living.

CON: A tax credit for research and development will reduce government tax revenue and may not increase research and development (R&D) expenditures very much since firms would get the credit for all the R&D dollars they would have spent without the tax credit.

c)   Standardized achievement tests

PRO: Making students pass standardized achievement tests would encourage them, their parents, and their teachers to make sure they received a better education than they now receive, which would raise productivity. The Solow model shows that a one-time increase in productivity will provide a one-time jump in the country's standard of living.

CON: Although it is probably true that we don't achieve higher academic standards than we demand, standardized achievement tests would not necessarily represent higher aggregate standards; they could cause standards to fall to minimum required levels in many schools. Much of the enriching, motivating diversity of American education would be lost in a homogenized education system even if Americans policymakers could agree on the desired standards and acceptable tests.

d)   A less democratic form of government

PRO: One of the problems with a broadly democratic, representative, popularly elected government is that government leaders are subject to a lot of short-run political pressures to fund the pet projects of special interest group lobbies. Avoiding these inefficient, politically inspired projects would increase productivity. The Solow model shows that a one-time productivity improvement would create a one-time jump in a country's living standard.

CON: Government by the people, of the people, and for the people must be sensitive to the will of the people if it is going to act in the interests of the people. A government that is sheltered or isolated from the will of the people is unlikely to be more efficient in satisfying the demands of the people.

e)   Industrial policy

PRO: Production subsidies to high-tech firms will enable them to increase production and lower their product prices. These subsidies may create a wave of technological innovations, including technological advances in capital goods that can be used to lower production costs in many industries. Output growth will spill over to firms in many other industries linked to these high-tech firms, as suppliers and as buyers of their outputs, causing employment and economic growth to rise.   The Solow model shows that increases in the quality and quantity of capital goods will increase the country's standard of living.

CON: Production subsidies to high-tech firms would need to be financed by raising taxes on other firms; increased taxes would cause the other firms to cut production. In the absence of spillover benefits, these subsidies would be unfair. The subsidies may be taken as higher profits rather than invested in creating new technological innovations. The subsidies may cause foreign competitors to charge the country with unfair trading practices; foreign countries may respond by imposing some new trade barriers that reduce the country's exports. If the allocation of the factors of production with the production subsidies is less economically efficient than without them, then productivity would fall, causing the standard of living to fall.

Answers to Mathematical Problem-Solving Questions

1.   **Productivity growth:**

The growth accounting equation is $\dfrac{\Delta Y}{Y} = \dfrac{\Delta A}{A} + a_k \cdot \dfrac{\Delta k}{k} + a_N \cdot \dfrac{\Delta N}{N}$.

Therefore productivity growth is $\dfrac{\Delta A}{A} = \dfrac{\Delta Y}{Y} - a_k \cdot \dfrac{\Delta k}{k} - a_N \cdot \dfrac{\Delta N}{N}$.

For the given values, productivity growth = .6% = 3.5% - (0.3)(5%) - (0.7)(2%).

2.   **Convergence of standards of living:**

One country starts with real GDP per capita = $15,000 and achieves 10% economic growth each year, with no population growth. Its real GDP per capita at the end of the first year is $15,000 x 1.1 = $16,500; at the end of the second year it is $16,500 x 1.1 = $18,150; at the end of the third year it is $18,150 x 1.1 = $19,965; and at the end of the fourth year it is $19,965 x 1.1 = $21,962.

The other country starts with real GDP per capita = $20,000 and achieves 1% economic growth each year, with no population growth. Its real GDP per capita at the end of the first year is $20,000 x 1.01 = $20,200; at the end of the second year it is $20,200 x 1.01 = $20,402; at the end of the third year it is $20,402 x 1.01 = $20,606; and at the end of the fourth year it's $20,606 x 1.01 = $20,812.   The $20,812 real GDP per capita for this country is now $1150 lower than the real GDP per capita of the competing country.

3.   **Steady state:**

The steady state equation is sf(k) = (n + d)k. Given s = 15% and f(k) = $20,000, then sf(k) = (.15)($20,000) = $3000 = saving per worker. Given n = 2% and d = 10%, then $3000 = (.02 +.10)k = .12k. Therefore k = $3000/.12 = $25,000 = the capital-labor ratio, and investment per worker = (.12)($25,000) = $3000. Consumption per worker = f(k) - (n + d)k = $20,000 - $3000 = $17,000.

CHAPTER 7: THE ASSET MARKET, MONEY, AND PRICES

A Fill-In-The-Blanks Review of Chapter Highlights: Use the following key terms to fill in the blanks. Each key term is used only once.

demand for money
interest elasticity of money demand
M2
money
open-market operations
risk
velocity

expected returns
liquidity
medium of exchange
money demand function
portfolio allocation decision
store of value

income elasticity of money demand
M1
monetary aggregates
money supply
quantity theory of money
unit of account

1. _Money_ is the set of assets that are widely used to make payments. Since many different assets have been used as money in different countries and in different time periods within one country, a conceptual definition of money has to be quite general. One conceptual approach is to provide a functional definition of money. Whatever functions as money is money.

Money has three principal functions: it serves as a medium of exchange, a unit of account, and a store of value. As a 2. _Medium of Exchange_, money is used to pay for items purchased. Using money as a payment mechanism lowers the costs of trading resources, products, and assets; thereby the use of money promotes exchange and production for exchange in a market economy. As a 3. _Unit of Account_, the value of resources, goods, and assets is denominated in money units; each unit costs so many dollars. Using money as a unit of account lowers trading costs by greatly reducing the number of exchange value calculations we need to make in a market economy. As a 4. _Store of Value_, money is one possible asset that can be used to hold wealth. For example, if a farmer wanted to save the market value of some of his or her apple crop for five years, it would be cheaper to sell the apples now and save the money than it would be to store the apples now and sell them in five years for money. In brief, money is a form of wealth that can be used for making payments.

Money is the set of financial instruments that are widely used as a medium of exchange and store of value in a country. The total amounts of money in measurable sets of money assets are called 5. _Monetary Aggregates_, examples are M1 and M2. 6. _M1_ is a monetary aggregate of the assets that are principally used to make payments; M1 consists of currency plus checkable deposits in banks and thrifts. 7. _M2_ is a monetary aggregate that includes M1 but also has a number of assets that are largely used for saving (i.e., storing value). M2 consists of M1 plus saving accounts, small time deposits, noninstitutional money market accounts, noninstitutional money market mutual funds, overnight repurchase agreements, and overnight Eurodollars. The 8. _Money Supply_, or stock of money, is the number of dollars in a particular monetary aggregate; for example, there is an M1 money supply and an M2 money supply.

The supply of money is controlled by the central bank of the United States, which is called the Federal Reserve. The Federal Reserve controls the supply of money primarily through 9 _Open Market Operations_. The Federal Reserve can increase the money supply by an open market purchase of government bonds and can reduce the money supply by an open market sale of government bonds.

People hold all their wealth in portfolios of money assets and nonmonetary assets. The decision by a wealthholder about how much wealth to hold in the form of money and how much to hold in the form of nonmonetary assets is called a 10._Portfolio Allocation decision_. The three most important determinants of portfolio allocation decisions are expected return, risk, and liquidity. 11.___Expected Return___ are the rates of return or interest rates that different assets are expected to earn per year. 12.___Risk___ is a measure of the degree of uncertainty about the actual rate of return. For a high-risk asset there is a high probability that the actual return will be significantly different from the expected return. 13.___liquidity___ is a measure of the trading costs that will be incurred if you quickly trade the asset for money. The trading costs may be high for an illiquid asset, such as a house. To sell an illiquid asset quickly, a wealth-holder may have to drop the selling price far below the asset's full market value. Wealth-holders prefer assets with higher expected returns, lower risk, and more liquidity. For assets with a given liquidity, they will demand more of those assets that pay higher risk-adjusted, expected returns.

In addition to the amount of money demanded for use as a medium of exchange, some money is demanded as a store of value, because money is the most liquid asset and it is a relatively low-risk asset when the inflation rate is low and stable even though the expected return on money is lower than the expected return on nonmonetary assets. The 14.___demand for money___ in the macroeconomy is the total amount of money people want to hold in their portfolios in some time period. Real money demand is nominal money demand divided by the price level. The principal determinants of real money demand are specified by the 15.___Money Demand Function___. The money demand function tells us that the demand for real money balances is positively related to real income but negatively related to the nominal interest rate on nonmonetary assets. The nominal interest rate is the sum of the real interest rate and the expected rate of inflation. The percent change in the quantity of money demanded divided by the percent change in real income is called the 16.___Income Elasticity of Money Demand___; it measures how responsive money demand is to a change in real income. The percent change in the quantity of money demanded divided by the percent change in the nominal interest rate is called the 17.___Interest Elasticity___; it measures how responsive money demand is to a change in the nominal interest rate.

For a given level of nominal income, an increase in the demand for money is a decline in the velocity of money. 18.___Velocity___ is the circulation rate, or rate at which money is spent in buying the national output produced. For example, a velocity of 12 means that each dollar is spent 12 times a year, buying $12 worth of GDP. The nominal money supply times velocity equals nominal income (MV = PY). The inverse of velocity is the portion of nominal income demanded as money [$1/V = k = M^d/(PY)$]. According to the classical 19.___Quantity Theory of Money___, velocity is a constant number, so the portion of nominal income demand as money is fixed and does not vary with changes in the interest rate. If velocity is constant, the interest elasticity of money demand is zero and a change in the nominal money supply is needed to change nominal income for a given level of real income. Data presented in Figure 7.1 in the textbook show empirically that the velocity of M1 was not constant over the 1959 - 1992 period, especially after 1980, although the velocity of M2 was more stable than the velocity of M1.

To simplify our analysis of the asset market, we aggregate all wealth into monetary assets and nonmonetary assets. Given this aggregation, asset market equilibrium is achieved if and only if money market equilibrium is achieved. Since the asset market is in equilibrium whenever the money market is in equilibrium, we can study changes in asset market equilibrium by studying changes in money market equilibrium without separately analyzing changes in nonmonetary asset conditions. An increase in the nominal money supply relative to real money demand is the principal cause of inflation. An increase in expected inflation will increase the nominal interest rate for a given real interest rate.

True-False Questions: Circle T for true statements and circle F for false statements.

T F   1.   Money is the only asset that is efficient as a store of value.

T (F) 2.   Comparing the money prices of products is using money as a medium of exchange.

(T) F 3.   Examples of nonmonetary assets include bonds, corporate stocks, and land as well as houses and consumer durable goods produced in former years.

(T) F 4.   Examples of money assets in M2 include currency as well as checkable deposits and savings deposits in banks and thrifts.

T (F) 5.   Since 1970 there has been no change in composition of assets included in the M1 and M2 measures of the money supply.

(T) F 6.   Changes in the money supply, as measured by M1 and M2, are reported weekly and monthly by the Federal Reserve; these data are regularly reported by the business media.

T (F) 7.   The U.S. president is principally responsible for deciding how much the money supply should change in any year.

(T) F 8.   As the real interest rate on nonmonetary assets declines, the quantity of money demanded increases.

T (F) 9.   Both the nominal demand for money and the real demand for money increase when the price level increases.

(T) F 10.   If the real money supply initially exceeds real money demand, the price level will rise just enough to achieve asset market equilibrium where $M/P = L$.

Multiple Choice Questions: Circle the letter corresponding to the correct answer to each question.

1.   Which of the following statements best defines money?
      a. Income is money.
      b. Wealth is money.
      c. Time is money.
      d. The root of all evil is money.
      (e) The set of assets that can be used to make payments is money.

2.   Which of the following best illustrates the medium of exchange function of money?
      a. The price of a new car is $25,000.
      b. A penny saved is a penny earned.
      c. A person owes $10,000 on his or her credit card.
      (d) You pay $3 to purchase a bag of apples.
      e. Time is money.

3.   The number of units of one good that trade for one unit of alternative goods can be determined most easily when
      (a) there is one unit of account.
      b. the goods all weigh about the same.
      c. the goods are all new.
      d. the goods are actively traded through barter.
      e. money is used as a medium of exchange.

4.   The most widely used money assets
      a. include government bonds.
      b. do not include bank deposits.
      c. include credit cards.
      d. and nonmonetary assets are used as a store of value.
      e. have zero risk.

5.   One of the criticisms of standard monetary aggregates is that
      a. they cannot be measured.
      b. the sum of the assets they contain is not weighted by the frequency of their use in making payments.
      c. they cannot be controlled by the central bank.
      d. fluctuations in their size are purely inflationary.
      e. they are never updated to include the assets actually used in modern transactions.

6.   Which of the following is not included in M1?
      a. Demand deposits
      b. NOW accounts
      c. Money market accounts
      d. Other checkable deposits
      e. Currency

7.   Compared to M1, the assets in M2
      a. are more liquid.
      b. are held more as a store of value.
      c. are more homogeneous.
      d. are more stable in value.
      e. have a higher velocity.

8.   The shortest reporting period for publication of data on the size of the money supply and on money supply growth is
      a. weekly.
      b. semimonthly.
      c. daily.
      d. monthly.
      e. annually.

9.   An open market purchase by the Federal Reserve will
      a. increase the nominal interest rate.
      b. reduce the price level.
      c. increase the supply of corporate bonds on the open market.
      d. reduce real GDP.
      e. increase the nominal money supply.

10.   Which of the following portfolio allocation decisions represents the best individual response to an increase in the interest rate on nonmonetary assets?
      a. Sell some stocks and use the money to buy bonds.
      b. Sell some bonds and use the money to buy stocks.
      c. Trade some money for nonmonetary assets.
      d. Sell some land and use the money to buy nonmonetary assets.
      e. Reduce your assets and increase your liabilities.

11.   Instability in money demand for M1 in the mid-1970s and since the early 1980s is most closely related to changes in
        a.   Federal Reserve chairmen.
        b.   the risks of nonmonetary assets.
        c.   real GNP.
        d.   deregulation, financial innovations, and payment technologies.
        e.   the liquidity of M1 assets.

12.   In part, money is demanded because
        a.   it usually has a higher expected return than nonmonetary assets.
        b.   it is relatively low risk when inflation is stable.
        c.   it is relatively high risk.
        d.   it usually has a lower expected return than nonmonetary assets.
        e.   money is relatively illiquid.

13.   The liquidity of an asset indicates
        a.   how many years before the asset matures.
        b.   how quickly the asset can be sold at market value.
        c.   how easily the asset is physically damaged by frequent exchange.
        d.   the costs of transporting the asset to market.
        e.   how much the purchasing power of the asset can be lowered by inflation.

14.   The nominal demand for money is proportional to
        a.   nominal income.
        b.   real income.
        c.   the nominal interest rate.
        d.   the nominal interest rate on money.
        e.   the price level.

15.   The money demand function specifies
        a.   the variables that determine how much money is held in a given time period.
        b.   the uses of money.
        c.   the value of money.
        d.   how much real income will increase if money demand increases by 5%.
        e.   which market actors demand money.

16.   According to the classical quantity theory of money, velocity
        a.   increases with nominal income.
        b.   is positively related to the real interest rate.
        c.   is a constant number.
        d.   is proportional to the price level.
        e.   is unstable.

17.   The income elasticity of money demand is the
        a.   increase in the quantity of money demanded per dollar increase in nominal income.
        b.   decrease in the quantity of money demanded per dollar increase in nominal income.
        c.   percent increase in the quantity of money demanded per dollar increase in nominal income.
        d.   percent decline in the quantity of money demanded per dollar increase in nominal income.
        e.   percent change in the quantity of money demanded divided by the percent change in real income.

18. Goldfeld estimated the interest elasticity of money demand to be in the range of
    a. -10% to -20%.
    b. -5% to -10%.
    c. -1% to -5%.
    d. -0.1% to -0.2%.
    e. -0.1% to -2%.

19. If real money demand remains constant, then a 10% increase in the nominal money supply will cause
    a. real income to rise.
    b. real interest rate to rise.
    c. expected inflation to rise by 10%.
    d. inflation to rise by 10%.
    e. the price level to rise by 10%.

20. If the real interest remains constant, an increase in expected inflation from 4% to 8% will cause the nominal interest rate to
    a. remain constant.
    b. rise to 8%.
    c. fall to 8%.
    d. rise by 4 percentage points.
    e. fall by 4 percentage points.

Short-Answer Essay Questions

1. **Money supply:** a) Identify and briefly describe the three principal uses of money. b) What overall economic benefit does money provide to a market economy? c) What are the major components of M1? d) What are the major components of M2? e) What determines the supply of money?

2. **Portfolio allocation:** a) Define portfolio allocation decision. b) Identify and briefly define the three principal determinants of portfolio allocation decisions. c) What is the principal economic goal of market actors in making portfolio allocation decisions? d) How often are portfolio allocation decisions made? e) Compare and contrast money and nonmonetary assets in terms of expected return, risk, and liquidity.

3. **Money demand:** a) What is the difference between nominal money demand and real money demand? b) State the money demand function. c) Identify three possible causes of an increase in money demand. d) Briefly explain how money demand and velocity are related. e) Do modern classicals and Keynesians accept the traditional quantity theory of money assumption that velocity is approximately constant? Briefly explain.

4. **Asset market equilibrium:** a) Define asset market equilibrium. b) State the asset market equilibrium equation. c) Explain why the nonmonetary asset market cannot be in disequilibrium when the money market is in equilibrium. d) In the classical model would changes in the nominal money supply or money demand create changes in employment, real income, the real interest rate, or real wealth? Briefly explain. e) In the classical model would a change in the nominal money supply change the real money supply?

5.   **Money supply growth and inflation**: a) Define inflation. b) State the inflation equation. c) In the classical model would a change in the nominal money supply change real income or change the income elasticity of money demand? Briefly explain. d) Use the inflation equation to identify two changes that would increase inflation. e) Explain how the Federal Reserve could use monetary policy to maintain price level stability.

Mathematical Problem-Solving Questions

1.   **Inflation rate**: Use the inflation rate equation to calculate the inflation rate for each of the following conditions, assuming that the income elasticity of money demand is 2/3: a) nominal money supply growth of 4% and real income growth of 6%; b) nominal money supply growth of 12% and real income growth of 6%; and c) nominal money supply growth of -2% and real income growth of -3%.

2.   **Interest elasticity of money demand**: Calculate the decline in money demand for each of the following changes in the interest rate, given that money demand is $500 billion at an interest rate of 5%: a) The interest rises to 8% and the interest elasticity of money demand is -0.1; and b) the interest rate rises to 8% and the interest elasticity of money demand is -0.2.

3.   **Expected inflation**: Calculate the expected rate of inflation for each of the following conditions: a) The nominal interest rate is 10% and the real interest rate is 4%; b) the nominal interest rate is 6% and the real interest rate is 3%; and c) the nominal interest rate is 4% and the real interest rate is -1%.

Answers to Fill-In-The-Blank Questions

1. money
2. medium of exchange
3. unit of account
4. store of value
5. monetary aggregates
6. M1
7. M2
8. money supply
9. open market operations
10. portfolio allocation decision
11. expected returns
12. risk
13. liquidity
14. demand for money
15. money demand function
16. income elasticity of money demand
17. interest elasticity of money demand
18. velocity
19. quantity theory of money

Answers to True-False Questions

1. F   Money is not unique in its function as a store of value or means of saving. Bonds and corporate stocks are other financial assets that are held by wealth-holders to store their wealth for future use. People also hold real assets, such as real estate, as a store of value.

2. F   Comparing the money prices of products is using money as a unit of account.

3. T   Bonds and corporate stocks are financial nonmonetary assets. Land is a real nonmonetary asset. Houses and consumer durables that were produced in former years are also real nonmonetary assets. Houses produced in the current year are investment goods, and consumer durables produced in the current year are consumer goods. Goods produced in the current year are part of national output, rather than wealth.

4. T   M2 includes all the money assets in M1, such as currency and checkable deposits, plus other assets, such as savings deposits in banks and thrifts.

5. F   What we call money today is substantially different from the composition of assets called money in 1970. For example, M1 did not include NOW accounts until the early 1980s. M2 became an official measure of money in 1971, but money market deposit accounts and money market mutual funds were not included until the mid-1970s. The particular mix of assets that we call money is likely to continue to change in the near future, in part because of deregulation of the banking industry and financial innovations.

6. T   Changes in the money supply, as measured by M1 and M2, are reported weekly and monthly by the Federal reserve; these data are regularly reported by the business media. Changes in the money supply are closely watched, mostly because of the Keynesian belief that changes in nominal money supply can create changes in the real interest rate, real output, and unemployment in the short run.

7. F   The central bank uses monetary policy to control the money supply. The central bank of the United States is called the Federal Reserve. The U.S. presidency is not part of the Federal Reserve.

8. T   Money demand is negatively related to the interest rate on nonmonetary assets. Goldfeld estimated the interest elasticity of real money demand to be in the range of -0.1 to -0.2; this suggests that real money demand is relatively insensitive to small changes in the real interest rate. For a given expected rate of inflation, a change in the nominal interest rate is a change in the real interest rate. For a given price level, a change in nominal money demand is a change in real money demand.

9. F   An increase in the price level will create a proportional increase in the nominal demand for money in the long run, but the real demand for money is independent of the price level in the long run.

10. T   If the real money supply initially exceeds real money demand, the price level will rise just enough to reduce the real money supply to the level of real money balances demanded. When money supply equals money demand, the asset market is in equilibrium.

Answers to Multiple Choice Questions

1. e	8. a	15. a
2. d	9. e	16. c
3. a	10. c	17. e
4. d	11. d	18. d
5. b	12. b	19. e
6. c	13. b	20. d
7. b	14. e	

Answers to Short-Answer Essay Questions

1. **Money supply**:

a)   The three principal uses of money are the following:

    1)   Medium of exchange. Money is used to pay for the factors of production, goods and services, and nonmonetary assets. For example, you may be able to buy a bag of apples for $3.

    2)   Unit of account. Money is the standard of value used to compare the market values of dissimilar resources, goods, and assets. For example, the dollar is the monetary standard for the United States; the value of other things is measured in dollar units.

    3)   Store of value. Money is used as a way of holding wealth. For example, keeping money in NOW account deposits and savings account deposits represents using money as a store of value.

b)   The principal economic benefit of using money in a market economy is that it lowers trading costs. By lowering trading costs, the use of money encourages people to allocate their factors of production to their highest valued uses to produce for exchange in a market economy, which increases real GDP.

c)   The principal components of M1 are currency, demand deposits, other checkable deposits, and traveler's checks. Currency includes coins and Federal Reserve notes (i.e., paper money). Other checkable deposits are checking accounts at banks and thrifts that earn interest (e.g., NOW accounts).

d)   The principal components of M2 are M1, savings account deposits including money market deposit accounts (MMDAs), small time deposits, money market mutual funds (MMMFs), overnight repurchase agreements, and overnight Eurodollars. Small time deposits are certificates of deposits (CDs) of less than $100,000 denomination.

e)   The Federal Reserve determines the supply of money. The Federal Reserve is the central bank of the United States.

2. **Portfolio allocation**:

a)   Definition: By making a portfolio allocation decision, a market actor determines how much of various assets to use to hold one's wealth.

b)   The three principal determinants of portfolio allocation decisions are the following:

    1)   Expected return - the predicted percent increase in value that an asset will pay on average when the actual rate of return is not known with certainty.

    2)   Risk - a measure of the likelihood that the actual return will significantly differ from the expected return. The higher the risk, the greater the probability that the actual return will significantly differ from the expected return.

    3)   Liquidity - a measure of the trading costs incurred when an asset has to be sold quickly. The more illiquid an asset is, the lower we have to drop the price below market value to achieve a quick sale.

c)   The principal goal of market actors in making portfolio allocation decisions is to maximize their income. Given their liquidity preferences, individuals and firms attempt to maximize their earnings by choosing the combination of assets that will provide the maximum risk-adjusted, expected return on the portfolio.

d)   Portfolio allocation decisions may be made whenever a market actor's preferences for risk or liquidity change and whenever the expected return, risk, and liquidity of one or more assets changes.

e)   Nonmonetary assets earn higher expected rates of return, are higher risk, and are less liquid than money.

3.   **Money demand:**

a)   Real versus nominal money demand:

1) Real money demand = L = amount of money held, measured in terms of the goods it will buy.

2) Nominal money demand = PL = market value of the money held = dollar value of goods and services that the money held could purchase.

b)   The money demand function is $M/P = L(Y, r + \pi^e)$.

The demand for real money balances is a function of real income (Y), the real interest rate (r), and the expected rate of inflation (π^e). A change in the value of Y, r, or π^e will change the real quantity of money demanded.

c)   The real quantity of money demanded would increase if real income increased, the real interest rate on nonmonetary assets declined, or expected inflation declined. The nominal interest rate equals the sum of the real interest rate and expected inflation (i.e., $i = r + \pi^e$). A increase in the nominal interest, created by an increase in the real interest rate or an increase in expected inflation, will reduce real money demand.

d)   Velocity is negatively related to real money demand. Velocity = PY/M = nominal income/nominal money supply = the number of times each dollar is spent in buying final goods and services produced in the current time period. In equilibrium, M/P = L; real money supply = real money demand. By replacing M/P with L, we see that velocity: V = Y/L. Velocity increases when real money demand declines for a given real income. If real demand for money increases relative to real income, velocity declines.

e)   No. Both classicals and Keynesians believe that real money demand (L) depends on Y, r, and π^e. For velocity to be constant, the ratio of real income to real money demand must be constant, since V = Y/L. This would require that the income elasticity of money demand = 1, and the interest elasticity of money demand = 0. However, empirical research suggests that the income elasticity of money demand is approximately 2/3, and the interest elasticity of money demand is between -0.1 and -0.2. Therefore velocity is not constant; it increases when income increases and when the interest rate increases.

4.   **Asset market equilibrium:**

a)   Asset market equilibrium exists when the quantity of assets supplied equals the quantity of assets demanded in a national economy in some time period. The aggregate net value of a country's assets is its wealth.

b)   The asset market equilibrium equation is $M/P = L(Y, r + \pi^e)$.

c)   All wealth is held in the form of money assets and nonmonetary assets. For a given level of national wealth, $(M^d - M) + (NM^d - NM) = 0$. If money market equilibrium exists, $(M^d - M) = 0$; therefore $(NM^d - NM) = 0$. If there is no excess supply or excess demand for money, then there is no excess supply or excess demand for nonmonetary assets, so the asset market clears.

d)   No. In the classical model, changes in the nominal money supply or money demand would not create changes in employment, real income, the real interest rate, or real wealth. Changes in the nominal money supply or money demand create changes in the price level, but do not affect the value of any real variable. Real variables are independent of the price level. Employment is determined by labor supply and labor demand. For a given level of employment, real income or output is determined by the production function. Desired saving and desired investment determine the real interest rate. Real wealth is the accumulated value of income saved in all previous time periods.

e)   No. In the classical model a change in the nominal money supply would not change the real money supply. M is the nominal money supply. P is the price level. M/P is the real money supply. An increase in M causes P to rise by the same percentage, so M/P doesn't change. For example, a 20% increase in the nominal money supply would increase the price level by 20%. Velocity and real output are both independent of the money supply. For a given velocity and real output, M/P is fixed because $M/P = Y/V$. Therefore a change in M cannot change M/P.

5.   **Money supply growth and inflation:**

a)   Inflation is the continuous increase in the price level in some time period. The percent increase in the price level in a year is the inflation rate.

b)   The inflation rate equation is $\pi = \dfrac{\Delta M}{M} + \eta_Y \cdot \dfrac{\Delta Y}{Y}$.

c)   No. In the classical model, real income and the income elasticity of money demand are not dependent on the nominal money supply, they are independent of the nominal money supply. Real income or output is determined by labor supply, labor demand, and the production function. The income elasticity of money demand shows the effect of a change in real income on the real demand for money.

d)   The inflation equation shows that an increase in nominal money supply growth would increase inflation for a given level of real money demand. Similarly, a decline in output growth would increase inflation for a given rate of nominal money supply growth. A decline in real output growth could increase inflation by reducing growth in the real demand for money, $\Delta L/L$.

e)   The inflation equation shows that the Federal Reserve could maintain price level stability by increasing the nominal money supply at the same rate of growth as real money demand; in the absence of inflation the increase in the nominal money supply is an increase in the real money supply. Any greater increase in the money supply would be inflationary; any lesser increase in the money supply would be deflationary.

Answers to Mathematical Problem-Solving Questions

1.   **Inflation rate**: The inflation rate equations for the three conditions are as follows:

   a) Inflation rate = 4% - 2/3(6%) = 4% - 4% = 0%.

   b) Inflation rate = 12% - 2/3(6%) = 12% - 4% = 8%.

   c) Inflation rate = -2% - 2/3(-3) = -2% + 2% = 0%.

2.   **Interest elasticity of money demand**: An increase in the interest rate reduces the demand for real money balances. An increase in the interest rate from 5% to 8% is a 60% increase in the interest rate.

   a) Change in real money demand = -0.1(60%)($500 billion) = (-6%)($500 billion) = -$30 billion.

   b) Change in real money demand = -0.2(60%)($500 billion) = (-12%)($500 billion) = -$60 billion.

3.   **Expected inflation**: The expected rate of inflation = the nominal interest rate - the real interest rate.

   a) Expected inflation = 10% - 4% = 6%.

   b) Expected inflation = 6% - 3% = 3%.

   c) Expected inflation = 4% - (-1%) = 5%.

CHAPTER 8: HOUSEHOLD DECISIONS TO CONSUME, SAVE, AND WORK: A MORE FORMAL TREATMENT

A Fill-In-The-Blanks Review of Chapter Highlights: Use the following key terms to fill in the blanks. Each key term is used only once.

bequest motive
budget constraint
consumption-smoothing motive
2 income effect (of the real interest rate on saving)
indifference curve
no-borrowing, no-lending point
present value
1 substitution effect (of the real interest rate on saving)
utility

borrowing constraint
budget line
income effect
4 income effect (of the real wage on labor supply)
life-cycle model
permanent income theory
present value of lifetime resources (PVLR)
3 substitution effect (of the real wage on labor supply)

Forward-looking consumers consider their current and future resources as well as their preferences for current and future consumption in making their consumption and saving decisions. For each possible level of current consumption the 1. *Budget Constraint* determines future consumption for given values of initial wealth, current income, expected future income, and the real interest rate. The 2. *Budget Line* is a graph of the budget constraint, depicting the set of current consumption and future consumption (c, c^f) combinations available to a consumer. The slope of the budget line is $- (1 + r)$; an increase in the real interest rate will cause the budget line to pivot clockwise at the 3. *No-Borrowing, No-Lending*

An 4. *Indifference Curve* depicts the set of alternative (c, c^f) choices that would provide a consumer with a fixed level of utility. The negative slope of an indifference curve illustrates the trade-off between current consumption and future consumption for a given level of consumer utility. Indifference curves are bowed toward the origin to illustrate the consumption-smoothing motive. Indifference curves that are higher and further to the right provide more utility than lower indifference curves; higher indifference curves are preferred but may not be attainable with a given budget constraint. A consumer maximizes utility by choosing the (c, c^f) point on the budget line that is tangent to an indifference curve.

The current resource value of income payments received in the future, for example $[y^f/(1 + r)]$, is called the 5. *Present Value* of these resources. The current resource value of initial wealth and current income is the same as their present value, since these economic resources are available in the present (i.e., current) time period. The 6. *PVLR* is the current dollar value of a consumer's initial wealth, current income, and expected future income. PVLR determines the budget constraint by determining the present value of lifetime consumption [i.e., $PVLC = c + c^f/(1+r) = y + y^f/(1 + r) + a$]. At any point on the budget line the present value of current and future consumption equals PVLR. For a given real interest rate an increase in PVLR causes the budget line to shift to the right by the amount of the increase.

Because of their 7. *Consumption-Smoothing Motive*, households (i.e., individuals and families) tend to spend a fairly stable share of their economic resources in each time period to maximize their 8. *Utility* (i.e., happiness, satisfaction, or well-being) intertemporally. Consistent with the consumption-smoothing motive, the

9. _Permanent Income Theory_ predicts that consumption spending will change more in response to permanent changes in one's income than in response to temporary changes in one's income. The 10. _Life-Cycle Model_ is also consistent with the consumption-smoothing motive; it predicts that consumption changes much less than income as individuals advance through life from the early working years, to the high-income years, to retirement years.

The 11. _Bequest Motive_ causes people to save more and consume less in each time period, so they can leave an estate of accumulated wealth for their heirs.

By restricting the amount of future income that can be borrowed, a 12. _Borrowing Constraint_ potentially affects the consumption and saving decision. A nonbinding borrowing constraint has no effect on an individual's consumption and saving decision because the person does not desire to borrow more than he or she is able to borrow. A binding borrowing constraint reduces current consumption and dissaving because it reduces the amount that can be borrowed against future income.

A change in the real interest rate has two opposing effects on desired saving for both net savers and borrowers; these are the substitution effect and the 13. _Income Effect_. The 14. _1_ of an increase in the real interest rate is an increase in desired saving. Households save more because the higher rate of return increases the reward to saving. For savers, the 15. _2_ of an increase in the real interest rate is a decline in desired saving. Households that save reduce their desired saving because an increase in the rate of return increases their wealth. For lenders, desired saving is positively related to the real interest rate if the substitution effect is stronger than the income effect. Empirical evidence suggests that the substitution effect does exceed the income effect for savers but not by much. For borrowers, an increase in the interest rate reduces their wealth; this negative income effect causes them to reduce their dissaving and current consumption. For borrowers, both the substitution effect and the income effect of an increase in the interest rate causes them to save more and consume less in the current period.

Assuming that the substitution effect is stronger than the income effect for savers, desired saving is negatively related to the tax rate on interest earnings. An increase in taxes reduces the after-tax real interest rate, causing savers to save less and consume more in the current period.

A change in the real wage has both a substitution effect and an income effect on the amount of labor supplied. An increase in the real wage is an increase in the rate of return to work relative to leisure; the 16. _3_ tells us that people tend to give up some leisure to work more when the real wage rises. However, an increase in the real wage also increases labor's real income for a given amount of work; the 17. _4_ tells us that people tend to give up some work for leisure when the real wage rises. Assuming that the positive substitution effect of a temporary increase in the real wage is more powerful than the negative income effect on labor supplied, more labor will be supplied at a temporarily higher wage. However, a permanent increase in the real wage, by making workers wealthier, is likely to reduce the amount of labor supplied.

True-False Questions: Circle T for true statements and F for false statements

T (F) 1. In the two-period model, every dollar spent today on consumption reduces future spending by a dollar in real terms.

T (F) 2. If c = y + a, the individual is not dissaving.

T (F) 3. The constant slope of the budget line shows that a consumer is willing to trade off future consumption for current consumption at a constant rate.

T F 4. For an individual, the present value of current consumption is c; the present value of wealth is a.

T (F) 5. An indifference curve depicts the set of (c, c^f) combinations that have the same total cost.

(T) F 6. For a given real interest rate, an increase in income or wealth will shift the budget line to the right. However, an increase in income will increase saving, an increase in wealth will reduce saving.

(T) F 7. According to the permanent income theory, consumers adjust to temporary business cycle fluctuations in their income mostly by reducing their saving rate during recessions and increasing their saving rate during expansions; changes in consumption spending are small relative to changes in current income.

(T) F 8. According to the Ricardian equivalence proposition, a temporary tax cut that raises each household's income by $1000 will not increase their consumption spending; households will save the $1000 to pay for the anticipated future tax increase needed to pay off the increase in government debt created by the tax cut.

T (F) 9. According to the life-cycle model, individuals should dissave in their early working years and during their retirement years.

(T) F 10. For a temporary change in the real interest rate or real wage, the substitution effect is likely to be greater than the income effect; but for a permanent change in the real interest rate or real wage, the income effect is likely to be greater than the substitution effect.

Multiple Choice Questions: Circle the letter corresponding to the correct answer to each question.

1. Which of the following behaviors is not characteristic of a forward-looking consumer?
   a. The individual reduces his or her saving when his or her expected future income increases.
   b. The individual dissaves during retirement years.
   c. The individual reduces saving during a temporary recession.
   d. The individual reduces saving during his or her middle-age, high-income years.
   e. The individual's saving decision is not affected by a nonbinding borrowing constraint.

2. Which of the following variables does not directly determine the budget constraint?
   a. Initial wealth
   b. Future consumption
   c. The real interest rate
   d. Current income
   e. Expected future income

3. The slope of the budget line is
   a. $-1/(1 + i)$.
   b. $1/(1 - i)$.
   c. $(1 + r)$.
   d. $-(1 + r)$.
   e. $1/(1 + r)$.

4.   Which of the following changes would reduce the present value of a given future real income payment?
a. The real interest rate increases.
b. The real interest rate declines.
c. The future payments will be received one year earlier than initially expected.
d. The individual learns that she or he will not be allowed to borrow against the future income.
e. Inflation will be higher than expected between the current period and the receipt of the future payment.

5.   For a given real interest rate an increase in the present value of lifetime resources (PVLR) will always
a. increase saving.
b. reduce consumption.
c. create a parallel shift to the right of the budget line by the amount of the increase in PVLR.
d. increase the slope of the budget line because it will allow for more future consumption at any given level of current consumption.
e. cause the individual's preference for current consumption relative to future consumption to increase.

6.   The fact that consumption is more stable than income over time is best explained by
a. the income effect.
b. utility maximization.
c. the consumption-smoothing motive.
d. binding borrowing constraints.
e. impatience.

7.   The principal reason consumers buy goods and services is that doing so increases their
a. real income.
b. wealth.
c. PVLR.
d. consumption opportunities.
e. utility.

8.   According to Friedman's permanent income theory, a temporary increase in income will
a. increase saving more than will a permanent increase in income.
b. increase consumption more than will a permanent increase in income.
c. increase an individual's PVLR more than will a permanent increase in income.
d. not affect current consumption and saving because these depend only on permanent income.
e. not increase the value of an individual's future assets.

9.   According to Modigliani's life-cycle model, individuals usually
a. dissave during their middle-age, high-income years.
b. dissave during their early working years and retirement years.
c. save for the future.
d. save throughout their working years but dissave during their retirement years.
e. have high saving rates through their lifetimes so they can provide large bequests.

10.   An increase in an individual's bequest motive would
a. increase the real interest rate.
b. increase inflation.
c. shift the budget line to the right.
d. reduce present values.
e. reduce current consumption.

11.   Which of the following best illustrates a borrowing constraint?
   a.   Your parents refuse to give you a no-interest loan.
   b.   A bank wants you to pay interest on a loan while you are going to school.
   c.   A bank wants to charge you a relatively high interest rate on a loan.
   d.   Your credit card permits you to borrow up to $5000.
   e.   A bank will give you a loan only if you appear able to pay it back.

12.   A nonbinding borrowing constraint
   a.   reduces saving.
   b.   creates a positive income effect.
   c.   does not affect the consumption and saving decision.
   d.   causes individuals to consume all their initial wealth and current income.
   e.   causes individuals to dissave.

13.   One reason why the Japanese had higher saving rates in the 1980s than Americans is that
   a.   unlike the Japanese, Americans are not forward-looking consumers.
   b.   unlike the Japanese culture, the American culture does not encourage saving.
   c.   the opportunity to buy low-cost housing, financed mostly by borrowing, was greater in the United States.
   d.   a higher percentage of American households provides large bequests.
   e.   during the 1980s temporary income declined in America while permanent income declined in Japan.

14.   According to the budget constraint equation, which of the following changes would reduce future consumption for a net saver?
   a. y^f increases.
   b.   c increases.
   c.   r increases.
   d.   a increases.
   e.   y increases.

15.   The present value calculations show that
   a.   at low interest rates there is no point in saving.
   b.   an increase in saving will lower the interest rate.
   c.   the longer you have to wait for a payment the lower its present value.
   d.   people should not borrow money at high interest rates.
   e.   present values increase with the interest rate.

16.   An alternative view of a person's budget constraint is that the present value of lifetime consumption equals
   a. $y + y^f/(1 + r) + a$.
   b. $y + y^f + a$.
   c. $y + y^f(1 + r) + a$.
   d. $c + c^f$.
   e. $c(1 + r) + c^f$.

17.   The substitution effect of a decline in the real interest rate would
   a.   at least partially offset the income effect for a saver.
   b.   cause desired saving to increase.
   c.   sometimes increase and sometimes decrease desired saving; the theoretical effect is ambiguous.
   d.   never be greater than the income effect.
   e.   have the same effect as the income effect for a saver.

18.   An increase in the personal income tax rate on interest income received by households will
       a.   unambiguously increase desired saving.
       b.   unambiguously decrease desired saving.
       c.   decrease saving if the income effect is larger than the substitution effect.
       d.   decrease saving if the income effect is smaller than the substitution effect.
       e.   not affect national saving.

19.   Which of the following does not illustrate leisure?
       a.   Repairing your home
       b.   A night out for dinner and dancing
       c.   Studying for an upcoming economics exam
       d.   Enjoying a productive day at the office
       e.   Figuring out how to pay your household bills on your limited income

20.   If an unexpected bonus temporarily increases your income, the income effect suggests that you will
       a.   postpone retirement.
       b.   continue working but reduce the number of hours worked.
       c.   continue working forty hours per week even if you could work more.
       d.   offer to increase the number of hours you work.
       e.   substitute toward leisure, whose relative rate of return has increased.

Short-Answer Essay Questions

1.   **Consumption and saving motives**: a) Why do individuals save? b) Can the consumption decision and saving decision be made separately? Briefly explain. c) Describe the behavior predicted by the consumption-smoothing motive. d) How would a decline in an individual's bequest motive affect the individual's consumption and saving? e) State the effects on consumption and saving of a binding borrowing constraint.

2.   **Present values**: a) Define present value. b) Write out the present value equation for payments to be received *n* years in the future. c) Assuming an interest rate of 5%, calculate the present values of a $1000 payment received in one year, in two years, and in three years. d) Identify four variables that determine the present value of lifetime resources. e) How would a decline in an individual's PVLR affect the individual's budget line and PVLC?

3.   **Budget constraints and preferences**: a) Draw a budget line diagram with an indifference curve for a two-period model. Label the axes, curves, and optimal consumption combination. b) What would cause the slope of the budget line to increase (i.e., become steeper)? c) Identify two variable changes that would cause the budget line to shift to the right. d) What economic cost of current consumption is illustrated by the budget line? e) Explain why an indifference curve is negatively sloped and bowed toward the origin.

4.   **Permanent income theory**: a) Define the terms temporary income and permanent income. b) Compare and contrast the effects on consumption and saving of an increase in temporary income and an increase in permanent income. c) Is the permanent income theory consistent with the consumption-smoothing motive? Briefly explain. d) How does the permanent income theory help us to understand why the effect of a recession on current consumption depends on whether the recession is expected to be temporary or permanent? e) State one advantage of the life-cycle model over the permanent income theory in explaining consumption.

5.   **Life-cycle model**: a) Identify the three principal stages of consumption and saving in Modigliani's life-cycle model. b) Briefly explain the hump-shaped pattern of saving in the life-cycle model. c) Is the life-cycle model consistent with the consumption-smoothing motive? Briefly explain. d) Does the life-cycle model explain the behavior of people who are forward-looking, or those who are relatively impatient, or both? Briefly explain. e) Does the life-cycle model explain the behavior of people with low bequest motives, high bequest motives, or both? Briefly explain.

6.   **Explaining the Japanese saving rate**: a) State and briefly explain four reasons why the Japanese saving rate exceeded the American saving rate in the 1980s. b) Which, if any, of these reasons is a determinant of individuals' opportunities to save? c) Which, if any, of these reasons is a determinant of individuals' incentives to save? d) Identify one change that would increase the aggregate saving rate in the United States. e) Evaluate the following statement: The American saving rate is far too low, thus government policymakers must do whatever is needed to raise the saving rate in America to equal the Japanese saving rate.

7.   **The real interest rate, taxes, and the saving decision**: a) Draw a budget line and indifference curve diagram for a person who chooses to consume at the no-borrowing, no-lending point. Label the axes, curves, and optimal consumption combination. b) Use the diagram to show the effect of an increase in the real interest rate on desired consumption. c) Briefly state the income effect and the substitution effect of an increase in the real interest rate for a saver. d) Would a tax increase on interest earnings reduce household saving? Briefly explain. e) Draw a budget line and indifference curve diagram for a borrower, and use the diagram to show the income effect and the substitution effect of an increase in the interest rate.

8.   **The real wage and the labor supply decision**: a) Define leisure. b) Describe the income-leisure trade-off encountered by workers. c) State the decision rule that an individual worker uses to determine how much labor to supply. d) Use marginal cost-benefit analysis to explain how a worker knows that he or she is working too much at a given number of hours worked and a given wage. e) State the substitution effect and income effect of an increase in the real wage on labor supply, and state which effect is likely to be stronger for a temporary and permanent wage increase.

Mathematical Problem-Solving Questions

1.   **Consumption combinations**: Calculate future consumption for each of the following levels of current consumption when current income = $30,000, expected future real income = $55,000, initial wealth = $10,000, and the real interest rate = 5%: a) current consumption = $92,381; b) current consumption = 0; c) current consumption = $24,000; d) current consumption = $36,000.

2.   **Present values**: Calculate the present value of $40,000 of nominal future income received in one year when a) the nominal interest rate is 15%; b) the nominal interest rate is 5%. Calculate the present value of $40,000 of real future income received in one year, when: c) the real interest rate is 4%; d) the real interest rate is -1%.

3.   **Life-cycle consumption and saving**: Assuming that the real interest rate is zero, calculate yearly consumption and saving for each stage of a person's life cycle, given that the person earns $25,000 per year for twenty years in the early working years, $55,000 per year for twenty years in the middle-age years, $20,000 per year for thirty years during the retirement years, consumes a fixed portion of PVLR each year, and makes a bequest of 10% of his or her lifetime income.

Answers to Fill-In-The-Blanks Questions

1. budget constraint
2. budget line
3. no-borrowing, no-lending point
4. indifference curve
5. present value
6. present value of lifetime resources (PVLR)
7. consumption-smoothing motive
8. utility
9. permanent income theory
10. life-cycle model
11. bequest motive
12. borrowing constraint
13. income effect
14. substitution effect (of the real interest rate on saving)
15. income effect (of the real interest rate on saving)
16. substitution effect (of the real wage on labor supply)
17. income effect (of the real wage on labor supply)

Answers to True-False Questions

1. F In the two-period model, every dollar spent today on consumption reduces future consumption by $(1 + r)$ dollars in real terms.

2. F If $c = y + a$, then $c > y$, which means the individual is dissaving. Spending part of current wealth on consumer products reduces wealth. Reducing wealth is dissaving. People dissave in their retirement years largely by spending part of the wealth each year that they accumulated from saving during their working years.

3. F The constant slope of the budget line shows that a consumer has the market opportunity to trade future consumption for current consumption at a fixed rate, but it does not show the consumer's willingness to trade one for the other. At a fixed level of utility the willingness of an individual to trade future consumption for current consumption is identified by the slope of an indifference curve. Because an indifference curve is bowed toward the origin, its slope decreases as we move down the curve; this decreasing slope means that the amount of future consumption an individual is willing to sacrifice to increase current consumption by one unit declines as current consumption increases.

4. T Present value is the current market value. For an individual, the present value of consumption is c; the present value of wealth is a.

5. F An indifference curve depicts various (c, c^f) combinations that would provide a consumer with a given amount of total utility; it does not identify the costs of these various combinations. A budget line depicts the set of (c, c^f) combinations that have the same total cost.

6. T For a given real interest rate, an increase in income or wealth will shift the budget line to the right. Part of any increase in household income is consumed and part is saved, so an increase in income increases saving. Consumption spending is positively related to wealth. At a given level of income, an increase in wealth increases consumption spending, thereby reducing saving.

7. T Consistent with the consumption-smoothing motive, the permanent income theory contends that consumers attempt to maintain a fairly stable level of consumption spending during business cycle fluctuations in income. To keep consumption spending fairly stable, individuals reduce their saving rate during recessions and increase their saving rate during business cycle expansions.

8. T   If government temporarily reduces taxes without reducing government outlays, it will have to borrow the amount of the tax cut by selling government bonds to the private sector. The tax cut creates a budget deficit, which reduces government saving. Households recognize that taxes will be raised in the future to pay off the government debt created by the temporary tax cut. In order to save just enough to pay off the government debt, households will have to save every dollar of the tax cut; the $(1 + r)$ future dollars earned from saving all the tax cut will just repay the $(1 + r)$ dollars of future government debt. Since the temporary tax cut is just equal to the present value of the expected future tax increase, the tax cut does not change an individual's PVLR; therefore it does not change current consumption spending. None of the temporary tax cut will be spent on current consumption; all of it will be saved. The increase in private saving will offset the decline in government saving; consequently, there is no change in national saving. Note that a temporary tax cut creates a temporary increase in after-tax household income; this gives people an opportunity to increase their current consumption spending at the expense of reducing future consumption. Yet in the absence of binding borrowing constraints, people already have the opportunity to do this by borrowing - the tax cut does not offer any new opportunity. The Ricardian equivalence proposition contends that the government's decision to temporarily reduce taxes will not change people's current consumption because it will not change their budget constraint (i.e., the budget line) and it will not change their preferences for current and future consumption (i.e., their indifference curves).   If households do face binding borrowing constraints and/or do not expect that their future taxes will be increased to finance the temporary tax cut, they may increase current consumption spending; under these conditions the Ricardian equivalence proposition may fail to accurately predict the effects of the tax cut on consumption and saving.

9. F   The life-cycle model of consumption and saving contends that as a general rule, people do usually dissave during their early working years and during their retirement years, but the model does not tell us that individuals should or should not do this. Economic theories, including the life-cycle model, do not represent normative statements about what people should or should not do; they are positive statements supported by the empirical evidence about what most people usually do in response to changes in market conditions. In general, economists contend that people as a general rule act in their own rational self-interest to improve their economic well-being in response to changes in market conditions.

10. T   For a temporary change in the real interest rate or real wage, the substitution effect is likely to be greater than the income effect. The net effect of a temporary increase in the real interest rate is to increase the amount of saving. The net effect of a temporary increase in the real wage is to increase the labor supply. The longer the increase in the real interest rate or real wage is expected to last, the greater the income effect. With an increase in the long-term real interest rate or a permanent increase in the real wage, the income effect is likely to be greater than the substitution effect, causing saving or labor supply to decline. If expected inflation remains unchanged, an increase in the nominal interest rate is an increase in the real interest rate. If the price level remains unchanged, an increase in the nominal wage is an increase in the real wage.

Answers to Multiple Choice Questions

1. d	8. a	15. c
2. b	9. b	16. a
3. d	10. e	17. a
4. a	11. d	18. d
5. c	12. c	19. d
6. c	13. c	20. b
7. e	14. b	

Answers to Short-Answer Essay Questions

1.   **Consumption and saving motives:**

a)   Individuals save to increase their future consumption and to provide bequests. Unless individuals save, their future consumption cannot exceed their future income. Individuals save to pay for expensive goods and services, such as cars, houses, and education. They save to pay for expenses during future possible periods of unemployment and to eventually achieve financial independence from work. By saving, they accumulate wealth that will pay for their consumption during retirement years. They save to earn interest income that can supplement or replace their labor income.

b)   No. The consumption decision cannot be made separately from the saving decision since saving is defined as the income that is not spent on consumer goods and services (i.e., y - c = s). We could call it the consumption and saving decision since the shares of our income allocated to consumption and saving at any point in time is made by one decision. By choosing how much to consume, we have chosen how much to save. Alternatively, by choosing how much to save, we have chosen how much to consume. In general, the economic benefits (i.e., utility) of consuming and saving are simultaneously considered in making each consumption-saving decision.

c)   The consumption-smoothing motive suggests that individuals prefer to have a fairly stable level of consumption across different time periods, so consumption varies less than income over the business cycle and over the life cycle. In terms of a budget line diagram, the consumption-smoothing motive predicts that people will generally choose a (c, c^f) combination that is near the middle of the budget line, rather than being near either end.

d)   A decline in an individual's bequest motive would increase his or her consumption and reduce his or her saving each year during the working years and retirement years.

e)   A binding borrowing constraint reduces current consumption because it reduces the amount an individual borrows against future income. The individual chooses to save nothing with or without the constraint, but the binding borrowing constraint reduces dissaving.

2.   **Present values:**

a)   Present value is the current dollar value of future payments. Present value calculations tell us how much future income payments are worth in today's dollars.

b)   For a nominal income payment received n years in the future, the present value is $[\text{nominal income}/(1 + i)^n]$, where i is the nominal interest rate. For a real income payment received n periods in the future, the present value is $y^f/(1 + r)^n$, where r is the real interest rate.

c)   Given a 5% interest rate, the present values of $1000 received one year, two years, and three years in the future are, respectively,

1) $\$1000/(1 + .05) = \$1000/1.05 = \$952.38.$
2) $\$1000/(1 + .05)^2 = \$1000/1.1025 = \$907.03.$
3) $\$1000/(1 + .05)^3 = \$1000/1.1576 = \$863.86.$

d)   The four variables that determine the present value of lifetime resources (PVLR) are current income, future income, the real interest rate, and initial wealth:

$$PVLR = y + y^f/(1 + r) + a$$

e)   A decline in an individual's PVLR would cause her or his budget line to shift to the left by the amount that PVLR declined.

3.   **Budget constraints and preferences:**

a)   Budget line diagram.

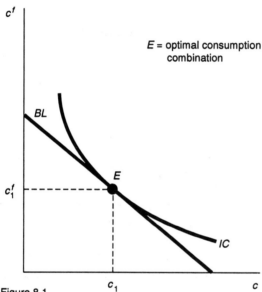

Figure 8.1

b)   The slope of the budget line is $-(1 + r)$, where r is the real interest rate. An increase in r would increase the slope by making it a larger negative number. The slope is defined as the change in the value of the variable on the vertical axis (c^f) per unit change in the value of the variable on the horizontal axis (c).

c)   Two variable changes that would make the budget line shift to the right are 1) an increase in current income (y); and 2) an increase in expected future income (y^f). A third possibility is an increase in wealth. This can be seen from the budget constraint equation, which defines the budget line: $c^f = (y + a - c)(1 + r) + y^f$. This can be rewritten as: $c^f = [(y + a)(1 + r) + y^f] - (1 + r)c$, where $-(1 + r)$ is the slope of the budget line and $[(y + a)(1 + r) + y^f]$ is the vertical intercept of the budget line, where c = 0.

d)   The slope of the budget line, $-(1 + r)$, is the per-unit cost of current consumption in terms of units of future consumption foregone. For every dollar of goods bought today, $(1 + r)$ dollars of future consumption of goods is given up. Likewise, the economic benefit (i.e., reward) for every dollar saved is $(1 + r)$ dollars of additional consumption spending in the future.

e) The negative slope of an indifference curve illustrates that there are a number of (c, c^f) combinations that would provide a consumer with a fixed amount of utility. At any given consumption point there is some relative price or rate of exchange at which the consumer is willing to trade off future consumption for current consumption. An indifference curve is bowed toward the origin because consumers prefer consumption combinations for which the difference between c and c^f is relatively small; this illustrates the consumption-smoothing motive.

4. **Permanent income theory:**

a) Definitions:

1) Temporary income is income that is transitory or short-lived. A temporary change in income changes current income but not future income.

2) Permanent income is income that is not transitory. A permanent change in income changes both current income and future income.

b) Current consumption and future consumption would increase more, while saving would increase less, for a given increase in permanent income compared to the same current period increase in temporary income. The temporary increase in income will be mostly saved, so future consumption will increase somewhat, even though the temporary increase in income does not increase expected future income.

c) Yes. Both the permanent income theory and the consumption-smoothing motive predict that individuals will choose to consume a fairly stable share of their current and future economic resources (i.e., PVLR) in each time period. Therefore temporary changes in income, as might occur in a recession, will mostly change saving, rather than current consumption.

d) The permanent-income theory predicts that current consumption will decline more in response to a recessionary decline in income that is expected to be permanent than for a recessionary decline in income that is expected to be temporary.

e) One advantage the life-cycle model has over the permanent income theory of consumption and saving is that unlike the permanent income theory, the life-cycle theory can show how changes in the age distribution of a country's population can cause the saving rate to change.

5. **Life-cycle model:**

a) The three stages of Modigliani's life-cycle model are the early working years (adults under 40), middle-age working years (ages 40 - 65), and retirement years (over 65).

b) Changes in saving over these three periods provide a "hump-shaped" saving pattern. A brief description and explanation follows.

1) In the early working years individuals dissave at declining rates until about age 35, when they achieve low but increasing saving rates as they age. During these relatively low-income years, adults are acquiring education, buying and furnishing their first homes, and raising their young children.

2) During the middle-age working years saving rates continue to increase with age until about age 55, when they begin to decline to a zero saving rate at age 65. During these relatively high-income years, adults are able to reduce their liabilities and increase their saving to finance their children's education and their retirement.

3) During the retirement years people again dissave at an increasing rate for several years, after which they dissave at a fairly constant rate during retirement. After a few years with no labor income, people usually learn to maintain a fairly stable standard of living during retirement.

c) Yes. Both the life-cycle model and the consumption-smoothing motive predict that individuals attempt to maintain a fairly stable standard of living over the different time periods of their lifetime. As a result, consumption changes less than income in different time periods.

d) Both. Like many economic theories, the life-cycle model is quite general; therefore it predicts the behavior of most people. Relatively impatient people are still forward-looking consumers, even though they save less of their income in any time period compared to more forward-looking consumers. Most people will exhibit the same hump-shaped pattern of saving over their life cycles.

e) Both. Compared to people with high bequest motives, individuals or families with low bequest motives will save more in any time period, so that they can leave an estate of accumulated wealth for their heirs. The life-cycle model is general enough to be used to predict the basic pattern of saving behavior of people with different bequest motives.

6. **Explaining the Japanese saving rate**:

a) The following factors help explain why the Japanese saving rate exceeded the American saving rate during the 1980s.

1) Population age structure: A higher percentage of Japanese were in their peak saving years, per the life-cycle model, and they generally expected to live longer than Americans.

2) Income growth: The growth rate of national income has been higher in Japan than in America over the past forty years, so the working adults in Japan saved relatively more than those in America, while the retired Japanese dissaved relatively less than Americans. Therefore the aggregate saving rate was higher in Japan than America.

3) Housing and land prices and mortgage markets: The Japanese must save more than Americans because Japanese land prices and housing prices are much higher and down payment requirements for their mortgages are higher than in America.

4) Bequest motive: Hayashi's research suggests that the Japanese have higher bequest motives than most Americans, so they must save more of their income in each time period.

b) Population age structure and income growth are two principal determinants of individuals' opportunities to save.

c) Housing and land prices and down payment requirements in mortgage markets, as well as bequest motives, are principal determinants of individuals' incentives to saving.

d)   The U.S. saving rate would increase if banks increased their down payment requirements for housing loans.

e)   Economists can show that the U.S. saving rate is low today compared to some other time periods or compared to some other countries. Economists can identify and measure the various economic costs and benefits of a low saving rate compared to a high saving rate. Furthermore, economists can identify the causes of a low saving rate. However, economic theory cannot tell us that the saving rate is too low or that it should or must be increased; these statements rely on social value judgments, which are beyond the scope of economic theory. Economists believe that American individuals and families are saving what they want to save, given their market opportunities and incentives to save. Government policies can change the U.S. saving rate by changing market opportunities or incentives to save. However, economic theory alone cannot tell us whether government policies should attempt to do this. It would be hard to prove that the current Japanese saving rate is the optimal saving rate for America. We can say that economists do not generally endorse "whatever it takes" kinds of policies; economists weigh the expected social benefits of any change against the expected social costs and generally endorse those policies that offer greater net benefits than could be achieved by alternative policy options.

7.   **The real interest rate, taxes, and the saving decision:**

a)   The following is a budget line and indifference curve diagram for a person who chooses to consume at the no-borrowing, no-lending point.

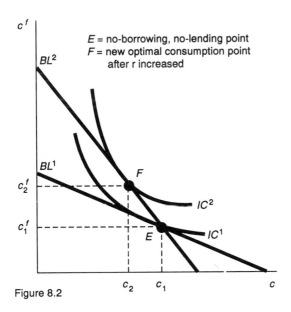

Figure 8.2

b)   As shown in part (a), an increase in the interest rate causes the budget line to pivot in a clockwise direction around the no-borrowing, no-lending point. The substitution effect of the interest rate increase causes current consumption to decline; c_1 declines to c_2. When an individual initially consumes at the no-borrowing, no-lending point, there is no income effect of a change in the interest rate.

c)   Income and substitution effects of an increase in the real interest rate for a saver are as follows:

1) Income effect: An increase in the real interest rate will cause an individual to reduce saving and increase current consumption, because the higher rate of return on saving means that the saver can reduce saving and still achieve his or her target level of future wealth.

2) Substitution effect: An increase in the real interest rate will cause an individual to increase saving and decrease current consumption, because the relative rate of return to saving has increased. An increase in the real interest rate reduces consumption because it increases the opportunity cost of consumption.

d)   An increase in the tax rate on interest earnings has the same effect on desired saving as a decline in the interest rate, since it reduces the after-tax real interest rate. Given the usual assumptions that most people are savers and that the substitution effect is stronger than the income effect, household saving would decline for the national economy. Individual savers, however, could choose to increase saving if the income effect is stronger than the substitution effect for them. For borrowers, both the substitution effect and the income effect of a decline in the after-tax real interest rate would cause them to decrease saving, assuming that interest payments are tax-deductible. Individuals who neither borrow nor lend would decrease saving because of the substitution effect.

e)   Budget line and indifference curve diagram for a borrower. Since both the income effect and the substitution effect cause a borrower to save more and consume less, current consumption declines from c_1 to c_2.

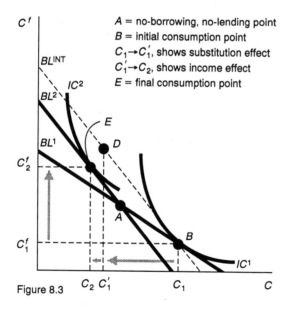

A = no-borrowing, no-lending point
B = initial consumption point
$C_1 \to C_1'$, shows substitution effect
$C_1' \to C_2$, shows income effect
E = final consumption point

Figure 8.3

8.   **The real wage and the labor supply decision:**

a)   Leisure is time spent not working to produce products for exchange in the market economy. Students studying, homemakers doing household chores, and people on vacation are all doing so during their leisure time.

b)   A worker encounters an income-leisure trade-off when in order to work more hours to increase income, the worker has to reduce his or her leisure time. Alternatively, by reducing the number of hours he or she works, the worker could increase his or her leisure time. In deciding how much to work to earn income, a person is deciding how much leisure time to enjoy; it is the same decision, because the opportunity cost of leisure is the utility of the income that could have been earned by working.

c)   Each worker attempts to maximize her or his utility from labor income and leisure by working the number of hours needed to equate the marginal utility of income to the marginal disutility of working. The marginal utility of income is the expected benefit of the last hour worked. The marginal disutility of working is the expected cost in terms of foregone happiness of the last hour of leisure traded for work. Where marginal utility = marginal utility, total utility exceeds total disutility by the maximum possible amount; so the net benefits of working are maximized.

d)   For a given number of hours worked and a given wage, if the utility of the last dollar earned from work is less than the disutility from the last hour of leisure foregone in order to work (i.e., marginal benefit < marginal cost), the person is working too much to maximize his or her utility (i.e., happiness). The worker would be happier if he or she worked less and enjoyed more leisure time.

e)   An increase in the real wage has an income effect and a substitution effect on the quantity of labor supplied. The income effect is that it increases labor's income for a given amount of work, which induces labor to work less. The substitution effect is that it increases the rate of return to work compared to leisure, which induces labor to work more. For a temporary real wage increase the substitution effect is likely to be stronger than the income effect; therefore more labor will be supplied at a temporarily higher wage. For a permanent real wage increase the income effect is likely to exceed the substitution effect; therefore less labor will be supplied at a permanently higher real wage.

Answers to Mathematical Problem-Solving Questions

1.   **Consumption combinations**: Future consumption can be calculated using the future consumption equation, given that y = \$30,000, y^f = \$55,000, a = \$10,000, and r = 5%.

$$c^f = (y + a - c)(1 + r) + y^f$$

a)   When c = \$92,381, c^f = (\$30,000 + \$10,000 - \$92,381)(1.05) + \$55,000 = 0.

b)   When c = 0, c^f = (\$30,000 + \$10,000 - 0)(1.05) + \$55,000 = \$97,000.

c)   When c = \$24,000, c^f = (\$30,000 + \$10,000 - \$24,000)(1.05) + \$55,000 = \$71,800.

d)   When c = \$36,000, c^f = (\$30,000 + \$10,000 - \$36,000)(1.05) + \$55,000 = \$59,200.

2.   **Present values:** The present value of real income to be received in one year = $y^f/(1 + r)$. The present value of nominal income to be received in one year = nominal income$/(1 + i)$.

   a) When i = 15%, the present value of $40,000 of nominal income to be received in one year = $40,000/1.15) = $34,783.

   b) When i = 5%, the present value of $40,000 of nominal income to be received in one year = ($40,000/1.05) = $38,095.

   c) When r = 4%, the present value of $40,000 of real income to be received in one year = ($40,000/1.04) = $38,462.

   d) When r = -1%, the present value of $40,000 of real income to be received in one year = ($40,000/.99) = $40,404.

3.   **Life-cycle consumption and saving:**

PVLR = ($25,000 x 20) + ($55,000 x 20) + ($20,000 x 30) = $2,200,000.

Bequest = 10% of PVLR = $2,200,000 x 10% = $220,000.

PVLC = PVLR - Bequest = $2,200,000 - $220,000 = $1,980,000.

Consumption per year at a constant level for 70 years of adult life = PVLC/70 = $1,980,000/70 = $28,286.

Saving in early working years = y - c = $25,000 - $28,286 = - $3,286.

Saving in middle-age years = y - c = $55,000 - $28,286 = $26,714.

Saving in retirement years = y - c = $20,000 - $28,286 = - $8,286

CHAPTER 9: BUSINESS CYCLES

A Fill-In-The-Blanks Review of Chapter Highlights: Use the following key terms to fill in the blanks. Each key term is used only once.

acyclical

business cycle chronology

contraction

countercyclical

leading variable

procyclical

turning point

boom

coincident variable

depression

index of leading indicators

peak

recession

business cycle

comovement

expansion

lagging variable

persistence

trough

The NBER's 1._Business Cycle Chronology_ gives the dates for the peaks and troughs and identifies the number of months of contraction and expansion for the thirty complete business cycles experienced by the United States since 1854.

A 2._Contraction_, also called a 3._Recession_, is a downturn in aggregate economic activity that follows a peak in the business cycle. A severe recession of long duration is called a 4._Depression_. A business cycle contraction bottoms out at a 5._trough_, followed by an 6._Expansion_ in aggregate economic activity. An expansion that includes rapid real GDP growth is called a 7._Boom_. An expansion rises to a 8._Peak_, which completes one cycle.

In addition to being measured from peak to peak, a 9._Business Cycle_ can also be measured from trough to trough. A peak is an upper 10._Turning Point_ and a trough is a lower turning point in a business cycle.

Business cycle fluctuations are deviations from the normal growth path of many aggregate economic variables, including changes in the economic growth rate, unemployment rate, inflation rate, and in other macroeconomic variables. The tendency for many economic variables to move together in a predictable way over business cycles is called 11._Comovement_. The tendency for both contractions and expansions to last a while is called 12._Persistence_.

Comovements of aggregate economic variables over the business cycles are called business cycle facts. We study the business cycle facts, in part, by analyzing the direction and timing of changes in the values of these economic variables over the business cycles.

An economic variable that moves in the same direction as aggregate economic activity over the cycle is 13._Procyclical_. An economic variable that moves in the opposite direction as aggregate economic activity over the cycle is 14._Countercyclical_. An 15._acyclical_ variable has no predictable pattern of change in value over the business cycle. The more sensitive a variable is to business cycles, the more it changes in value over a cycle; changes in a mildly procyclical variable are smaller than changes in a strongly procyclical variable over the business cycle. Although the real interest rate is an acyclical variable, it is not necessarily insensitive to business cycles; the fact that it is not consistently procyclical or countercyclical may be because different cycles are caused by different types of shocks. Some types of shocks cause the real interest rate to rise, while other types cause it to fall.

A variable that reaches its peak and trough before the respective peak and trough in aggregate economic activity is a 16. _Leading Variable_ . A variable that reaches its peak and trough at about the same time as aggregate economic activity is a 17. _Coincident Variable_ . A variable that reaches its peak and trough after the respective peak and trough in aggregate economic activity is a 18. _Lagging Variable_ . Movements in leading variables lead the cycle, movements in coincident variables coincide with movements in the cycle, and movements in lagging variables lag behind the cycle. The 19. _Index of Leading Indicators_ is a weighted average of eleven leading variables; it is used to forecast business cycles.

True-False Questions: Circle T for true statements and F for false statements.

T (F)   1.   Macroeconomists agree that business cycles are the economy's best response to disturbances in production or spending, so it is not efficient for government to attempt to reduce business cycles.

T (F)   2.   Deviations in real GDP growth from its normal growth path adequately measure business cycles.

(T) F   3.   Business cycle contractions are sometimes called recessions; business cycle expansions are sometimes called booms.

(T) F   4.   Business cycles are persistent and recurrent but not periodic.

T (F)   5.   Over the 1929-1933 period of the Great Depression and the 1939-1944 period of World War II, the U.S. economy maintained full employment and output grew at its potential growth rate.

T (F)   6.   Economic researchers agree that economic policies used since 1945 to reduce business cycle fluctuations have been successful.

(T) F   7.   Most business cycles in the United States and in foreign countries exhibit the same comovements of macroeconomic variables in terms of direction and timing.

T (F)   8.   Changes in leading variables cause business cycles; changes in lagging economic variables are the effects of business cycles.

(T) F   9.   The average productivity of labor and the real wage are mildly procyclical, while employment growth is strongly procyclical, and the unemployment rate is strongly countercyclical.

(T) F   10.   In most recessions, investment, consumption, nominal money supply growth, the nominal interest rate, inflation, and output decline, while the real interest rate may rise or fall.

Multiple Choice Questions: Circle the letter corresponding to the correct answer to each question.

1. The NBER's business cycle chronology for the United States shows that
    a. there were no business cycles after 1961.
    b. there were no business cycles prior to 1929.
    c. there was no business cycle expansion in the 1930s.
    d. the onset of major wars usually has caused the economy to contract.
    e. compared to the 1854-1929 period, the post-1945 period was characterized by fewer months in contraction and more months in expansion.

2. A business cycle contraction is best described as
    a. a decline in aggregate economic variables below their normal growth path.
    b. a decline in real GNP growth.
    c. an increase in the unemployment rate.
    d. a decline in the inflation rate.
    e. a decline in nominal interest rates.

3. The 1973-1975 period showed that
    a. business cycles are easy to accurately forecast.
    b. business cycles are dead.
    c. stabilization policies have tamed business cycles.
    d. Keynesian stabilization policies can quickly offset business cycle contractions without creating inflation.
    e. business cycle recessions are not entirely temporary events, they sometimes create long-run losses of output.

4. During the Great Depression,
    a. Roosevelt's "New Deal" was completely ineffective in pulling the economy out of a contraction.
    b. Roosevelt proposed a government program of annually balanced budgets and minimal government intervention in economic activity.
    c. planned investment spending declined substantially.
    d. output fell but the economy continued to provide full employment.
    e. the financial market remained healthy despite the collapse of the goods market.

5. After reaching a trough in November 1982, the U.S. economy expanded until
    a. the recession of 1985.
    b. the recession of 1990.
    c. the recession of 1988.
    d. reaching a peak in 1985.
    e. reaching a peak in 1988.

6. Which of the following will not likely occur during an expansion?
    a. Real GNP growth
    b. Declining money supply growth
    c. Declining unemployment rate
    d. Increasing average labor productivity
    e. Increasing consumption expenditures

7.   One negative aspect of a business cycle boom is
        a. a declining rate of unemployment.
        b. a declining rate of inventory investment.
        c. a reduction in government budget deficits.
        d. increasing real wages.
        e. increasing rate of inflation.

8.   A peak in a business cycle
        a. exhibits persistence.
        b. is where real GNP has stopped growing.
        c. is an upper turning point.
        d. is where unemployment peaks.
        e. occurs periodically.

9.   Listed in order, the phases of a complete business cycle are
        a. contraction, trough, expansion, peak.
        b. contraction, recession, depression, expansion.
        c. trough, expansion, boom, bust.
        d. expansion, contraction, trough, peak.
        e. peak, expansion, contraction, trough.

10.   The lower turning point in a business cycle is reached by
        a. lagging variables before being reached by coincident variables.
        b. lagging variables before being reached by leading variables.
        c. coincident variables before being reached by leading variables.
        d. leading variables before being reached by coincident variables.
        e. all cyclical variables simultaneously.

11.   The comovements of cyclical economic variables
        a. identify the cause-effect relationships between the variables.
        b. enable economists to accurately forecast the duration of most business cycle contractions.
        c. enable economists to accurately forecast the severity of most business cycle contractions.
        d. are all procyclical.
        e. are called business cycle facts.

12.   Persistence of a business cycle expansion is best measured by
        a. the number of months from trough to peak.
        b. the degree of periodicity in the expansion.
        c. the rate at which real GNP increases during the expansion.
        d. the degree of comovement of economic variables during the expansion.
        e. continuing high rates of unemployment during the expansion.

13.   Which of the following is not a procyclical variable?
        a. Unemployment rate
        b. Business fixed investment
        c. Average labor productivity
        d. Real wage
        e. Stock prices

14.   In theory, stabilization policies
a. are procyclical.
b. are acyclical.
c. are countercyclical.
d. are both countercyclical and procyclical.
e. exhibit no comovement.

15.   Real interest rates are
a. procyclical, just like nominal interest rates.
b. acyclical, while nominal interest rates are procyclical.
c. acyclical, just like nominal interest rates.
d. countercyclical, while nominal interest rates are procyclical.
e. not part of the business cycle facts.

16.   Which of the following is not a leading variable?
a. Nominal money supply growth
b. Stock prices
c. Average labor productivity
d. Residential investment
e. Inflation

17.   When the values of coincident variables are declining, aggregate economic activity
a. will begin to decline within six months.
b. might start to decline in the next year.
c. has been declining for at least six months.
d. is declining.
e. has just reached a trough.

18.   Lagging variables are aggregate economic variables that
a. reach a peak after leading variables but before coincident variables reach a peak.
b. reach a peak after coincident variables reach a peak.
c. reach a peak two or more years after aggregate economic activity reaches a peak.
d. are insensitive to business cycles.
e. are countercyclical variables.

19.   Consecutive increases in the index of leading indicators during the most recent few months of a recession suggest that
a. the severity of the recession will increase.
b. the recession will be of long duration.
c. the recession will become a depression.
d. within six months, the economy will be in an expansion.
e. the economy will soon recover if the index is rising by at least 5%; otherwise the recession will continue.

20.   Business cycles
a. are unique to the United States.
b. are unique to North America.
c. occur in all industrialized market economies, as illustrated by the worldwide recessions in about 1975, 1982, and 1991.
d. do not occur in Asian countries.
e. first occurred in this century.

Short-Answer Essay Questions

1.   **Characteristics of business cycles**: a) Define a business cycle. b) Define the following characteristics of business cycles: recurrence and persistence. c) Are business cycles periodic? Briefly explain. d) Identify and briefly describe the three types of possible comovement of economic variables in terms of direction and timing.

2.   **Comovements**: Identify the comovements (i.e., direction and timing) of the following variables over a business cycle: a) industrial production; b) unemployment; c) nominal interest rates; d) nominal money supply growth; and e) investment.

3.   **Effects of business cycles**: a) Compare and contrast the effects of the following business cycle contractions on national output and unemployment: 1) 1929-1933; (2) 1973-1975; 3) 1981-1982. b) Are business cycle contractions purely temporary events with only short-run real effects? Briefly explain. c) Identify two industries that are particularly sensitive to business cycles. d) Identify one negative effect of a booming expansion.

4.   **Index of Leading Indicators**: a) Define the Index of Leading Indicators. b) Briefly describe how the index would forecast a contraction. c) What is the measurement problem of the index? d) Can the index accurately predict the severity and duration of a recession? Briefly explain. e) How reliable is the index in predicting upper and lower turning points in business cycles? Briefly explain.

5.   **Business cycle research**:   State one important contribution that each of the following economic researchers has made to our current knowledge of business cycles: a) Arthur Burns and Wesley Mitchell; b) Charles Nelson and Charles Plosser; c) Simon Kuznets; d) Nathan Balke and Robert Gordon; e) Robert Lucas, Jr.

Mathematical Problem-Solving Questions

1.   **Duration of business cycles**: Use the NBER data in Table 9.1 in the textbook on U.S. business cycle turning points to calculate: a) the shortest business cycle for peak to peak; b) the shortest business cycle from trough to trough; c) the longest business cycle from peak to peak; and d) the longest business cycle from trough to trough.

2.   **Changes in the unemployment rate**: Calculate the percent increase in the U.S. unemployment rate for: a) the 1929-1933 recession, when the unemployment rate increased from 3% to 25%; b) the 1973-1975 recession, when the unemployment rate increased from 4% to 9%; and c) the 1981-1982 recession, when the unemployment rate increased from 7% to 11%.

Answers to Fill-In-The-Blanks Questions

1. business cycle chronology
2. contraction
3. recession
4. depression
5. trough
6. expansion
7. boom
8. peak
9. business cycle
10. turning point
11. comovement
12. persistence
13. procyclical
14. countercyclical
15. acyclical
16. leading variable
17. coincident variable
18. lagging variable
19. index of leading indicators

Answers to True-False Questions

1. F   Classical economists agree with this statement, but Keynesians believe that government fiscal and monetary policies can be used to reduce the inefficiencies and high economic costs of large business cycle fluctuations.

2. F   Real GDP growth is a measure of output growth. Deviations in output growth from potential output growth are an important measure of business cycle activity, but changes in any single variable provide an inadequate measure of the changes in many important macroeconomic variables during business cycles.

3. T   A recession is a business cycle contraction; a boom is a business cycle expansion.

4. T   Once the economy has entered a business cycle contraction or expansion, that phase tends to continue for a number of months, quarters, and sometimes years; this tendency of any phase to continue is called persistence. Business cycles are recurrent in that each cycle is soon followed by another cycle; aggregate economic activity is cyclical. Business cycles are not periodic because they differ in severity and duration; some recessions are short-lived and mild, while others last for years and are severe.

5. F   The contrast between these two periods illustrates how important business cycles can be. The 1929-1933 period was the first cyclical contraction in the Great Depression; the unemployment rate peaked at approximately 25% and output declined by approximately 30% over this time period. By contrast, the 1939-1944 period was a cyclical expansion during World War II; the unemployment rate reached a trough of 1.2% and output nearly doubled over this time period.

6. F   Economic researchers disagree about how much smaller post-1945 business cycles are than previous cycles and about how effective or ineffective government policies have been in moderating business cycles. Christina Romer's recent research suggests that Simon Kuznets's prior economic research estimates overstated the size of pre-Depression business cycles, but recent research by Nathan Balke and Robert Gordon lends support to Kuznets's conclusion that business cycles have been much smaller since 1945. While Keynesians believe that post-1945 business cycles have been moderated by government policy attempts to reduce business cycle fluctuations, classical economists contend that any moderation in business cycles that has occurred was not caused by these government policy attempts to moderate them.

7. T   Although the duration and magnitude of business cycle fluctuations can vary substantially, most business cycles in the world economy have historically demonstrated a stable pattern of comovements of macroeconomic variables in terms of direction and timing.

8. F   Correlation does not prove causation. Leading variables are potential causes of business cycles and lagging variables are potential effects, but the timing of these changes does not prove that a cause and effect relationship exits among them. For example, classical economists contend that a decline in nominal money supply growth will not cause a recession even though nominal money supply growth is a procyclical, leading variable. Likewise, Keynesians contend that a decline in investment spending will cause a recession even though business fixed investment is a procyclical, coincident variable.

9. T   These are business cycle facts. In a typical recession, the decline in the average productivity of labor and the real wage are small relative to the decline in employment growth and the increase in the unemployment rate. Classical economists highlight that the decline in average labor productivity is consistent with their belief that most recessions are caused by adverse productivity shocks. Keynesians highlight that the sharp increase in the unemployment rate is consistent with their belief that wages and prices do not adjust quickly enough to keep the economy at or near full-employment output during recessions.

10. T   These are business cycle facts. Classical and Keynesian economists offer different explanations of why these particular comovements occur. In the classical model, an adverse supply shock causes output to fall, and the decline in output causes consumption, investment, and the money supply to decline. In the Keynesian model, it is the decline in investment, consumption, and money supply that causes output to decline.

Answers to Multiple Choice Questions

1. e	8. c	15. b
2. a	9. a	16. e
3. e	10. d	17. d
4. c	11. e	18. b
5. b	12. a	19. d
6. b	13. a	20. c
7. e	14. c	

Answers to Short-Answer Essay Questions

1.   **Characteristics of business cycles:**

   a)   Business cycles are recurrent fluctuations in aggregate economic variables away from their potential growth path. A complete business cycle may start at a peak or at a trough. A peak is followed by a contraction that ends in a trough, which is followed by an expansion that rises to another peak to begin the next cycle.

   b)   Business cycles exhibit recurrence and persistence:

      1)   Recurrence means that each complete cycle is followed by another complete cycle.

      2)   Persistence means that, once begun, each contraction tends to continue. Likewise, once begun, each expansion tends to continue. For example, the 1981-1982 contraction lasted for 16 months, and the 1982-1990 expansion lasted for 93 months. These are persistent events.

   c)   No. Business cycles are not periodic. Contractions vary in length and severity; expansions are also irregular in their duration and intensity.

   d)   Comovements: Over the business cycle, the values of some variables move together in terms of direction and timing.

      1)   Direction: Variables may be procyclical, countercyclical, or acyclical. Procyclical variables change in the same direction as changes in business cycles. Countercyclical variables change in the opposite direction as changes in business cycles. Acyclical variables do not show any consistent directional movement over business cycles.

      2)   Timing: Variables may be leading, coincident, or lagging. Leading variables reach their respective peaks and troughs before business cycle peaks and troughs. Coincident variables reach their respective peaks and troughs at the same time as business cycle peaks and troughs. Lagging variables reach their respective peaks and troughs after business cycle peaks and troughs.

2.   **Comovements:**

a)   Industrial production is a procyclical and coincident variable.

b)   Unemployment is a countercyclical variable whose timing is unclassified by the NBER.

c)   Nominal interest rates are procyclical and lagging.

d)   Nominal money supply growth is a procyclical and leading variable.

e)   Investment includes inventory investment and residential investment, which are procyclical and leading variables; it also includes business fixed investment, which is a procyclical and coincident variable.

3.   **Effects of business cycles:**

a)   Among these particular contractions, the effects on output and employment were largest for the 1929-1933 contraction. The 1973-1975 contraction had the second largest output effect, but the 1981-1982 contraction had the second largest unemployment effect. At their troughs, the effects were:

	Decline in Output	Unemployment Rate
1929-1933	30.0%	25%
1973-1975	4.3%	9%
1981-1982	3.2%	11%

b)   No. At least some contractions have long-run permanent effects, in that the economy does not return to its prerecession growth path. An example is the 1973-1975 recession. One researcher concluded that, on average, 70% of the output effects of contraction is temporary and 30% is permanent.

c)   Consumer durables and investment goods industries are particularly sensitive to business cycle fluctuations. The auto industry is an example of an industry producing a consumer durable. The steel industry is an example of an industry producing an investment good.

d)   A booming expansion tends to overheat the economy, creating an increase in inflation. Booms are also likely to be followed by busts.

4.   **Index of Leading Indicators:**

a)   The Index of Leading Indicators is a weighted average of eleven economic variables that tend to reach their peaks and troughs before respective business cycle peaks and troughs.

b)   A decline in the index for three consecutive months during an expansion forecasts that a contraction will begin in the next three to six months.

c) The measurement problem is that the measures of the variables in the index are revised two months after being initially reported, and revised again two months later. These revisions, however, may be large enough to change the directional movement of the index from that initially reported. These errors in measurement may give off false alarms and therefore are troublesome.

d) No. The Index of Leading Indicators does not forecast the severity and length (i.e., duration) of recessions. During a contraction, it tells us only that the contraction will continue beyond or end in the next several months, but it does not tell us how long it may continue beyond the next quarterly period.

e) Partly because of measurement problems and partly because of the ever-changing structure of the U.S. economy, the Index of Leading Indicators is not perfectly reliable in forecasting peaks and troughs, but it is a valuable tool for predicting these business cycle turning points.

5. **Business cycle research**:

a) Arthur Burns and Wesley Mitchell wrote a book entitled *Measuring Business Cycles*, published in 1946. Their research was among the first to identify and analyze the business cycle facts.

b) Charles Nelson and Charles Plosser, in a 1982 economics journal article, showed that business cycles were not entirely temporary events. Their research showed that with the exception of the unemployment rate, part of the changes in the values of business cycle variables are permanent for a typical recession.

c) Simon Kuznets compiled the early national income data on real GDP of the United States. His pre-1929 real GDP estimates were in part based on William Shaw's earlier estimates of goods output for this time period. His real GDP figures were not considered to be controversial until research in the late 1980s by Christina Romer questioned their accuracy. Romer contended errors in Kuznets' real GDP estimates greatly exaggerated pre-1929 business cycle fluctuations.

d) Nathan Balke and Robert Gordon, in a 1989 economics journal article, answered Christina Romer's critique of Kuznets's real GDP data. Balke and Gordon added previously unused data on output of services to the Shaw-Kuznets data on output of goods to construct new estimates of pre-1929 real GDP. These estimates are closer to Kuznets's original estimates than to Romer's estimates; therefore they support the view that pre-1929 business cycle fluctuations were more severe than later, post-1945 business cycles.

e) Robert Lucas, Jr.'s research, published in a book on business cycles in 1977, showed that most business cycles are qualitatively very similar in terms of the comovements of macroeconomic variables, even though they are sometimes quantitatively very different.

Answers to Mathematical Problem-Solving Questions

1. **Duration of business cycles**: Per Table 9.1 in the textbook, the shortest and longest business cycles are as follows.

    a) The shortest business cycle from peak to peak is 17 months, which extended from August 1918 to December 1919. This includes 7 months of contraction followed by 10 months of expansion.

    b) The shortest business cycle from trough to trough is 28 months, which extended from July 1980 to October 1982. This includes 12 months of expansion followed by 16 months of contraction.

    c) The longest business cycle from peak to peak is 116 months, which extended from April 1960 to November 1969. This includes 10 months of contraction followed by 106 months of expansion.

    d) The longest business cycle from trough to trough is 117 months, which extended from February 1961 to October 1970. This includes 106 months of expansion followed by 11 months of contraction.

2. **Changes in the unemployment rate**: The percent increase in the unemployment rate for each time period follows.

    a) During the 1929-1933 recession the unemployment rate increased by 733% = (25% - 3%)/3%.

    b) During the 1973-1975 recession the unemployment rate increased by 125% = (9% - 4%)/4%.

    c) During the 1981-1982 recession the unemployment rate increased by 57% = (11% - 7%)/7%.

CHAPTER 10 : THE IS-LM MODEL: A GENERAL FRAMEWORK FOR MACROECONOMIC ANALYSIS

A Fill-In-The-Blanks Review of Chapter Highlights: Use the following key terms to fill in the blanks. Each key term is used only once.

full-employment line   general equilibrium   IS curve

LM curve   monetary neutrality

      The IS-LM model is a macroeconomic model of a national economy. In the IS-LM model, there are three markets: the labor market, the goods market, and the asset market. In a graph of the IS-LM model, a line or a curve shows the set of possible real income and real interest rate (Y, r) points at which each market is in equilibrium for fixed values of all other determinants of supply and demand for that market . The 1. _full- Employment Line_ depicts equilibrium in the labor market. The 2. _IS Curve_ depicts equilibrium in the goods market. The 3. _LM Curve_ depicts equilibrium in the asset market. Equilibrium in one market is called partial equilibrium; equilibrium in all three markets simultaneously is called 4. _General EQuilibrium_ .

      In the IS-LM model of an economy, 5. _Monetary Neutrality_ exists if a change in the nominal money supply causes the price level to change proportionally, so that there is no change in the real money supply. When a monetary policy change in the nominal money supply does not change the real money supply, it does not shift the LM curve; therefore it does not have real effects on the macroeconomy. Given the classical assumption of flexible prices, money is neutral in the IS-LM model, but money is not neutral in the short run under the Keynesian assumption of slow price adjustments.

True-False Questions: Circle T for true statements and F for false statements.

T (F) 1.   Classical economists believe that output is jointly determined by the labor market, goods market, and asset market.

(T) F   2.   Keynesians believe that output can be less than full-employment output for short-run periods that can last for several years.

(T) F   3.   Technological progress that increases the productivity of capital is a beneficial productivity shock that causes output and employment to increase.

T (F) 4.   An increase in desired investment will increase the capital stock, which causes the FE line to shift to the right, thereby causing output to increase.

T (F) 5.   Economists agree that an increase in desired saving will reduce the aggregate demand for output, causing output to decline and unemployment to increase.

T F 6.   Given full-employment output, any change in desired saving relative to desired investment causes the real interest rate to adjust to clear the goods market.

T F 7.   From a classical perspective, a financial crisis that created a sudden decline in wealth would not affect output.

T F 8.   The IS curve is negatively sloped, because an increase in income increases saving relative to investment, which causes the real interest rate to fall.

T F 9.   As the economy moves up along a fixed LM curve, the equilibrium quantity of money supplied and demanded increases, while the demand for nonmonetary assets falls.

T F 10.   In the IS-LM model, the price level adjusts to clear the asset market and return the economy to general equilibrium, but economists disagree about how quickly it adjusts.

Multiple Choice Questions: Circle the letter corresponding to the correct answer to each question.

1.   Classical economists believe that a market economy will normally
   a.   suffer from extended periods of sustained unemployment.
   b.   achieve full-employment output.
   c.   degenerate into pure monopolies in most industries.
   d.   suffer from expectations errors in predicting the price level.
   e.   eliminate the problems of economic scarcity.

2.   The full-employment line
   a.   determines the level of aggregate demand.
   b.   increases with the price level.
   c.   determines the equilibrium level of output.
   d.   is independent of labor supply.
   e.   would increase if the unemployment rate declined.

3.   Which of the following would not shift the FE line to the right?
   a.   A beneficial supply shock
   b.   An increase in the productivity of labor
   c.   An increase in the productivity of capital
   d.   An increase in the supply of labor
   e.   A decline in the capital stock

4.   The IS curve illustrates that when income increases, the
   a.   interest rate must fall to restore equilibrium in the goods market.
   b.   interest rate must rise to restore equilibrium in the goods market.
   c.   interest rate must fall to restore equilibrium in the asset market.
   d.   interest rate must rise to restore equilibrium in the asset market.
   e.   price level must rise to restore equilibrium in the asset market.

5.   As we move down along the Keynesian IS curve,
   a.   investment spending declines but savings increases.
   b.   investment spending and savings both decline.
   c.   investment spending and savings both increase.
   d.   investment spending increases but savings does not change.
   e.   the interest rate and national income both decline.

6.   The IS curve will shift to the left when
   a.   desired saving declines.
   b.   government purchases increase.
   c.   consumption increases.
   d.   expected future marginal product of capital declines.
   e.   desired investment increases.

7.   The LM curve is
   a.   negatively sloped in (Y, r) space.
   b.   negatively sloped in (Y, P) space.
   c.   negatively sloped in (N, Y) space.
   d.   positively sloped in (Y, P) space.
   e.   positively sloped in (Y, r) space.

8.   The LM curve illustrates that when income increases, the
   a.   price level must increase to clear the money market.
   b.   nominal interest rate on money must increase to clear the asset market.
   c.   price level must increase to clear the goods market.
   d.   real interest must increase to clear the goods market.
   e.   real interest rate on nonmonetary assets must increase to clear the asset market.

9.   The LM curve will shift to the right when the
   a.   nominal money supply declines.
   b.   price level rises.
   c.   real money demand declines.
   d.   expected inflation declines.
   e.   wealth increases.

10.   In Keynesian IS-LM analysis, a rightward shift in the FE line will
   a.   not affect the position of the IS curve or LM curve in the short run.
   b.   cause the IS curve to shift to the left in the short run.
   c.   cause the IS curve to shift to the right in the short run.
   d.   cause the LM curve to shift to the right in the short run.
   e.   cause the LM curve to shift to the left in the short run.

11.   Which of the following would not produce an adverse supply shock?
   a.   An increase in the personal income tax rate
   b.   A decline in the productivity of labor
   c.   An increase in saving
   d.   A decline in the supply of capital
   e.   An increase in wage demands by labor

12. In classical IS-LM analysis, which of the following is not an effect of an adverse productivity shock?
    a. Employment declines.
    b. The real wage increases.
    c. The real interest rate increases.
    d. Output declines.
    e. Consumption declines.

13. In Keynesian IS-LM analysis, the short-run effects of a decline in desired investment do not include
    a. an increase in the unemployment rate.
    b. a decline in desired saving.
    c. a decline in the real interest rate.
    d. a decline in the price level.
    e. a decline in output.

14. In classical IS-LM analysis, the effects of a decline in desired investment include
    a. a decline in output.
    b. a decline in employment.
    c. a decline in the real interest rate.
    d. an increase in unemployment.
    e. an increase in the price level.

15. Keynesians contend that in a recession caused by a decline in aggregate demand, a policy of increasing the nominal money supply would
    a. raise the level of aggregate demand, which would help return the economy to full-employment output.
    b. lower the level of aggregate demand, which would help return the economy to full-employment output.
    c. shift the LM curve to left, which would help return the economy to full-employment output.
    d. not affect the position of the LM curve, because the real money supply would not change.
    e. shift the FE line to the right, which would help return the economy to full-employment output.

16. Classical economists contend that an increase in the nominal money supply will
    a. shift the LM curve to the right, causing output to increase.
    b. shift the LM curve to the left, causing output to increase.
    c. shift the LM curve to the left, causing output to decline.
    d. shift the FE line to the right, causing output to increase.
    e. not increase the real money supply.

17. The theory of monetary neutrality suggests that
    a. a barter economy is just as economically efficient as a money economy.
    b. changes in the real money supply will not affect the real interest rate.
    c. money is not an asset.
    d. a decline in nominal money supply growth could create a recession.
    e. inefficient monetary policies that create high and unstable rates of inflation over several years will not affect the performance of the real economy.

18.   In the Keynesian IS-LM model, improvements in the expected future productivity of capital investments
       will not increase
       a. the price level in the long run.
       b. the real interest rate.
       c. desired investment.
       d. unemployment in the short run.
       e. output.

19.   At a given output level, a reduction in government purchases will
       a. increase desired saving, causing the IS curve to shift to the left, which causes the real interest rate to fall.
       b. increase desired saving, causing the IS curve to shift to the left, which causes the real interest rate to rise.
       c. increase desired saving, causing the IS curve to shift to the right, which causes the real interest rate to rise.
       d. decrease desired saving, causing the IS curve to shift to the left, which causes the real interest rate to rise.
       e. decrease desired saving, causing the IS curve to shift to the right, which causes the real interest rate to rise.

20.   The best-known forecasting firms, including Chase Econometrics, Data Resources, and Wharton Econometric
       Forecasting, typically forecast the future values of about
       a. 10 to 20 economic variables.
       b. 100 to 200 economic variables.
       c. 500 to 1000 economic variables.
       d. 700 to 1200 economic variables.
       e. 10,000 to 15,000 economic variables.

Short-Answer Essay Questions

1.   **The full-employment (FE) line:** a) Draw an FE line diagram. Label the axes and curves. b) Briefly
      describe the relationship between output and the interest rate in this diagram and explain why this
      relationship exists. c) Identify changes in three variables that would cause the FE line to shift to the right.
      d) Give an example of an adverse productivity shock. e) Briefly explain the importance in this model of the
      classical assumption that wages are perfectly flexible.

2.   **IS curve representation of goods market equilibrium:** a) Draw a saving-investment diagram. Label the
      axes and curves. b) Show how to use your S^d - I^d diagram to construct an IS curve diagram. Label the axes
      and curve. c) Identify two variables that are changing in value as we move down the IS curve and state the
      direction in which they are changing. d) Draw another IS diagram and use the diagram to show the effect
      on the equilibrium level of desired investment (I^d) of a decline in desired investment. e) Is the IS curve a
      supply curve? Briefly explain.

3.   **Equilibrium in the goods and labor markets:** a) Draw an IS curve and FE line diagram. Label the axes,
      curves, and equilibrium values. b) What markets are in equilibrium in this diagram? c) How important is the
      position of the IS curve in determining the equilibrium level of output? Briefly explain. d) Use the diagram
      to show the effects of a temporary increase in energy prices. Label the new equilibrium values.

4. **Productivity (supply) shocks**: Use the following diagrams to show the effects - if any exist - of human capital investments in education in some previous time period that now create a beneficial productivity shock: a) a production function diagram, for which labor is the variable factor of production; b) a labor market diagram; c) a saving-investment diagram; d) an IS curve-FE line diagram. e) Why would an increase in energy prices in this time period reduce our ability to measure the economic benefits of the human capital investments in education?

5. **The LM curve**: a) Draw a money supply and money demand diagram. Label the axes and curves. b) Show how to use the money supply and money demand diagram to construct an LM curve diagram. c) Define the LM curve. d) Draw another LM curve diagram and use the diagram to show the effects of an increase in money demand.

6. **Supply shocks, demand shocks, monetary policy, and inflation in a IS-LM model of the economy**: In answering the following questions, assume that prices are flexible: a) Draw a complete IS-LM model diagram and use it to show the effects of an adverse supply shock. b) Draw a IS-LM model diagram and use it to show the effects of an increase in money demand. c) Draw a IS-LM model diagram and use it to show the real effects of a decline in desired investment. d) Given flexible prices, could monetary policy be used to offset the real interest rate effects of an adverse supply shock or a decline in desired investment? Briefly explain. e) Identify two causes of inflation.

Mathematical Problem-Solving Questions

1. **Nonmonetary asset price and nominal interest rate**: Calculate the present discounted price of a bond that pays no interest but pays its face value of $1000 at maturity in one year for each of the following nominal interest rates: a) 3%; b) 6%; c) 9%.

2. **Nominal and real money supply growth**: Calculate the real money supply growth rate when the nominal money supply increases by 10% and the price level increases by each of the following percentages: a) 2%; b) 8%; c) 10%; d) 15%.

Answers to Fill-In-The-Blanks Questions

1. full-employment line   2. IS curve   3. LM curve
4. general equilibrium   5. monetary neutrality

Answers to True-False Questions

1. **F** In the classical approach, output is completely determined by equilibrium in the labor market, as illustrated by the full-employment line. If wages and prices adjust quickly, then the economy is always operating on the full-employment line at full-employment output. Changes in goods market conditions, as illustrated by shifts in the IS curve, and changes in asset market conditions, as illustrated by the shifts in the LM curve, change the aggregate demand for output, which causes the price level to adjust to return the economy to general equilibrium without changing output in the classical model.

2. T A leftward shift in the IS curve and/or LM curve creates a decline in the aggregate demand for goods and services, causing supply to exceed demand at the initial price level. Keynesians contend that output will decline to the level of output demanded for the short-run period in which the price level fails to adjust completely. Given the Keynesian belief that wages and prices adjust slowly, the short run may last for several years.

3. T A technological change that increases the productivity of capital shifts the production function up except at the origin and shifts the labor demand schedule to the right, so that more labor is employed and more output is produced at a higher level of employment on the higher production function.

4. F An increase in desired investment shifts the IS curve to the right, but does not affect the position of the FE line. Since the FE line and IS curve are independent, a shift in one does not cause the other to shift. Although an increase in desired investment is an increase in the purchase of capital stock, this new capital stock is not part of the capital stock used to produce current output; this new capital stock will be added to future production, causing future output to exceed current output. Although an increase in desired investment does not increase current output, it does increase economic growth.

5. F An increase in desired saving causes the IS curve to shift to the left, which causes the aggregate demand for output to fall below the full-employment output. In the Keynesian view, output falls to the level of output demanded, in the absence of quick wage and price adjustments. Firms can produce the lower level of output demanded with fewer workers, so they lay off workers and the unemployment rate increases. In the classical view, a decline in aggregate demand causes the price level to fall, which causes the LM curve to shift to the right enough to maintain full-employment output on the FE line at a lower price level. Classical economists contend that a decline in desired saving will not create a short-run period in which output declines and unemployment increases.

6. T The real interest rate is the market price that adjusts to maintain equilibrium in the goods market, holding output constant at full-employment output. An increase in desired investment shifts the investment curve to the right along the positively sloped saving curve to a higher interest rate at which desired saving equals desired investment. The interest rate is the price of credit paid by borrowers to lenders. Savers lend their savings to businesses, which borrow it to buy investment goods.

7. F A financial crisis that created a sudden decline in wealth would increase labor supply, which causes the FE line to shift to the right, which causes output to rise. A financial crisis would also shift the IS curve and the LM curve, but price-level adjustments would prevent these shifts from affecting full-employment output.

8. T An increase in income shifts the saving curve to the right along a fixed investment curve, causing the real interest rate to fall enough to equate desired saving to desired investment. A change in national income does not shift the investment curve in the IS-LM model, but it causes the real interest rate to fall, which increases the equilibrium level of investment spending.

9. F As the economy moves up along a fixed LM curve, the equilibrium level of money supplied and demanded remains unchanged, while the demand for nonmonetary assets rises. Along a given LM curve, the money supply is fixed; an increase in income increases the quantity of money demanded, which causes the interest rate to rise enough to reduce the quantity of money demand to the fixed quantity of money supplied. The interest rate is the rate of return on nonmonetary assets; at a higher interest rate, people will demand more nonmonetary assets and less money. The demand for both nonmonetary assets and money increases with income.

10. T In the IS-LM model, it is the price level that adjusts to clear the asset market and return the macroeconomy to general equilibrium in response to some supply or demand shock. Classical economists believe that the price level adjusts quickly enough to keep the economy continuously operating at full-employment output despite these shocks. Keynesians contend that the price level adjusts slowly, creating short-run periods of disequilibrium in which some markets do not clear. In the Keynesian view, a series of economic shocks, one following another, could keep the economy in disequilibrium for a long time. Economists agree that the price level will adjust to return the economy to general equilibrium, but they disagree about how quickly it adjusts. In the long run, general equilibrium is achieved, where all markets simultaneously clear.

Answers to Multiple Choice Questions

1. b	8. e	15. a
2. c	9. c	16. e
3. e	10. a	17. e
4. a	11. c	18. d
5. c	12. b	19. a
6. d	13. d	20. d
7. e	14. c	

Answers to Short-Answer Essay Questions

1.   **The full-employment (FE) line:**

   a)

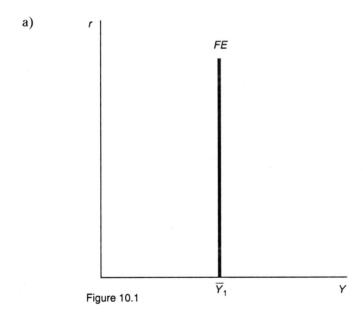

Figure 10.1

   b)   Output is independent of the current interest rate, as shown by the vertical FE line. In the short run, by definition, the amount of capital (K) employed in production is fixed at some given amount and the productivity of resources (A) is also fixed at some given level.   Given these assumptions, output depends only on the amount of labor employed, and equilibrium employment, determined in the labor market, is independent of the interest rate.   The interest rate does partly determine the amount of capital goods purchased, which we've seen in the goods market diagram.   However, the current level of output does not depend on the amount of capital goods bought, since that capital will not be added to production until some future time period.

c)   An increase in productivity, an increase in the supply of capital, or an increase in the supply of labor would increase the full-employment level of output, as illustrated by a rightward shift in the FE line.

d)   A decline in the productivity of labor is an example of an adverse productivity shock.

e)   Full employment exists only at the equilibrium wage.   If wages were not perfectly flexible, then the actual wage may be above the equilibrium wage or below it.   At any wage above the equilibrium wage, labor supply exceeds demand; so the economy is not operating at a point on the FE line.   At any wage below the equilibrium wage, labor demand exceeds supply, so the economy is not operating at a point on the FE line. Only when wages are perfectly flexible can we expect the economy to maintain full-employment output.

2.   **IS curve representation of goods market equilibrium:**

a)

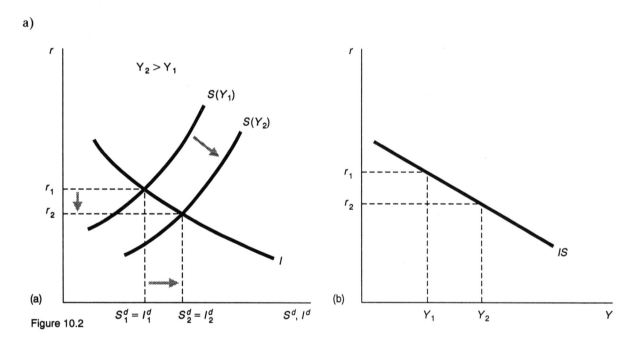

Figure 10.2

b)   As shown above in Fig. 10.2, the IS curve is constructed by showing that an increase in Y shifts S to the right, which causes r to decline.   The IS curve is the schedule of (Y, r) points where $I^d = S^d$.

c)   As we move down an IS curve, national output (Y, also called national income) increases and the real interest rate (r) declines.

d)

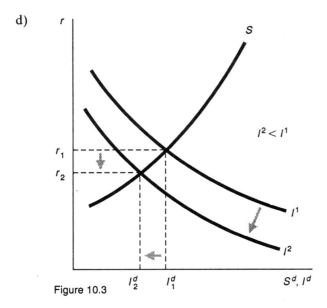

Figure 10.3

e)   The IS curve is not a supply curve; it is a goods market equilibrium curve. At every point along the IS curve, the quantity of goods supplied equals the quantity of goods demanded. As we move down an IS curve to a higher income level and lower real interest rate, desired saving and desired investment increase.

3.   **Equilibrium in the goods and labor markets:**

a)

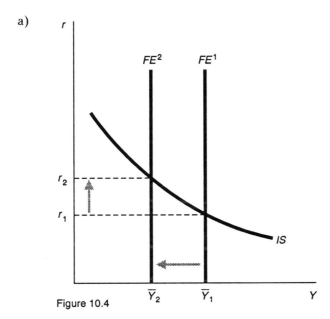

Figure 10.4

b)   Both the labor market and the goods market are in equilibrium in this diagram at (Y_1, r_1). Any point on the FE line represents labor market equilibrium. Any point on the IS curve represents goods market equilibrium. The equilibrium point in the IS curve-FE line diagram is on both curves.

c)   In this long-run, market-clearing model, the position of the IS curve is not even a partial determinant of the equilibrium level of output. Output is completely determined by the production function for a given equilibrium level of employment, as determined by the labor market. Output is independent of the IS curve. Even if the IS curve were to shift, output would remain unchanged.

d)   A temporary increase in energy prices causes the FE line to decline to FE^2, which causes output to fall to Y_2 and the market interest rate to rise to r_2.

4.   **Productivity (supply) shocks:**

a-d)

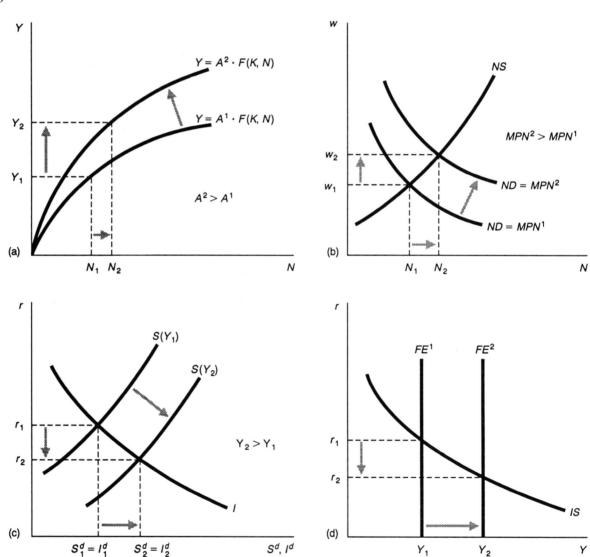

Figure 10.5

e)   An increase in energy prices in this time period would cause an adverse productivity (i.e., supply) shock, which would tend to offset the beneficial productivity shock of increases in labor's education level. We would observe only the net effects of both events. We would not be able to measure the effects of each event separately if they occurred at the same time and affected the values of the same market variables.

5.   **The LM curve**:

a)   A money supply (MS) and money demand (MD) diagram. The second money demand curve is added to help answer part (b).

$$MS = M/P \qquad MD = L(Y, i, i^m) \qquad Y_2 > Y_1$$

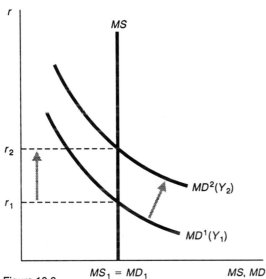

Figure 10.6

b)   Constructing an LM curve: The LM curve is drawn in (Y, r) space by connecting the (Y, r) equilibrium points in the above money supply and money demand diagram with a money demand curve for each level of real GDP.

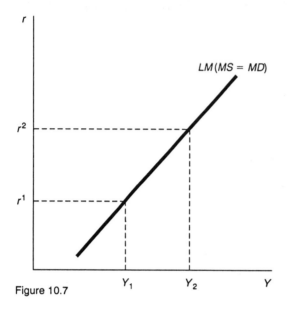

Figure 10.7

c)   LM is the set of (Y, r) points that clear the asset market. At points along the LM curve the money market is in equilibrium and the nonmonetary asset market is in equilibrium.

d)   Effect of an increase in MD on the asset market: r increases at a given level of real GNP.
        $MD_2 > MD_1$

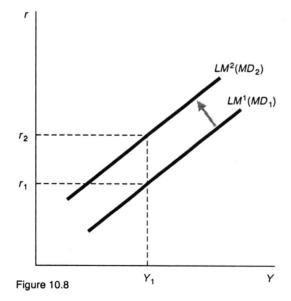

Figure 10.8

6.   **Supply shocks, demand shocks, monetary policy, and inflation in a IS-LM model of the economy**: Answers assume that prices are flexible.

a)   Effects of an adverse supply shock: Y decreases, r increases, P increases. $P_2 > P_1$

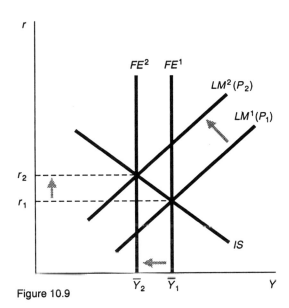

Figure 10.9

b)   Effects of an increase in money demand: P decreases. $L_2 > L_1$ $P_2 < P_1$

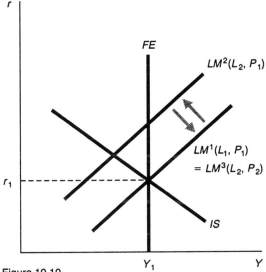

Figure 10.10

c)   Effects of a decline in investment: P decreases and r decreases. $I_2 < I_1$ $P_2 < P_1$

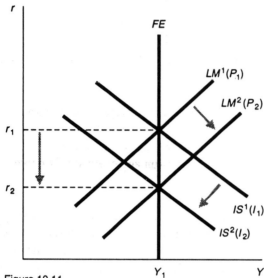

Figure 10.11

d)   No. Given flexible prices, monetary policy cannot shift the LM curve; therefore, it cannot offset either of these changes. Although the Federal Reserve can change the nominal money supply, any change in M creates a proportional change in P, so that the real money supply, M/P, does not change.

e)   Two causes of inflation are adverse supply shocks and increases in the nominal money supply.

Answers to Mathematical Problem-Solving Questions

1.   **Nonmonetary asset price and nominal interest rate**: If P_b is the present discount price or present value of the bond, i is the nominal interest rate, and FV is the face value or future value of the bond, then $P_b(1 + i) = FV$. Likewise, $[(FV - P_b)/P_b]$ = annual percent increase in the value of the bond, and $P_b = FV/(1 + i)$. Therefore, for FV = $1000, and:
a) i = 3%, P_b = $970 = $1000/1.03.
b) i = 6%, P_b = $943.39 = $1000/1.06.
c) i = 9%, Pb = $917.43 = $1000/1.09.

2.   **Nominal and real money supply growth**: The real money supply growth rate = the nominal money supply growth rate minus the price level growth rate. Alternatively stated, the percent increase in (M/P) = the percent increase in M minus the percent increase in P, where M/P is the real money supply, M is the nominal money supply, and P is the price level. The price level growth rate is the inflation rate. For a nominal money supply growth rate of 10% and a price level growth rate of:

a) 2%, the real money supply growth rate = 8% = 10% - 2%.
b) 8%, the real money supply growth rate = 2% = 10% - 8%.
c) 10%, the real money supply growth rate = 0% = 10% - 10%.
d) 15%, the real money supply growth rate = -5% = 10% - 15%.

CHAPTER 11: CLASSICAL BUSINESS CYCLE ANALYSIS: MARKET-CLEARING MACROECONOMICS

A Fill-In-The-Blanks Review of Chapter Highlights: Use the following key terms to fill in the blanks. Each key term is used only once.

aggregate demand curve   aggregate supply curve   long-run aggregate supply curve
misperceptions theory   nominal shocks   productivity shocks
propagation mechanism   rational expectations   real business cycle theory
real shocks   reverse causation   short-run aggregate supply curve

1. _Real Business Cycle theory_ is a version of the classical model that contends that business cycle fluctuations in aggregate economic activity are principally caused by real shocks, especially productivity shocks. All shocks to the economy are either real shocks or nominal shocks. 2._Real Shocks_, such as a change in aggregate labor supply or a change in aggregate saving, are changes that originate in the labor market or the goods market. 3._Nominal Shocks_, such as a change in the aggregate money supply or money demand, are changes that originate in the asset market. There are many different kinds of adverse and beneficial 4. _Productivity Shocks_, and any productivity shock will change the full-employment level of output.

One critique of the real business cycle model is that some business cycles are caused by changes in the money supply, which are nominal shocks. One business cycle fact that appears to support this critique is the fact that the money supply is a leading and procyclical variable. However, correlation does not prove causation; the fact that a decline in the nominal money supply usually precedes a contraction in the business cycle does not prove that money supply reductions cause these contractions. RBC theorists believe that the leading, procyclical nature of the nominal money supply illustrates 5. _Reverse Causation_, which means that an anticipated change in the business cycle causes the Federal Reserve to change the money supply in a procyclical, leading fashion to achieve its long-run policy goal of maintaining price level stability.

The classical aggregate demand and aggregate supply diagram illustrates general equilibrium. The 6._Aggregate Demand Curve_ shows that the amount of real output demanded is negatively related to the price level. Each point on the aggregate demand curve represents equilibrium in both the goods market and the asset market at one price level, which corresponds to an equilibrium point in an IS-LM diagram. Since a decline in the price level shifts the LM to the right along a negatively sloped IS curve to a higher equilibrium level of real output, the aggregate demand curve is negatively sloped. The vertical 7._Aggregate Supply Curve_ shows that employment and output in the macroeconomy are independent of the price level. Each point on the aggregate supply curve represents equilibrium in the labor market at one price level. Just as the FE line shows that full-employment output is independent of the real interest rate, the AS curve shows that full-employment output is independent of the price level. From a classical view, changes in the real interest rate and the price level do not cause output to deviate from full-employment output.

The basic classical model assumes that market actors have perfect information. One implication of the perfect information assumption is that the general public, including producers, usually know the price level, even if the price level is frequently changing. An alternative way of stating that producers know the price level is to say that the actual price level (P) is the expected price level (P^e), so that producers' expectations are correct.   The vertical aggregate supply curve is, in part, based on this assumption of perfect information; at any point on the vertical aggregate supply curve, producers' expectations are correct (i.e., $P = P^e$) at each possible price level.

The 8. <u>Misperceptions Theory</u> critiques the classical model assumption of perfect information by market actors. According to the misperceptions theory, producers' expectations do not quickly adjust to changes in the price level; therefore, there are short-run periods of time during which the price level does not equal the expected price level. In the short run, businesses misperceive a change in the price level as being a change in the price of their products relative to the price level, which causes them to change their output level.

The extended classical model is an extension of the classical model based on the misperceptions theory. The positively sloped 9. <u>Short-Run Aggregate Supply Curve</u> of the extended classical model shows that firms will produce more than the full-employment level of output when ($P > P^e$), and they will produce less than the full-employment level of output when ($P < P^e$). The vertical 10. <u>Long-Run Aggregate Supply Curve</u> of the extended classical model shows that firms will produce the full-employment level of output when their price level expectations are correct (i.e., $P = P^e$). The long-run aggregate supply curve in the extended classical model is identical to the aggregate supply curve in the basic classical model.

Although the basic classical model shows that money is neutral, this conclusion depends on the assumption that producers anticipate any changes in the money supply and understand the price level effects of any changes in the money supply. In contrast, the extended classical model shows that money is not neutral in the short run, because producers do not anticipate changes in the money supply or do not understand the price level effects of changes in the money supply. In both models, however, money is neutral in the long run.

According to the 11. <u>Rational Expectations</u> hypothesis, market actors are rational, which means that they will efficiently use all available information when forming expectations about changes in the values of economic variables. One implication of the rational expectations hypothesis is that producers will anticipate any systematic changes in the money supply and they will understand the price level effects of these changes; only nonsystematic changes in the money supply (i.e., monetary surprises) will be unanticipated. Consequently, money is neutral even in the short run, except in the unusual case of a monetary surprise. Therefore a change in the money supply normally has no real economic effect; it simply moves us along the vertical long-run aggregate supply curve, in both the short run and the long run, to a different price level.

Although the misperceptions theory shows how aggregate output could deviate from the full-employment output during the short-run misperceptions period, it does not explain the persistence of these business cycle deviations. Since money supply data is published weekly and price level data is published monthly, producers' expected price level errors appear to be short-lived. However, short-lived expectations errors could have longer-term real economic effects, if there is some 12. <u>Propagation Mechanism</u> at work in the economy.   The output effect of firms adjusting their inventory levels after an expectations error has been corrected provides one example of a propagation mechanism at work in the economy.

True-False Questions: Circle T for true statements and F for false statements.

Ⓣ F 1.   In the classical model, changes in the nominal money supply and money demand do not have any real economic effects.

Ⓣ F 2.   Classical economists contend that fiscal policies cannot be efficiently used to reduce the severity and duration of business cycle fluctuations.

T (F) 3.   Classical economists believe that the unemployment and inflation effects of business cycle contractions are very costly to the macroeconomy.

T (F) 4.   Technological progress is the only important cause of beneficial productivity shocks.

(T) F 5.   According to real business cycle theory, a decline in government purchases could create a recession.

(T) F 6.   In the classical view, unemployment does not increase above the natural rate of unemployment during recessions, which is consistent with full-employment output and general equilibrium.

T (F) 7.   Unlike classical economists, proponents of the extended classical model would propose using a nonsystematic increase in the nominal money supply during a recession to increase output and employment.

(T) F 8.   When the economy is operating at some point on an aggregate demand curve, both the goods market and the asset market are in equilibrium.

(T) F 9.   In the extended classical model, if the price level unexpectedly declines, output will temporarily decline below full-employment output.

T (F) 10.   Extended classical model theorists agree that slow wage and price adjustments provide a good example of a propagation mechanism needed to explain the persistence of recessions.

Multiple Choice Questions: Circle the letter corresponding to the correct answer to each question.

1.   According to real business cycle theory, which of the following events is least likely to cause a recession?
    (a) A decline in the money supply
    b.   A decline in the capital stock
    c.   A decline in productivity
    d.   A decline in labor supply
    e.   An increase in government spending and taxes

2.   Real shocks are disturbances in the
    a.   labor market only.
    b.   asset market only.
    c.   goods market and asset market.
    d.   asset market and labor market.
    (e) labor market and goods market.

3.   According to the basic classical model, an increase in the money supply will cause
    a.   employment to increase.
    b.   output to increase.
    c.   investment to increase.
    (d) the price level to increase.
    e.   saving to decline.

4.   Research on productivity shocks has shown that
       a. productivity shocks have only nominal effects.
       b. there have been no identifiable productivity shocks in the U.S. economy since World War II.
       c. small productivity shocks can explain large business cycle fluctuations.
       d. large productivity shocks produce only small deviations in aggregate output.
       e. productivity shocks have real effects but they don't have nominal effects.

5.   A decline in the money supply usually precedes a decline in business cycle activity; according to RBC
       theorists, this shows that the Federal Reserve
       a. intentionally causes most recessions.
       b. should not be allowed to control the money supply.
       c. does not know what it is doing.
       d. often creates productivity shocks.
       e. reduces the money supply when it forecasts a recession and increases the money supply when it
           forecasts a boom.

6.   An increase in saving will shift the IS curve to the
       a. left, but will not shift the AD curve.
       b. left, and shift the AD curve to the left.
       c. left, and shift the AD curve to the right.
       d. right, and shift the AD curve to the left.
       e. right, and shift the FE line to the right.

7.   If full-employment output declines, the aggregate supply curve
       a. shifts to the left, and the IS curve shifts to the left.
       b. shifts to the left, and the LM curve shifts to the left.
       c. does not shift, but the FE line shifts to the left.
       d. shifts to right, and the FE line shifts to the right.
       e. shifts to the right, and the IS curve shifts to the left.

8.   Misperceptions theory best explains why
       a. the aggregate demand curve is negatively sloped.
       b. the aggregate supply curve is vertical.
       c. the SRAS curve is positively sloped.
       d. the LM curve is positively sloped.
       e. money is neutral.

9.   In the extended classical model, a 5% decline in the money supply that is unanticipated will
       a. cause output to increase in the short run.
       b. cause output to increase in the long run.
       c. cause employment to decline in the long run.
       d. not change employment in the short run or long run.
       e. cause both output and employment to decline in the short run.

10. In the extended classical model, the economy is operating on the long-run aggregate supply curve when
   a. output = employment.
   b. the real wage = the real interest rate.
   c. $P = P^e$, at various price levels.
   d. there is no frictional nor structural unemployment.
   e. output exceeds the full-employment level of output.

11. The misperceptions theory and the rational expectations hypothesis together suggest that systematic attempts by the Federal Reserve to increase aggregate output will
   a. cause $(P > P^e)$ in the short run.
   b. not have any real economic effects.
   c. not increase the price level.
   d. cause the AD curve to shift to the right along a fixed SRAS curve.
   e. cause employment to increase more than the real wage.

12. In the extended classical model, some kind of propagation mechanism is needed to explain
   a. the persistence of a recession caused by a nominal shock.
   b. imperfect information.
   c. why money is neutral.
   d. the difference between correlation and causation.
   e. why producers are rational.

13. A classical IS-LM diagram can be used to develop an AD curve by analyzing the effect of
   a. an increase in the price level on real output.
   b. an increase in the real interest rate on the price level.
   c. an increase in real output on the real interest rate.
   d. a rightward shift in the IS curve on real output.
   e. a leftward shift in the IS curve on the real interest rate.

14. If money is neutral, then a 5% decline in the money supply causes
   a. the price level to change, but does not change absolute product prices.
   b. the price level to change, but does not change the nominal wage.
   c. the price level to change, but does not change nominal income.
   d. the price level to decrease, and nominal income to decline.
   e. the price level to increase by 5%, but has no real economic effects.

15. In the classical IS-LM diagram, a temporary increase in government purchases causes the
   a. IS curve to shift down to the left along a fixed FE line.
   b. IS curve to shift up to the right along a fixed FE line.
   c. LM curve to shift down to the right along a fixed IS curve.
   d. LM curve to shift up to the left along a fixed IS curve.
   e. FE line to shift to the right and the IS curve to shift up to the right.

16. In the extended classical model, an unexpected increase in the money supply causes the economy to
   a. move up the LRAS curve in the short run and long run.
   b. move down the LRAS curve in the long run, but not in the short run.
   c. move up the SRAS curve in the short run, and move up along the LRAS curve in the long run.
   d. shift the SRAS curve down along the LRAS curve in the short run, but not in the long run.
   e. move down the LRAS curve in the short run and long run.

17.   General equilibrium in the classical AD-AS diagram represents equilibrium in
   a. the goods market, but not in the labor market.
   b. the goods market, but not in the asset market.
   c. all markets simultaneously.
   d. the labor market and goods market, but not in the asset market.
   e. the asset market and goods market, but not in the labor market.

18.   Computer simulations of Edward Prescott's calibrated RBC model, using data for the post-World War II U.S. economy, show that his model substantially overestimated the correlation of output and
   a. investment.
   b. consumption.
   c. inventory stocks.
   d. productivity.
   e. total hours worked.

19.   According to classical economists, which of the following is not an important practical difficulty in using fiscal policies to reduce business cycle fluctuations?
   a. Changes in fiscal policy do not have any output and employment effects.
   b. Fiscal policy lags make it unlikely that the timing of fiscal policy changes will be efficient.
   c. Changes in fiscal policy could be too expansionary or too contractionary.
   d. Economists who advise fiscal policymakers are unable to accurately forecast the future path of business cycle fluctuations.
   e. Fiscal policymakers disagree about what changes in taxes and government purchases would be best for the economy.

20.   Research by Friedman and Schwartz on the monetary history of the United States for 1867-1960, and the recent updating of this research by Romer and Romer suggests that
   a. reverse causality can explain why the nominal money supply is a leading, procyclical variable.
   b. the Federal Reserve can accurately forecast turning points in the business cycle created by small, random changes in productivity.
   c. money is often nonneutral in the short run.
   d. money is often nonneutral in the long run.
   e. changes in the nominal monetary supply are systematic and anticipated by market participants with rational expectations, so money is neutral.

Short-Answer Essay Questions

1.   **General equilibrium in the classical IS-LM model:** a) Draw a classical IS-LM diagram. Label the axes, curves, and equilibrium values. b) Identify and briefly explain the slope of each curve. c) Do classical economists believe that the economy usually operates in equilibrium? Briefly explain. d) Identify one variable that will cause each curve to shift, state the direction of the shift for a decline in each variable, and determine the effects on equilibrium values.

2.   **General equilibrium in the classical AD-AS model:** a) Show how to use an IS-LM diagram to construct an AD-AS diagram. b) Identify and explain the slopes of the AD curve and the AS curve. c) Draw an AD-AS diagram and use the diagram to show the effects of a decline in aggregate demand. d) Draw an AD-AS diagram and use the diagram to show the effects of a beneficial supply shock. e) Draw an AD-AS diagram and use the diagram to show the effects of a decline in the expected rate of inflation.

3.   **Real business cycle (RBC) theory:** a) According to the real business cycle theory, what is the principal cause of business cycle fluctuations? b) Define real shocks, define nominal shocks, and give an example of each. c) How do RBC theorists answer the objection that there have been few examples of large and easily measurable real shocks to the U.S. economy in recent decades? d) How do RBC theorists answer the objection that the money supply is a leading, procyclical variable? e) What problem does the empirical evidence of a steep labor supply curve pose for RBC theorists?

4.   **Fiscal and monetary policy in the classical model:** a) Draw a classical IS-LM diagram and a corresponding AD-AS diagram, then use the diagrams to show the effects of an increase in government purchases. b) During a recession, would classical economists propose that changes in government spending or taxes be used to improve economic conditions? Briefly explain. c) Draw a classical IS-LM diagram and a corresponding AD-AS diagram, then use the diagrams to show the effects of an increase in the money supply. d) During a recession, would classical economists propose that changes in the money supply be used to improve economic conditions? Briefly explain.

5.   **The extended classical model:** a) State the short-run aggregate supply equation and use the equation to explain the slope of the SRAS curve. b) Draw an AD-AS diagram for the extended classical model and use the diagram to show the effects of an unanticipated decline in the money supply in the short run and long run. c) Draw an AD-AS diagram for the extended classical model and use the diagram to show the effects of an anticipated decline in the money supply in the short run and the long run. d) In the extended classical model is money neutral, and can nominal shocks create business cycle fluctuations? Briefly explain. e) Does the extended classical model explain the persistence of business cycle contractions and expansions? Briefly explain.

6.   **Rational expectations hypothesis (REH):** a) Briefly state the rational expectations hypothesis. b) If producers are rational will they anticipate changes in the money supply? Briefly explain. c) Why do REH theorists believe that any monetary policy attempt to increase output during a recession will be systematic, rather than a monetary surprise? d) How do producers know how much the price level will increase when the money supply increases by 5%?

Mathematical Problem-Solving Questions

1.   **Correlation of macroeconomic variables:** Suppose that consumption = constant term + a x GDP + random error. Assuming that GDP = $7000 billion and consumption = $4200 initially, calculate the expected change in consumption when GDP declines by 3% for each of the following values of a: a) 1.0; b) .9; c) .8.

2.   **Net jobs creation or destruction:** Table 11.1 in the textbook shows the percentages of job creation and job destruction in manufacturing in the United Sates each year for the 1973-1986 period. Use the data in the table to calculate the year and cumulative net job loss over the 1980-1983 period, assuming there were 30 million jobs at the beginning of 1980.

Answers to Fill-In-The-Blanks Questions

1. real business cycle theory	2. real shocks	3. nominal shocks
4. productivity shocks	5. reverse causation	6. aggregate demand curve
7. aggregate supply curve	8. misperceptions theory	9. short-run aggregate supply curve
10. long-run aggregate supply curve	11. rational expectations	12. propagation mechanism

Answers to True-False Questions

1. **T**   Money is neutral in the classical model, which means that changes in money market conditions do not have any real economic effects.

2. **T**   Expansionary fiscal policies include temporary tax cuts and/or temporary increases in government purchases. The Ricardian equivalence proposition is part of the classical model; this proposition shows that a temporary tax cut would not have any real effects on the economy, so it would not reduce business cycle fluctuations. Real business cycle theory is also part of the classical model; this theory shows that a temporary increase in government purchases would increase output and employment, but these expected benefits would be exceeded by the expected costs of this policy. According to RBC theory, a temporary increase in government purchases reduces workers' wealth because it necessitates a future tax increase; the decline in wealth increases labor supply, which increases employment and output, but also reduces the real wage. A temporary increase in government purchases also reduces government saving, which reduces desired saving, which increases the interest rate, which reduces desired investment. The increase in labor supply creates an increase in aggregate supply. The decline in desired saving creates an increase in aggregate demand. If the increase in government purchases causes aggregate demand to increase relative to aggregate supply, it will cause the price level to rise, which is inflationary. An increase in output and employment at the expense of higher future taxes, more work, a lower real wage, less desired saving and investment, and possibly higher inflation would not be economically efficient or desirable.

3. **F**   In the classical view, business cycle contractions are economically efficient in that they represent the optimal macroeconomic adjustments to unavoidable real shocks. Since changes in the price level, represented by inflation, do not affect output, employment, or any other real economic variable in the classical model, the cost of inflation or deflation is very small. It is a business cycle fact that inflation declines in a recession, but in the classical model, inflation doesn't matter. It is also a business cycle fact that unemployment increases during recessions, but in the classical model it doesn't increase above the natural rate of unemployment; this suggests that the increase in unemployment is also not very costly from a macroeconomic perspective. The classical view that the economy normally operates in the long run with general equilibrium conditions also suggests that any cyclical disequilibrium changes in inflation and unemployment are expected to be small and short-lived. The economic costs of these contractions appear to be small and cannot be efficiently reduced.

4. **F**   There are many possible causes of beneficial productivity shocks. Anything that increases the amount of output produced for a given amount of capital and labor employed is a beneficial productivity shock. In addition to technological progress, a decline in oil prices, human capital investments in education by labor, and improvements in business management practices would create beneficial productivity shocks.

5. **T**   According to real business cycle theory, recessions are caused by negative real shocks, which include changes in labor market conditions and goods market conditions. RBC theory is part of the classical model. In the classical model, a temporary decline in government purchases will cause government to cut taxes in the future, which increases wealth, which reduces labor supply, which causes the FE line and the aggregate supply curve to shift to the left, causing output and employment to decline, creating a recession. A temporary decline in government purchases also increases government saving, which increases desired saving, which causes the IS curve to shift to the left, which causes the real interest rate to decline, and causes the aggregate demand curve to shift to the left. The leftward shift in the AS curve is inflationary, but the leftward shift in the AD curve is deflationary, so whether inflation increases or decreases depends on the size of the shifts in the two curves.

6. T   In the classical model, recessions represent a general equilibrium decline in output and employment, so that the economy continues to operate at full-employment output throughout business cycle contractions and expansions. It is a business cycle fact that unemployment rises during recessions. Classical economists contend that the increase in unemployment during a recession just matches the increase in the natural rate of unemployment during recessions. With full-employment defined as the natural rate of unemployment, there is no unemployment above the natural rate of unemployment in a recession. The natural rate of unemployment includes frictional and structural unemployment.   At the natural rate of unemployment, there is no cyclical unemployment.

7. F   Unlike the classical model, the extended classical model shows that a nonsystematic increase in the nominal money supply would increase output and employment. Yet, classical and extended classical economists both agree that the government should not undertake such an expansionary monetary policy, since it would not be economically beneficial to the macroeconomy. In the classical model, money is neutral, so a nominal increase in the money supply has no real economic effect. In the extended classical model, a nonsystematic monetary policy increase in nominal money supply, given misperceptions, causes output and employment to increase in the short run, but it achieves this by fooling businesses into underestimating the price level, which causes them to employ more workers and produce more output than is economically efficient, thereby making them worse off. Economists do not endorse government policies that are expected to make market participants worse off.

8. T   The aggregate demand curve depicts the set of (Y, P) points at which the goods market and asset market clear, when all the other determinants of desired saving, desired investment, money supply, and money demand remain constant. The aggregate demand curve shows that when output increases, the price level must decline to maintain equilibrium in the aggregate demand for output, everything else remaining constant.

9. T   As the economy moves down a given short-run aggregate supply curve in the extended classical model, the price level (P) declines but the expected price level (P^e) remains constant. If P^e remains constant in the short run and P unexpectedly declines, then $P < P^e$; this misperception causes output to decline below full-employment output in the short run .

10. F   Extended classical economists reject the Keynesian belief that wages and prices adjust slowly; extended classical theorists propose other propagation mechanisms to explain the persistence of contractions and expansions created by misperceptions of the price level.

Answers to Multiple Choice Questions

1. a	8. c	15. e
2. e	9. e	16. c
3. d	10. c	17. c
4. c	11. b	18. d
5. e	12. a	19. a
6. b	13. a	20. c
7. b	14. d	

Answers to Short-Answer Essay Questions

1.   **General equilibrium in the classical IS-LM model**:

    a)   A classical IS-LM diagram follows.

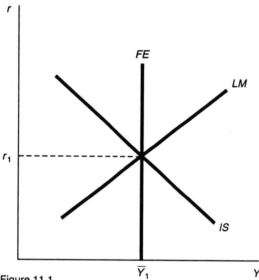

Figure 11.1

    b)   Slopes of the curves:

        1) The FE line is vertical at the full-employment level of output, indicating that output is independent of the real interest rate and independent of the price level.

        2) The IS curve is negatively sloped, because an increase in output increases saving, creating an excess supply of saving at the initial interest rate; therefore the interest rate must decline to reduce desired saving and increase desired investment, to restore equilibrium at the higher output level.

        3) The LM curve is positively sloped, because an increase in income increases the quantity of money demanded, creating excess demand for money at the initial interest rate; therefore the interest rate must rise to reduce the amount demanded, to restore equilibrium at the higher output level.

    c)   Yes, classical economists believe that the economy normally operates in equilibrium in all markets, which is called general equilibrium. Flexible prices quickly adjust to their equilibrium (i.e., market-clearing) values and, once there, there is no further tendency for these values to change. If there is some change in supply or demand in a market, flexible price adjustments quickly return the market and the economy to equilibrium.

d)   Examples of shift variables:

1)   Productivity: A decline in productivity will shift the FE line to the left, causing output to decline, employment to decline, the real interest rate to increase, and the price level to increase.

2)   Government purchases: A decline in government purchases causes the IS curve to shift down to the left and causes the FE line to shift to the left, causing output to decline, employment to decline, the interest rate to decline, and the price level to decline.

3)   Expected rate of inflation: A decline in the expected rate of inflation causes the LM curve to shift up to the left. In the classical model, the price level falls, shifting the LM curve back to its initial position so that equilibrium output, employment, and the real interest rate are unchanged.

2.   **General equilibrium in the classical AD-AS model:**

a)   An IS-LM diagram is used below to construct an AD-AS diagram. The (Y, P) points labeled A and B are used to construct the AD curve. The (Y, P) points labeled A and C are used to construct the AS curve.

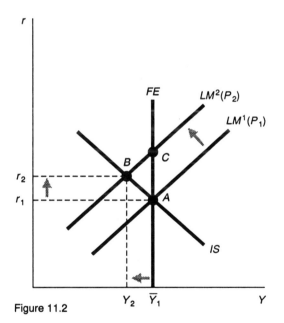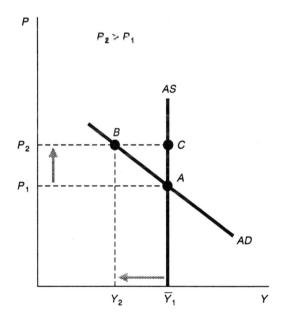

Figure 11.2

b)   The slopes of AD and AS curves:

1)   The AD curve is negatively sloped, because a decline in price level shifts the LM curve down to the right along a negatively sloped IS curve, causing the amount of output demanded to increase. The negatively sloped aggregate demand curve reflects this increase in output demanded at a lower price level.

2)   The AS curve is vertical, because a decline in the price level shifts the LM curve down to the right along the vertical FE line, which does not change the full-employment level of output supplied. The aggregate supply curve shows that the full-employment level of output is independent of the price level.

c)   In the following classical AD-AS diagram, a decline in AD lowers the equilibrium price level.

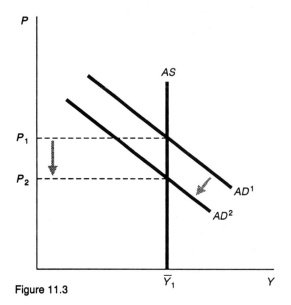

Figure 11.3

d)   In the following classical AD-AS diagram, a beneficial supply shock increases the level of output and lowers the price level.

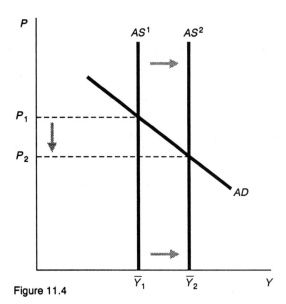

Figure 11.4

e)   A decline in the expected rate of inflation increases the demand for money, which shifts the
      LM curve to the left, which causes the AD curve to shift down to the left. In the classical AD-
      AS model, a decline in AD causes the price level to decline.

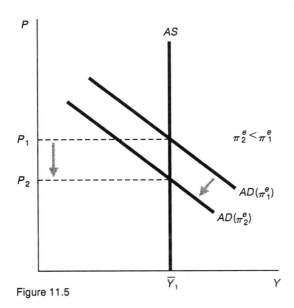

Figure 11.5

3.   **Real business cycle (RBC) theory:**

   a)   According to the real business cycle theory, real shocks, especially productivity shocks, are the
         principal cause of business cycle fluctuations in aggregate economic activity.

   b)   Real shocks are changes that disturb labor market equilibrium or goods market equilibrium. Nominal
         shocks are changes that disturb the asset market. A change in aggregate saving is an example of a
         real shock. A change in the money supply is an example of a nominal shock.

   c)   Computer simulations of RBC statistical models have shown that frequent, small, randomly generated
         productivity shocks can produce large business cycle fluctuations. Therefore large business cycle
         fluctuations occur even in the absence of large productivity shocks.

   d)   The money supply is a leading, procyclical variable, but correlation does not prove causation. One
         plausible explanation is that the Federal Reserve anticipates changes in the business cycle, then
         reduces the money supply prior to a recession, and increases it prior to an expansion to achieve its
         policy goal of maintaining price level stability.

   e)   RBC theory suggests that productivity shocks are the principal cause of business cycle fluctuations.
         In the labor market, temporary productivity shocks shift the labor demand curve along a fixed labor
         supply curve. If the labor supply curve is steep, movements along the labor supply curve would
         create larger changes in the real wage than in employment levels. Therefore a steep labor supply
         curve suggests that productivity shocks cannot create large fluctuations in employment and output.
         Some other kind of shock is needed to explain these large fluctuations in employment and output.

However, RBC theorists contend that the labor supply curve may be much flatter than previous research suggests. If the labor supply curve is relatively flat, then productivity shocks could be the principal cause of most business cycles.

4.   **Fiscal and monetary policy in the classical model:**

a)   In the classical IS-LM diagram, a temporary increase in government purchases causes the FE line to shift to the right and the IS curve to shift up to the right. Price level adjustments cause the LM curve to shift up to the left to restore general equilibrium at a higher real interest rate, a higher level of output, and at a higher price level. In the classical AD-AS model, the AD curve shifts up to the right and the AS curve shifts to the right; equilibrium is restored at a higher output and price level.

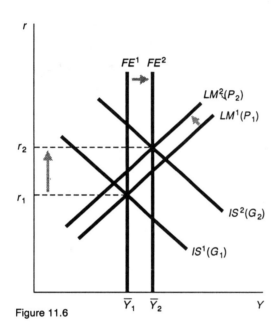 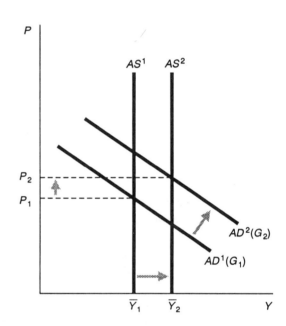

Figure 11.6

b)   No. Classical economists do not endorse changes in government spending or taxes designed to offset business cycle fluctuations; the classical model shows that such policy attempts are not likely to improve macroeconomic conditions. From a classical viewpoint, government spending and tax decisions should be long-run decisions based on cost-benefit analysis.

c)   In a classical IS-LM diagram, an increase in the money supply does not shift any curve, because the change in the nominal money supply creates a proportional change in the price level, so that the real money supply does not change. Therefore the LM curve does not shift. In the classical AD-AS diagram, an increase in the money supply shifts the AD curve up to the right along the vertical AS curve, causing the price level to increase.

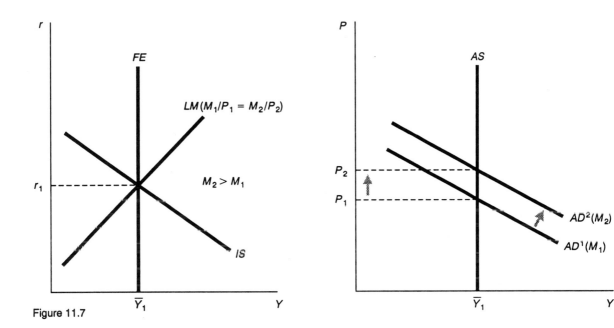

Figure 11.7

d)   No. In the classical model, an increase in the money supply cannot improve economic conditions, because it has no real economic effects. Money is neutral in the classical model.

5.   **The extended classical model:**

a)   The short-run aggregate supply equation is $Y = \overline{Y} + b(P - P^e)$, where $b > 0$. This equation states the SRAS curve is a set of (Y,P) points where: 1) Output equals the full-employment level of output when the actual price level equals the expected price level. 2) Output exceeds the full-employment level of output when the price level exceeds the expected price level. 3) Output is less than the full-employment level of output when the price level is less than the expected price level.

b)   In the extended classical model, an unanticipated decline in the money supply causes the price level to decline and output to decline, as shown by the movement from A to B. In the long run, the price level declines further, as the expected price level declines, but there is no output effect in the long run, as shown by the movement from A to C.

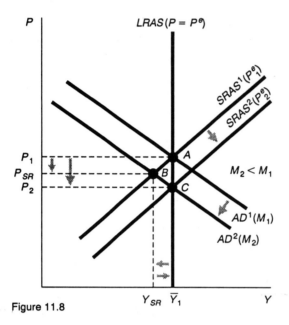

Figure 11.8

c)   In the extended classical model, an anticipated decline in the money supply causes the price level and the expected price level to immediately decline without producing any change in real output. The neutrality of money is shown by the movement from A to B in the diagram.

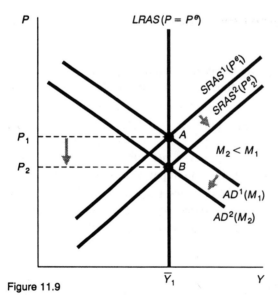

Figure 11.9

d)   In the extended classical model, money is neutral in the long run. In the short run, anticipated changes in the money supply are neutral, but unanticipated changes in the money supply are nonneutral. Changes in the money supply are nominal shocks. Only unanticipated nominal shocks can create business cycle fluctuations in the extended classical model.

e)   No. Although the model shows that a monetary surprise can create short-run business cycle fluctuations in aggregate economic activity, the frequent publication of money supply data and price level data suggests that these errors will not persist. The persistence of a business cycle contraction requires some additional propagation mechanism to explain it. One such propagation mechanism is the process of adjusting inventories to their desired level once misperceptions have been corrected.

6.   **Rational expectations hypothesis (REH):**

a)   The rational expectations hypothesis states that market actors will use all available information in predicting the values of important economic variables, and they will learn to improve the accuracy of their predictions over time.

b)   Rational producers will learn to anticipate any systematic changes in the money supply, but they cannot anticipate nonsystematic monetary surprises.

c)   REH theorists argue that the public will learn to understand the Federal Reserve's behavior and will expect the Federal Reserve to increase the money supply when the economy is in a recession. But if the public anticipates the increase in the money supply, output will be unaffected by the increase in the money supply.

d)   Producers know that classical economic theory predicts that a 5% increase in the money supply will cause the price level to increase by 5%, because price level changes are proportional to money supply changes in the long run.

Answers to Mathematical Problem-Solving Questions

1.   **Correlation of macroeconomic variables**: Initially, output = $7000 billion, and consumption = $4200 billion. When output declines by 3%, it falls to $6790 billion. When the coefficient for output, a, is

a) 1.0, then consumption declines on average by 3%, declining to $4074 billion.
b) .9, then consumption usually declines on average by 3% x .9 = 2.7%, declining to $4087.
c) .8, then consumption declines on average by 3% x .8 = 2.4%, declining to $4099.

2.   **Net jobs creation or destruction**: Using the data from Table 11.1 in the textbook, we subtract the percentage of jobs created from the percentage of jobs destroyed to obtain the net percentage of jobs destroyed. To obtain the net jobs lost in a year, we can multiply the number of jobs available at the beginning of the year by the percentage of net jobs lost. It is assumed that there are 30 million jobs at the beginning of 1980. The calculations follow.

In 1980, 9.3% - 8.0% = 1.3% of jobs destroyed x 30 million jobs = 390,000 jobs destroyed.
In 1981, 11.8% - 7.0% = 4.8% of jobs destroyed x (30 million - 390,000) jobs = 1,421,280 jobs destroyed.
In 1982, 15.2% - 6.4% = 8.8% of jobs destroyed x (29,610,000 - 1,421,280) jobs = 2,480,607 jobs destroyed.
For 1980-1983, the total jobs destroyed = 390,000 + 1,421,280 + 2,480,607 = 4,291,887 jobs destroyed.

CHAPTER 12: KEYNESIANISM: THE MACROECONOMICS OF WAGE AND PRICE RIGIDITY

A Fill-In-The-Blanks Review of Chapter Highlights: Use the following key terms to fill in the blanks. Each key term is used only once.

aggregate demand management	aggregate demand shocks	effective labor demand curve
efficiency wage	efficiency wage model	effort curve
labor hoarding	macroeconomic stabilization	marginal cost
markup	menu cost	monopolistic competition
multiplier	perfect competition	price stickiness
real-wage rigidity	turnover costs	

1. _Real Wage Rigidity_ in the short run is an important feature of the Keynesian model of the labor market. Real-wage rigidity means that the real wage does not change when firms' aggregate demand for labor increases or declines. The assumption of real-wage rigidity in the Keynesian model contrasts with the assumption of perfectly flexible real wages in the classical model.

The Keynesian model of the labor market is also an 2. _Efficiency Wage Model_ in which the point on the 3. _Effort Curve_ that maximizes each worker's effort per dollar of wages is the 4. _Efficiency wage_. In the Keynesian model of the labor market, firms can hire all the labor they want at the efficiency wage. At the efficiency wage, there is an excess supply of labor; changes in labor supply do not affect the efficiency wage or employment. The efficiency wage in the Keynesian model contrasts with the market-clearing wage in the classical model.

5. _Price Stickiness_ in the short run is another important feature of the Keynesian model. Price stickiness means that firms do not change the price at which they supply goods when the aggregate demand for goods either increases or declines. Given price stickiness, the short-run aggregate supply curve is horizontal at a fixed price level for all levels of output. The assumption of price stickiness in the Keynesian model contrasts with the assumption of perfectly flexible prices in the classical model.

Another contrast is that individual firms are price takers in the classical model, whereas individual firms are price setters in the Keynesian model. This difference arises because the classical model assumes 6. _Perfect Competition_ among firms, but the Keynesian model assumes 7. _Monopolistic Competition_ among firms. A perfectly competitive firm is a price taker, which cannot increase its selling price without losing all its customers to competing firms. In contrast, a monopolistically competitive firm is a price setter, which can vary its price by a small margin without greatly affecting its market share.

The cost incurred by a firm in changing its price is called its 8. _Menu Cost_. To maximize profits, a firm will change its price only if the change is large enough to create an increase in revenue minus production costs large enough to pay for the menu cost. Keynesians believe that although menu costs are small, they are large enough for monopolistically competitive firms to prevent them from frequently changing their prices; therefore prices are sticky.

For the perfectly competitive firms of the classical model, operating under long-run, general equilibrium market conditions, price equals marginal cost. For an individual firm, the 9. _Marginal Cost_ is the cost of producing the last unit of output. In contrast, the monopolistically competitive firms of the Keynesian model in the short run may charge a price that exceeds marginal cost. The 10. _Markup_ is the percentage by which price exceeds marginal cost (e.g., 10%).

In the Keynesian model, employment is independent of labor supply; labor demand depends on the quantity of goods demanded. Firms demand just enough labor to produce the level of output demanded. The 11 _Effective labor Demand Curve_ shows that more labor will be demanded and employed as output increases. In the short run, output may exceed or be less than the full-employment level of output.

The Keynesian model offers an explanation for the Great Depression. It shows how a short-run period of recession and high unemployment can continue for several years. Keynesians propose that national government policymakers attempt to pull the economy out of recessions by using expansionary 12. _MacroEconomic Stabilization_ policies, such as increasing the money supply or increasing government purchases. Macroeconomic stabilization policies attempt to maintain the level of aggregate demand at the full-employment level of output; they represent 13. _Aggregate Demand Mgmt_ , in that they are attempts to reduce business cycle fluctuations in aggregate demand in order to improve the performance of the macroeconomy. Keynesians contend that an increase in government purchases or any other type of spending on output has a 14. _Multiplier_ effect in increasing output, which means that output increases by more than the initial increase in spending.

The Keynesian model highlights the importance of aggregate demand in the determination of output and employment. Changes in the goods market and the asset market create changes in aggregate demand, called 15. _Aggregate Demand Shocks_ Aggregate demand shocks, in turn, create changes in output, employment, and unemployment. The early Keynesians believed that most recessions were caused by some aggregate demand shock.

Although the basic Keynesian model can explain many of the business cycle facts, it requires the additional assumption of 16. _Labor Hoarding_ to explain why the average productivity of labor is procyclical. Average labor productivity declines during recessions because high 17. _Turnover Costs_ cause firms to retain more labor than is needed to produce output during these short-run contractions. Turnover costs are the costs of firing, hiring, and training workers.

True-False Questions: Circle T for true statements and F for false statements.

(T) F 1.   Keynesians contend that the minimum wage law, union contracts, and turnover costs help to create some real-wage rigidity in the short run.

(T) F 2.   The gift exchange motive and the shirking model help to explain why it may be profitable for monopolistically competitive firms to pay labor a real wage that exceeds the market-clearing wage.

T (F) 3.   Full-employment output in the Keynesian efficiency wage model provides the same level of employment and output in the long run as provided by full-employment output in the classical model.

(T) F 4.   When a decline in the aggregate demand for output creates a recession, monopolistically competitive firms tend to reduce output and lay off workers rather than reduce the prices of their goods and services.

T (F) 5.   In both the Keynesian efficiency wage model and the classical model, output is completely determined by labor demand, labor supply, and the production function.

T (F) 6.   Economists agree that money is neutral.

(T) F 7.   Economists agree that any change that causes the IS curve or LM curve to shift to the right will also cause the aggregate demand curve to shift to the right.

(T) F 8.   In the Keynesian efficiency wage model, a temporary increase in government purchases will not shift the FE line to the right, but it will increase output in the short run.

(T) F 9.   In the Keynesian efficiency wage model, a temporary tax cut has a multiplier effect in increasing output.

(T) F 10.   Keynesians contend that a decline in desired investment or an increase in desired saving can create a recession, and macroeconomic stabilization policies may be needed to prevent a long, severe recession.

Multiple Choice Questions: Circle the letter corresponding to the correct answer to each question.

1.   Real-wage rigidity in the Keynesian efficiency wage diagram of the labor market is depicted by
       a. a vertical labor supply curve at the efficient level of employment.
       b. a vertical labor demand curve at the efficient level of employment.
       (c) a horizontal wage curve at the efficiency wage.
       d. a steep, positively sloped labor supply curve depicting various efficiency wages at various employment levels.
       e. an equilibrium wage, where the quantity of labor demanded equals the quantity of labor supplied.

2.   At full employment in the Keynesian efficiency wage model,
       a. the real wage is the market-clearing wage.
       b. there is an excess demand for labor.
       c. $MPN^* < w^*$.
       (d) there is an excess supply of labor.
       e. there is no structural or frictional unemployment.

3.   The effort curve is
       a. horizontal, because work effort is independent of the real wage.
       b. negatively sloped, because of diminishing marginal returns to labor.
       c. positively sloped, because of the law of increasing cost.
       (d) s-shaped, because a small increase in the real wage will increase work effort more at an intermediate wage than at a low wage or at a high wage.
       e. positively sloped at low wages, because of the substitution effect, but negatively sloped at high wages because of the income effect.

4. The efficiency wage is the real wage that
   a. maximizes labor income.
   b. maximizes profits.
   c. maximizes employment.
   d. maximizes labor supply.
   e. clears the labor market.

5. Because of price stickiness in the Keynesian model, a decline in investment demand will not cause the
   a. LM curve to shift down to the right in the short run.
   b. LM curve to shift in the long run.
   c. IS curve to shift down in the short run.
   d. IS curve to shift in the long run.
   e. FE line to shift to the left in the long run.

6. A firm is a price taker if it
   a. always sells its output at the industry-determined price.
   b. takes consumer demand into consideration in setting its price.
   c. takes its production costs into consideration in setting its price.
   d. uses a pricing strategy to gain market share.
   e. sells its output at a fixed price despite short-run fluctuations in industry demand, but adjusts its price to the market-clearing price in the long run.

7. If firms are price setters, a small decline in the demand for their outputs will cause them to
   a. reduce price and reduce the level of output produced.
   b. reduce output in the short run, but reduce price in the long run.
   c. reduce output and price in the short run, but reduce output only in the long run.
   d. increase price in the short run to offset the effect on profits of a decline in output.
   e. hold price and output constant in the short run, since price setters do not have to respond to changing market conditions in the short run.

8. In an economy where firms in most industries are purely competitive firms, individual firms in each industry would produce
   a. differentiated products and a large share of industry output.
   b. differentiated products and a small share of industry output.
   c. standardized products and a large share of industry output.
   d. standardized products, but a few firms would produce a large share of industry output while most firms produced a small share.
   e. standardized products and a small share of industry output.

9. In the Keynesian model, firms are best characterized as
   a. perfectly competitive.
   b. irrational.
   c. small producers.
   d. price takers.
   e. monopolistically competitive.

10.   In the Keynesian model, a firm's high menu cost causes
        a.   real-wage rigidity.
        b.   full employment.
        c.   price stickiness.
        d.   efficiency wages.
        e.   perfectly flexible price adjustments.

11.   The cost to a firm of producing one more unit of output
        a.   usually exceeds the firm's price.
        b.   is significantly less than the firm's price for purely competitive firms operating in long-run equilibrium.
        c.   usually equals the firm's price for monopolistically competitive firms.
        d.   is the firm's marginal cost.
        e.   declines as more output is produced in the short run.

12.   Firms that charge a price for their output in excess of marginal cost in the short run
        a.   are not maximizing profits.
        b.   cannot find buyers for their output.
        c.   are charging a markup.
        d.   will suffer huge losses.
        e.   are purely competitive firms.

13.   As the economy moves down an effective labor demand curve,
        a.   output declines and employment declines.
        b.   the price level declines and employment increases.
        c.   the real wage declines and employment increases.
        d.   goods demand increases and employment declines.
        e.   the efficiency wage declines and employment increases.

14.   During a severe and persistent recession, Keynesians would most likely propose
        a.   tax increases.
        b.   a tight money policy.
        c.   annually balanced federal budgets.
        d.   no government intervention into the economy.
        e.   macroeconomic stabilization.

15.   In practice, one of the principal problems with aggregate demand management is that
        a.   changes in aggregate demand do not affect output.
        b.   changes in aggregate demand cannot reduce unemployment.
        c.   changes in aggregate demand are highly inflationary.
        d.   stabilization policies could increase aggregate demand too much and at the wrong times.
        e.   the price level is sticky in the short run.

16.   In a short-run Keynesian IS-LM diagram, an aggregate demand shock could not cause
        a.   the real interest rate to change.
        b.   output to change.
        c.   the IS curve to shift.
        d.   the FE curve to shift.
        e.   the LM curve to shift.

17.   The Keynesian model can be extended to explain why average labor productivity is procyclical by assuming
       a.   labor hoarding by firms.
       b.   that the production function does not shift during the business cycle.
       c.   that the wage is procyclical.
       d.   that prices are perfectly flexible.
       e.   that firms are perfectly competitive.

18.   In the Keynesian model, the full-employment level of output is the amount of output produced when
       a.   the quantity of labor demanded equals the quantity of labor supplied.
       b.   the market wage exceeds the efficiency wage.
       c.   labor is paid an efficiency wage, and the real wage equals the marginal product of labor.
       d.   the real wage exceeds the nominal wage.
       e.   there are no productivity shocks.

19.   In the Keynesian IS-LM diagram, if aggregate demand is less than the full-employment level of output in
       the short run,
       a.   the price level will rise in the long run.
       b.   the price level will decline in the long run.
       c.   the LM curve will shift up to the right in the long run.
       d.   the FE line will shift to the left in the long run.
       e.   the IS curve will shift up to the right in the long run.

20.   In the Keynesian AD-AS diagram, the short-run aggregate supply curve is
       a.   horizontal at one price level.
       b.   horizontal at the full-employment level of output.
       c.   horizontal at the efficiency wage.
       d.   vertical at the full-employment level of output.
       e.   negatively sloped, because of diminishing marginal returns to labor.

Short-Answer Essay Questions

1.   **The efficiency wage model:** a) How do Keynesians explain real-wage rigidity during a recession? b) Why
      might firms pay an efficiency wage rather than a market-clearing wage? c) Draw a labor demand-labor
      supply diagram for the efficiency wage model and draw a corresponding effective labor demand curve
      diagram. Label the axes, curves, and equilibrium values. d) State the full-employment output equation for
      the efficiency wage model, and define the variables. e) Why might Keynesians want to specify also that the
      unemployment rate is a determinant of labor effort?

2.   **Price stickiness:** a) Briefly define price stickiness. b) Briefly explain how monopolistic competition and high
      menu costs can explain price stickiness. c) Why does price stickiness not occur in the classical model?
      d) How is price stickiness illustrated in the Keynesian IS-LM diagram and in the AD-AS diagram? e) Do the
      real effects of aggregate demand shocks differ in the short run and long run in the Keynesian sticky-price
      model from the effects of these shocks in the classical model of perfectly flexible prices? Briefly explain.

3.   **Fiscal stabilization policy**: a) Draw a Keynesian IS-LM diagram, an effective labor demand curve diagram, and a corresponding AD-AS diagram. Label the axes, curves, and equilibrium values. b) Use the diagrams to show the short-run effects and long-run effects of a temporary decline in investment spending. c) What is the principal goal of macroeconomic stabilization, and how can fiscal policy be used to achieve this goal? d) Do Keynesians and classicals agree on the effectiveness and desirability of macroeconomic stabilization? Briefly explain.

4.   **Monetary stabilization policy**: a) Draw a Keynesian IS-LM diagram, an effective labor demand curve diagram, and a corresponding AD-AS diagram. Label the axes, curves, and equilibrium values. b) Use the diagrams to show the short-run effects and long-run effects of a temporary decline in consumption spending. c) Could monetary stabilization policy be used to reduce or offset the negative short-run output effect of a temporary decline in consumption spending? Briefly explain. d) Is money neutral in both the classical model and the Keynesian model? Briefly explain. e) Do Keynesians believe that aggregate demand management policies should be used to "fine-tune" the economy? Briefly explain.

5.   **Supply shocks and other critiques**: a) What critique does the real business cycle theory make of the Keynesian belief that most recessions are caused by aggregate demand shocks? b) What critique does the real business cycle theory make of macroeconomic stabilization? c) Draw a Keynesian IS-LM diagram and a corresponding AD-AS diagram, and use the diagrams to show the effects of an adverse productivity (i.e., aggregate supply) shock. d) Can macroeconomic stabilization policies effectively reduce the negative effects of a temporary supply shock? Briefly explain. e) Compare and contrast the effects of a tax cut on the positions of the FE line and the IS curve in the Keynesian and classical models.

6.   **Business cycle facts and other empirical evidence**: State and briefly explain whether or not the business cycle facts and other empirical evidence appear to support the following characteristics of the Keynesian model: a) efficiency wage; b) real-wage rigidity; c) price stickiness; d) effective labor demand; and e) labor hoarding.

Mathematical Problem-Solving Questions

1.   **Markup pricing**: Calculate the selling price of a consumer good for a firm whose marginal cost is $10 at its desired output level for the following markups: a) 0%; b) 10%; c) 50%; d) 100%.

2.   **Efficiency wage**: A firm pays an efficiency wage, w^*. Given that it pays w^*, it has the following marginal productivity of labor schedule for a particular specialized type of labor: MPN is 20 units per hour when 5 workers are employed, and MPN declines by 1 unit per hour for each additional worker hired. The firm employs 13 workers and its product price is $3 per unit. Find w^*.

Answers to Fill-In-The-Blanks Questions

1. real-wage rigidity	2. efficiency wage model	3. effort curve
4. efficiency wage	5. price stickiness	6. perfect competition
7. monopolistic competition	8. menu cost	9. marginal cost
10. markup	11. effective labor demand curve	12. macroeconomic stabilization
13. aggregate demand management	14. multiplier	15. aggregate demand shocks
16. labor hoarding	17. turnover costs	

Answers to True-False Questions

1. **T** Turnover costs are the costs of firing, hiring, and training workers; firms expect to reduce the costs of unwanted employee turnover by paying an efficiency wage, which makes employees happier than they would be at a market-clearing wage. However, an efficiency wage tends to be rigid or inflexible. A minimum wage law prevents the nominal wage for low-skilled workers from falling below some legal minimum wage; this would prevent the real wage from falling in a recession. Union contracts include contract terms that fix the nominal or real wage over the period of the labor contract, which may last for several years; contractual wages create rigidities in the wage rate.

2. **T** Both the gift exchange motive and the shirking model suggest that firms may be able to reduce their labor costs and increase their profits by paying an efficiency wage somewhat above the market wage, because the increase in labor productivity will exceed the increase in the real wage. Firms could buy all the labor they want at a market wage, but the workers would have little incentive to be productive. An efficiency wage rewards workers for being very productive and increases the potential cost of shirking. In most economic models, market-clearing wages and prices are considered to be efficient, but the market-clearing wage is not efficient in the efficiency wage model.

3. **F** Since the efficiency wage is a higher wage than the market-clearing wage, firms in the efficiency wage model demand and employ less labor than do firms in the classical model. If the efficiency wage raises the productivity of labor sufficiently, it is possible that full-employment output could be higher than in the classical model, even though there are fewer workers employed at the efficiency wage. Because the efficiency wage exceeds the market-clearing wage, there is always more unemployment at full-employment output in the Keynesian efficiency wage model than suggested by the classical model. Keynesians contend that the classical model underestimates the actual unemployment rate at full-employment output.

4. **T** In the Keynesian efficiency wage model most recessions are caused by demand shocks, and monopolistically competitive firms tend to reduce employment and output in recessions rather than reduce the real wage and their product prices. Prices are sticky, so product prices tend to remain fixed in the short run. In contrast, in the classical model most recessions are caused by supply shocks, and perfectly competitive firms tend to reduce product prices and the real wage to maintain full-employment output.

5. **F** In the classical model, output is completely determined by labor demand, labor supply, and the production function; these variables determine the position of the FE line and the aggregate supply curve at which there is full-employment output. In the classical model, output is independent of the aggregate demand for output. In the Keynesian efficiency wage model the aggregate demand for output determines output. The effective labor demand curve is a production function, but it is output that determines employment in this model rather than employment determining output. Firms plan to produce the level of output that is demanded and hire the number of workers needed to produce that amount of output. Labor supply does not determine employment in the efficiency wage model, since there is always an excess supply of labor at the efficiency wage. Changes in labor supply reduce or increase the excess supply of labor, but don't affect the level of employment.

6. **F** Economists agree that money is neutral in the long run. Classical economists believe that money is also neutral in the short run. In the extended classical model, unanticipated changes in the nominal money supply are not neutral in the short run. In the Keynesian model with slow wage and price adjustments, money is not neutral in the short run.

7. T   Economists agree than any change that causes the IS curve or LM curve to shift to the right will also cause the aggregate demand curve to shift to the right.   However, classical economists and Keynesians disagree about what variable changes will shift the IS and LM curves.   For example, the Ricardian equivalence proposition of the classical model suggests that a temporary tax cut will not change desired saving, so it will not shift the IS curve to the right. Keynesians reject the Ricardian equivalence proposition; they contend that a temporary tax cut will shift the IS curve to the right. For another example, classical economists contend that an increase in the nominal money supply will not shift the LM curve to the right, because the price level will increase proportionally. Given price stickiness, Keynesians contend that an increase in the nominal money supply will increase the real money supply in the short run; consequently, it will cause the LM to shift to the right.

8. T   Although a temporary increase in government purchases does increase labor supply, employment is independent of labor supply; consequently an increase in labor supply does not shift the FE line in the efficiency wage model. An increase in government purchases reduces desired saving, which causes the IS curve to shift to the right, which causes the AD curve to shift to the right, which causes output to increase in the short-run.

9. T   In the Keynesian model, a temporary tax reduces desired saving and increases desired consumption. An increase in any type of spending, including consumption, increases output more than the initial increase in spending; this is called the multiplier effect.

10. T   A decline in desired investment or an increase in desired saving will cause the IS curve to shift to the left, which causes the aggregate demand curve to shift to the left, which causes output to decline below the level of full-employment output, which is a recession. Keynesians contend that, because wages and prices adjust slowly, recessions may be long enough and severe enough to justify the use of macroeconomic stabilization policies to shift the AD curve to the right, causing output to increase, which more quickly moves the economy back toward full-employment output.

Answers to Multiple Choice Questions

1. c	8. e	15. d
2. d	9. e	16. d
3. d	10. c	17. a
4. b	11. d	18. c
5. a	12. c	19. b
6. a	13. a	20. a
7. b	14. e	

Answers to Short-Answer Essay Questions

1. **The efficiency wage model:**

    a)   In the Keynesian efficiency wage model, firms pay each worker the efficiency wage. A recession reduces labor demand, which causes employment to decline, but firms do not lower the efficiency wage. Since the efficiency wage is the wage that maximizes effort per dollar of real wage paid to labor, reducing the real wage would reduce the productivity of labor, which would increase production cost. Another problem with lowering the wage enough to induce the desired number of workers to quit during a recession is that the most productive workers are the most likely workers to quit.

b)   An efficiency wage is better than a market-clearing wage in that it maximizes effort per dollar of wage income paid to labor. This means that labor productivity per dollar spent on labor is maximized, which means that labor cost per unit of output is minimized. The *gift-exchange motive* and the *shirking model* provide two explanations for why an efficiency wage that is above the market-clearing wage may increase productivity per wage dollar. The gift-exchange motive views the higher wage as a gift to the workers who, in exchange, give the firm a gift of higher labor productivity. The shirking model views the wage as the reward that workers risk losing if they are so unproductive that they get fired; a higher wage increases productivity by increasing the expected cost of shirking (i.e., having low productivity).

c)   A labor demand and labor supply diagram for the efficiency wage model and a corresponding effective labor demand curve diagram follow.

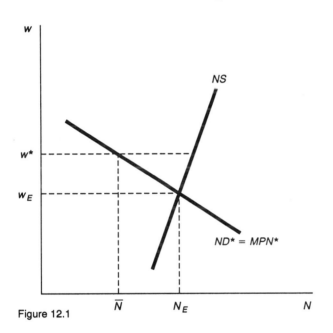
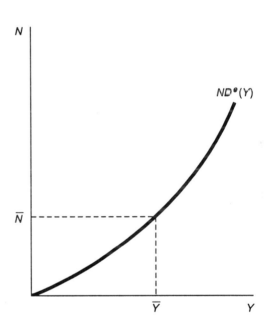

Figure 12.1

d)   The full-employment output equation for the efficiency wage model:

$$\overline{Y} = AF(K, E^*\overline{N})$$

$E^*\overline{N}$ = The quantity of effort-hours worked when labor is paid the efficiency wage.

$\overline{N}$ = The full-employment level of employment at which the efficiency wage (w^*) equals the marginal product of labor (MPN^*), with effort per effort-hour held constant at the maximum effort per real wage dollar (E^*).

$\overline{Y}$ = full-employment level of output in the efficiency wage model.
A = overall productivity.
K = capital stock employed.

e)   The basic efficiency wage model suggests that the real wage is rigid over the business cycle; this is inconsistent with the business cycle fact that the real wage is mildly procyclical. By adding the unemployment rate as a determinant of labor effort, the extended model can explain this business cycle fact. The efficiency wage can be lower in a recession because a high unemployment rate already encourages workers to be productive to avoid being fired. At a lower unemployment rate, in an expansion, the efficiency wage would need to be higher to reduce shirking.

2.   **Price stickiness:**

a)   Price stickiness means that prices are not perfectly flexible; they do not quickly adjust to long-run market-clearing levels. If prices are slow to adjust to changes in market conditions, they may be viewed, for analytic purposes, as fixed or rigid for some short-run time period.

b)   Monopolistic competition and menu costs explanations of price stickiness:

1)   Monopolistic competition: Unlike perfectly competitive firms, monopolistically competitive firms may be able to sell about the same volume of output at prices slightly above or slightly below the equilibrium price, because there are fewer competing firms in the market selling an identical product. Monopolistically competitive firms each produce a larger share of industry output and typically produce differentiated products rather than standardized products. Compared to perfectly competitive firms, they engage in more nonprice competition (e.g., advertising) and less price competition. If all monopolistically competitive firms in each industry held their prices constant during a recession and reduced their output levels, the market share of each firm may not change. Therefore prices can be sticky.

2)   Menu costs: To maximize profits a firm would not change its price unless the menu cost of changing the price were less than the expected benefit (i.e., the increase in revenue minus production cost) of the price change. Compared to perfectly competitive firms, monopolistically competitive firms obtain smaller benefits from price changes. Consequently, changes in market conditions tend to produce fewer price changes. Prices and the price level tend to be sticky.

c)   In the classical model, prices are perfectly flexible because firms are assumed to be perfectly competitive and because the model abstracts from the transactions cost (i.e., menu cost) of price changes. In the classical model, menu costs are assumed to be negligible.

d)   A change in prices creates a change in the price level. A change in the price level shifts the LM curve. Price stickiness is illustrated in the Keynesian IS-LM diagram by the absence of any price-induced shift in the LM curve in the short run.. Price stickiness is illustrated in the Keynesian AD-AS diagram by a horizontal SRAS curve at one price level, with the position of the curve being fixed in the short run.

e)   Yes, in the short run. In the Keynesian model, aggregate demand shocks affect real output, employment, and unemployment in the short run. There is no short-run adjustment period in the classical model, since economic shocks cause prices to adjust immediately to their long-run, general equilibrium values. Keynesian and classical economists agree that aggregate demand shocks have no real output or employment effects in the long run.

3.   **Fiscal stabilization policy**:

a)   A Keynesian IS-LM diagram, an effective labor demand curve diagram, and a corresponding AD-AS diagram follow.

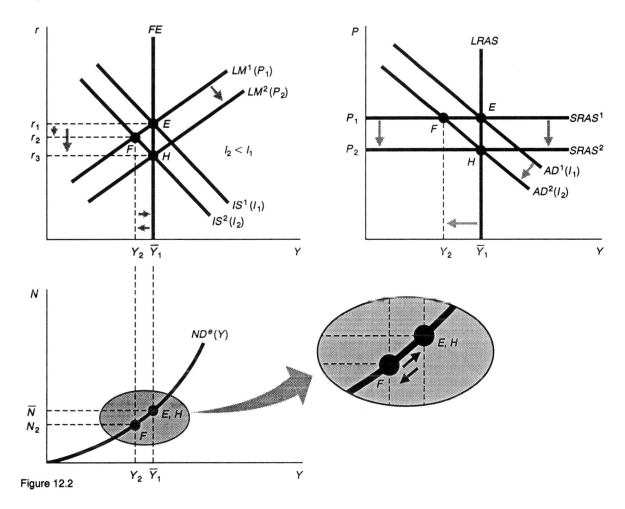

Figure 12.2

b)   The effects of a decline in investment spending, as shown in the diagrams are:

1)   Short-run effects: Y declines, r declines, and N declines, as the economy moves from E to F.

2)   Long-run effects: r declines and P declines, as the economy moves from E to H.

c)   The principal goal of macroeconomic stabilization is to maintain aggregate demand (AD) at the full-employment level of output. Countercyclical changes in government purchases, and possibly taxes, can be used to offset the output effects of private sector AD shocks, to maintain AD at the full-employment level of output. For example, the downward shift in IS and AD, caused by a decline in investment spending, can be offset by a temporary increase in government purchases, causing IS and AD to shift back to their original positions.

d)   No, Keynesians and classical economists disagree on the effectiveness and desirability of macroeconomic stabilization.

   1) In the classical model, business cycles fluctuations are the optimal response of the economy to various shocks that hit the economy; thus they should not be offset by macroeconomic policy.

   2) In the Keynesian model, large and persistent business cycle fluctuations are usually caused by aggregate demand shocks in the presence of price stickiness. Macroeconomic stabilization policies can effectively reduce business cycle fluctuations, so these policies are desirable in that they can help the economy to maintain output at the full-employment level.

4.   **Monetary stabilization policy**:

a)   A Keynesian IS-LM diagram, an effective labor demand curve diagram, and a corresponding AD-AS diagram follow.

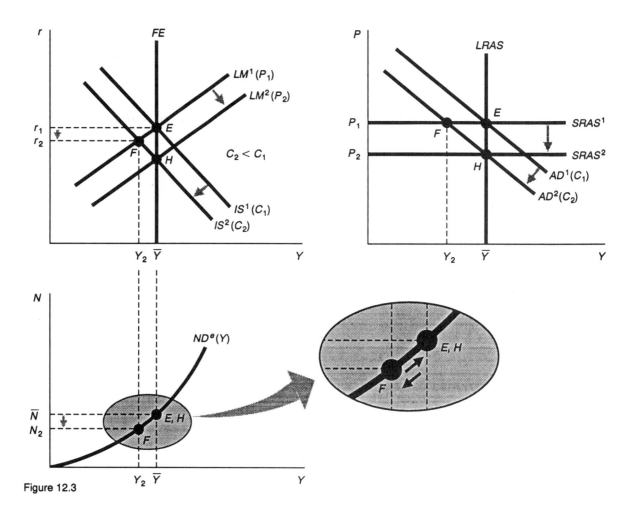

Figure 12.3

b)   As shown in the diagrams, the effects of a temporary decline in consumer spending are:

   1)   Short-run effects: Y declines, N declines, and r declines, as the economy moves from E to F.

   2)   Long-run effects: r declines and P declines, as the economy moves from E to H.

c)   Yes, an increase in the money supply would shift the LM curve down to the right and shift AD up to the right to offset the output effect of a decline in consumer spending. The increase in the money supply returns the AD curve to its original position, at the full-employment level of output.

d)   Money is neutral in the classical model, which is a long-run model with perfectly flexible wages and prices. In the Keynesian model of imperfectly flexible wages and prices, money is nonneutral in the short run, but it is still neutral in the long run. In the Keynesian model, quantities adjust in the short run (e.g., employment and output), rather than wages and prices.

e)   No. Modern Keynesians do not typically endorse policy attempts to "fine-tune" the level of aggregate demand over small, short-term business cycle deviations in output and employment from their full-employment levels. Arguments against fine-tuning include the practical problems of dosage and timing. The problem of dosage is that fine-tuning attempts to offset small fluctuations could easily destabilize the economy by increasing or reducing AD too much. The problem of timing is that fine-tuning attempts to stabilize the economy could easily destabilize it by increasing AD when AD is already too high or decreasing it when AD is already too low. However, Keynesians do propose that macroeconomic stabilization be used to reduce large, persistent business cycle deviations from the full-employment level of output.

5.   **Supply shocks and other critiques:**

a)   As classical economists, real business cycle (RBC) theorists believe that aggregate supply shocks cause most business cycle fluctuations. RBC theorists highlight the importance of productivity shocks. RBC theorists believe that Keynesians are wrong in their contention that aggregate demand shocks cause most recessions, because aggregate demand shocks would cause productivity to be countercyclical, when in fact it is procyclical.

b)   RBC theory suggests that small, random productivity shocks create business cycle fluctuations in aggregate economic activity, which represent the economy's best response to these unpredictable supply shocks. Macroeconomic stabilization policies are ineffective in offsetting aggregate supply shocks, and therefore these policies are undesirable.

c)   A Keynesian IS-LM diagram and corresponding AD-AS diagram showing the effects of a temporary
        adverse productivity shock follow. The short-run effects: Output and employment decline; the
        interest rate and the price level increase. The long-run effects: The interest rate and the price level
        increase.

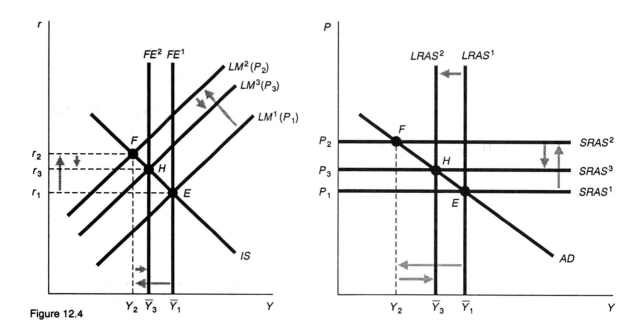

Figure 12.4

d)   No, Keynesian macroeconomic stabilization policies cannot effectively reduce the effects of a
        temporary supply shock. Stabilization policies are attempts to offset undesirable shifts in the
        aggregate demand curve, but they cannot offset undesirable supply-side shifts in the FE line and in
        the aggregate supply curves. In the short run, expansionary macroeconomic stabilization policies
        could offset the negative output effect of an adverse supply shock; in the long run, however, this
        would increase the price level.

e)   The effects of a lump-sum, temporary tax cut on

        1)   the FE line: It will not affect the FE line in the classical model, because the present value of
             taxes is unchanged. Keynesians do not believe that a tax cut will significantly increase labor
             supply, but even if it did, it would not increase employment nor shift the FE line, since
             employment is determined by output along the effective demand curve for labor.

        2)   the IS curve: Classical economists, relying on the Ricardian equivalence proposition, do not
             believe that a temporary tax cut will shift the IS curve in the absence of borrowing constraints.
             If a sufficiently large share of the population does face borrowing constraints, then a tax cut could
             increase consumption spending, causing the IS curve to shift to the right. Keynesians believe that
             a temporary tax cut will significantly increase consumption spending, causing the IS curve to shift
             up to the right.

6.   **Business cycle facts and other empirical evidence:**

a)   Efficiency wage: The case study example of Henry Ford paying an efficiency wage (which significantly increased productivity and profits for Ford Motor Company and was subsequently adopted by other auto producers) provides supporting empirical evidence of the Keynesian view that firms pay an efficiency wage.

b)   Real-wage rigidity: The business cycle fact that the real wage is mildly procyclical is evidence against real-wage rigidity. However, by adding the unemployment rate as a determinant of labor effort, Keynesians can explain why the effort-maximizing efficiency wage is mildly procyclical.

c)   Price stickiness: Carlton's research on price changes by manufacturing firms over the 1957-1966 period provides empirical evidence that supports the Keynesian belief that firms exhibit considerable price stickiness. Cecchetti's study of newsstand magazine prices and Kashyap's study of catalogue prices also found considerable price stickiness.

d)   Effective labor demand: Empirical evidence in support of the efficiency wage and in support of real wage rigidity also supports the Keynesian view that effective labor demand determines employment. Evidence in favor of price stickiness also supports the Keynesian view that the amount of labor effectively demanded depends on the amount of aggregate output demanded.

e)   Labor hoarding: Empirical research by Fay and Medoff found that manufacturing firms do retain a significant amount of redundant labor during recessions; this empirical evidence supports the Keynesian assumption of labor hoarding. The assumption of labor hoarding also enables the Keynesian model to explain the business cycle fact that the average productivity of labor is procyclical.

Answers to Mathematical Problem-Solving Questions

1.   **Markup pricing:** The constant markup rule is that the firm's product price is $P = (1 + \text{markup})MC$. With a marginal cost of $10 at the desired output level and a markup of:

a) 0%, $P = (1 + 0\%) \times \$10 = \$10$.

b) 10%, $P = (1 + .10) \times \$10 = \$11$.

c) 50%, $P = (1 + .50) \times \$10 = \$15$.

d) 100%, $P = (1 + 1.0) \times \$10 = \$20$.

2.   **Efficiency wage:** It is given that MPN = 20 units per hour when 5 workers are employed, and that MPN declines by 1 unit per hour for each additional worker hired. The firm would have to hire 8 workers to have a total of 13 workers; with 13 workers employed, MPN would be 12 units, which is 20 units - 8 units. We also know that the efficiency wage is the real wage, $w^* = MPN$, so the efficiency wage = 12 units per hour. The nominal wage, $W = P \times MPN = \$3 \times 12$ units per hour = $36 per hour, when $P = \$3$ per unit.

CHAPTER 13: UNEMPLOYMENT AND INFLATION

A Fill-In-The-Blanks Review of Chapter Highlights: Use the following key terms to fill in the blanks. Each key term is used only once.

cold turkey

gradualism

insider-outsider theory

shoe leather costs

disinflation

hyperinflation

long-run Phillips curve

expectations-augmented Phillips curve

hysteresis

Phillips curve

The 1. _Phillips Curve_ depicts a fixed trade-off between the unemployment rate and the inflation rate. As we move down the Phillips curve to a higher unemployment rate, the inflation rate declines. Following the work of Friedman and Phelps, the Phillips curve has been replaced by the 2. _Expectations #3_, which relates unanticipated inflation to the cyclical unemployment rate. The expectations-augmented Phillips curve shows the trade-off between the unemployment rate and the inflation rate during the short-run period in which the expected inflation rate is fixed. For each possible expected inflation rate, there exists a negatively sloped expectations-augmented Phillips curve depicting the possible (unemployment rate, inflation rate) points that could exist in the economy. At the natural unemployment rate on any expectations-augmented Phillips curve, the expected inflation rate equals the inflation rate; at this point inflation is anticipated and the economy is operating at full-employment output.

The 3. _Long-Run Phillips Curve_ is vertical at the natural unemployment rate. At each point on the long-run Phillips curve inflation is anticipated, so the expected inflation rate equals the inflation rate. When anticipated inflation increases, the economy moves up the long-run Phillips curve. The vertical long-run Phillips curve illustrates that output and the natural unemployment rate are independent of the inflation rate in the long run. If market participants' expectation of the inflation rate is wrong, then unanticipated inflation exists and the economy is not operating on the long-run Phillips curve. When inflation unexpectedly increases, the unemployment rate falls below the natural unemployment rate. When inflation unexpectedly declines, the unemployment rate rises above the natural unemployment rate. Once market participants have adjusted their expected inflation rate to match the inflation rate, the unemployment rate will return to the natural unemployment rate and the economy will return to some point on the long-run Phillips curve.

In the long run, there are no misperceptions, so expectations are correct; the expected price level equals the price level, and the expected inflation rate equals the inflation rate. In the long run, inflation doesn't matter, because inflation is anticipated and changes in anticipated inflation do not affect real economic variables, including output, employment, and unemployment. In the long run, the macroeconomy is operating in general equilibrium at the natural unemployment rate and at full-employment output. Classical economists contend that most of the time the economy maintains long-run, general equilibrium conditions; in their view, short-run periods of unanticipated inflation are short-lived and create only small deviations from full-employment output because wages and prices adjust quickly to their market-clearing levels. However, Keynesians contend that short-run periods of unanticipated inflation are not uncommon, can last for several years, and can create large deviations from full employment because wages and prices adjust slowly.

The theory of 4. _Hysteris_ tells us that an increase in the unemployment rate causes the natural unemployment rate to increase. Similarly, a decline in the unemployment rate causes the natural unemployment rate to decline. Therefore the natural unemployment rate is positively related to the unemployment rate. The theory of hysteresis explains why a recession-induced increase in the unemployment rate does not quickly decline to the prerecession unemployment rate as soon as the recession is over. 5. insider-outsider theory explains how hysteresis could be caused by labor union attempts to maximize wages for inside labor (i.e., current employees) during recessions, without regard to outside labor (i.e., potential future employees). When the recession ends, firms will be reluctant to hire more labor at the high union wage.

The principal costs of anticipated inflation are menu costs and shoe leather costs. Menu costs are the costs incurred by businesses in changing their product prices, such as the costs incurred by a restaurant in changing the food prices on its menu. 6. Shoe leather costs are the transactions costs incurred by market participants in trading some of their money for other goods or assets. If people expect the rate of inflation to increase, they will reduce their demand for money because inflation reduces the exchange value (i.e., purchasing power) of money. The principal costs of unanticipated inflation are the costs of the arbitrary redistribution of wealth and the relative price distortions that it creates.

7. Hyperinflation is an extremely high inflation rate (e.g., above 50% per month) over a sustained period of time (e.g., a year or more). When hyperinflation is unanticipated, the costs of hyperinflation include the costs of both anticipated and unanticipated inflation, and these economic costs could potentially be very high.

Economists agree that a persistently high inflation rate is mostly caused by excess money supply growth; reducing nominal money supply growth will reduce inflation in the long run. A decline in the inflation rate is called 8. Disinflation. Over the 1980-1983 period, for example, the United States experienced disinflation; inflation declined from 13.5% to 3.2%.

If the inflation rate is unacceptably high, classical economists propose that it be reduced quickly to an acceptable inflation rate; this approach to achieving disinflation is the 9. Cold Turkey approach. Keynesians believe that the cold turkey approach will produce high unemployment in the short run. Keynesians believe that it would be more economically efficient to reduce the high inflation rate gradually over several years; this approach is called 10. Gradualism. The difference in the classical and Keynesian approaches to achieving disinflation is explained by differences in their views about the price-adjustment process and the credibility of government policies to reduce inflation. Credible monetary policy reductions in the inflation rate will be less costly, because the disinflation will be anticipated rather than unanticipated. Classical economists believe that wages, prices, and expected inflation quickly adjust to credible policy reductions in the inflation rate, but only a cold turkey approach is credible. Keynesians believe that wages, prices, and expected inflation slowly adjust to credible reductions in the inflation rate, and that gradualism is a credible approach to achieving disinflation. The longer the short-run adjustment period and the greater the unanticipated disinflation, the larger the output and unemployment costs of disinflation will be.

True-False Questions: Circle T for true statements and F for false statements.

T (F) 1.   The Phillips curve trade-off between inflation and unemployment is consistent with the classical view that increases in nominal money supply growth do not have any real economic effect.

T (F) 2.   The Phillips curve trade-off between inflation and unemployment is consistent with the classical view that adverse supply shocks do not increase unemployment above the natural unemployment rate, assuming that the natural unemployment rate is fixed.

T (F) 3.   The inflation and unemployment data for the United States in the 1970-1990 period supports the Phillips curve view that there is a stable trade-off between inflation and unemployment.

T (F) 4.   The only shift variable for the long-run Phillips curve is the expected inflation rate.

(T) F 5.   Keynesians contend that expansionary macroeconomic stabilization policies can help reduce high unemployment in recessions without creating much inflation.

(T) F 6.   Okun's law states that each 1% increase in cyclical unemployment will reduce output by 2.5% of full-employment output.

T (F) 7.   The macroeconomic costs of inflation nearly always exceed the macroeconomic costs of unemployment.

(T) F 8.   Gender is not a determinant of unemployment in the United States, since women have about the same unemployment rate as men.

(T) F 9.   Government could reduce the natural unemployment rate by reducing its regulation of labor market conditions and by cutting unemployment insurance benefits.

(T) F 10.   Economists agree that the short-run economic costs of a credible disinflationary policy will be smaller than they would be for a policy that is not credible.

Multiple Choice Questions: Circle the letter corresponding to the correct answer to each question.

1.   In the United States, the natural unemployment rate
      a. has been fixed at about 2% since 1960.
      b. has been fixed at about 4% since 1960.
      c. has been fixed at about 6% since 1960.
      (d) is higher than it was in 1960.
      e. is lower than it was in 1960.

2.   Cyclical unemployment is caused by
      a. people entering the labor force to search for jobs.
      b. technological progress, which causes some industries to expand employment and others to reduce employment.
      c. reducing international trade barriers, which causes some industries to expand employment and others to reduce employment.
      d. the deindustrialization of America.
      (e) business cycle recessions.

3.   Okun's law predicts that when 2% of the labor force is cyclically unemployed in an economy where full-employment output is $7000 billion, this unemployment will cause output to decline by about
      a. 6% of full-employment output.
      b. 4% of full-employment output.
      c. 0% of full-employment output.
      (d) $350 billion.
      e. $175 billion.

4.   The Phillips curve suggests that monetary policymakers could use monetary policy to
   a. reduce the unemployment rate at the expense of higher inflation.
   b. reduce the unemployment rate while reducing inflation.
   c. reduce the unemployment rate without affecting the inflation rate.
   d. reduce inflation without affecting the unemployment rate.
   e. increase the inflation rate while increasing the unemployment rate.

5.   Which of the following changes will cause the expectations-augmented Phillips curve to shift down to the left?
   a. An increase in the price level
   b. A decline in the unemployment rate
   c. A decline in the expected inflation rate
   d. An unanticipated decline in the money supply
   e. A decline in taxes

6.   If the expected inflation rate is 15%, the expectations-augmented Phillips curve will
   a. be the same as the Phillips curve.
   b. be the same as the long-run Phillips curve.
   c. intersect the long-run Phillips curve at the natural unemployment rate, when the inflation rate is 15%.
   d. be parallel to the long-run Phillips curve.
   e. be horizontal at an expected inflation rate of 15%.

7.   The long-run Phillips curve
   a. will shift down to the left, as a result of expansionary monetary policy.
   b. will shift to a lower natural unemployment rate, as a result of expansionary monetary policy.
   c. will shift up to the right, as a result of expansionary monetary policy.
   d. will shift vertically to a higher inflation rate and expected inflation, as a result of expansionary monetary policy.
   e. is vertical at the natural unemployment rate, and its position is independent of monetary policy.

8.   In the 1980-1982 period in the United States, a tight money policy
   a. reduced inflation without increasing unemployment.
   b. reduced expected inflation without reducing inflation.
   c. reduced unemployment without increasing inflation.
   d. increased unemployment by creating unanticipated disinflation.
   e. reduced expected inflation without increasing unemployment.

9.   The theory of hysteresis explains why
   a. inflationary expectations do not adjust quickly to changes in the inflation rate.
   b. the long-run Phillips curve is vertical at the natural unemployment rate.
   c. a recession increases the natural unemployment rate.
   d. a change in the demographics of the labor force can cause the natural unemployment rate to change.
   e. cyclical unemployment has trivial output costs.

10.   According to the insider-outsider theory of labor markets,
   a. firms prefer to hire workers who can give them inside information about the plans of competing firms.
   b. firms prefer to promote workers inside their organization rather than hire more productive people from outside.
   c. within each firm, each level in the hierarchy of managers has insiders and outsiders.
   d. labor unions attempt to maximize the wage of currently employed workers while ignoring outsiders.
   e. firms will quickly replace striking workers with nonunion outsiders.

11.   The costs of quickly trading money for nonmonetary assets to reduce one's holdings of money are the
       a. menu costs of anticipated inflation.
       b. menu costs of unanticipated inflation.
       c. shoe-leather costs of anticipated inflation.
       d. shoe-leather costs of unanticipated inflation.
       e. relative price distortion costs of unanticipated inflation.

12.   If the inflationary effect of an increase in the money supply is anticipated, money is neutral in the short run
       a. in the basic classical model, but not in the extended classical model.
       b. in both the classical and Keynesian models.
       c. in the extended classical model, but not in the basic classical model.
       d. in both the basic classical and extended classical model, but not in the Keynesian model.
       e. in the Keynesian model, but not in the classical model.

13.   Most economists would agree that the best way to reduce hyperinflation is to
       a. wipe out labor unions.
       b. increase transfer payments.
       c. institute wage-price controls.
       d. reduce taxes.
       e. reduce the nominal money supply growth rate.

14.   If disinflation is unanticipated, it causes
       a. inflation to initially decline along an expectations-augmented Phillips curve in the short run, followed by a decline in expected inflation in the long run.
       b. inflation to rise along an expectations-augmented Phillips curve in the short run, followed by an increase in expected inflation in the long run.
       c. no short-run real economic effects, because money is neutral in the extended classical model.
       d. inflationary expectations to decline immediately, with no real economic effects.
       e. unemployment and output to fall in the short run with no long-run price level effect in the Keynesian model.

15.   In analyzing the disinflationary period of the early 1980s in the United States, Keynesians concluded that
       a. political business cycle theory best explains this monetary policy attempt to reduce unemployment just prior to the 1980 presidential election.
       b. the rational expectations hypothesis correctly predicts that systematic monetary policies are anticipated and are neutral.
       c. the basic classical model is correct in showing that changes in the money supply have only price effects.
       d. real business cycle theory correctly predicted that the disinflation resulted from small, random beneficial supply shocks.
       e. the cold turkey approach to reducing inflation can create a costly recession with a sharp increase in cyclical unemployment.

16.   Which of the following disinflationary monetary policies would classical economists prefer?
       a. A dramatic monetary surprise.
       b. A cold turkey approach that is announced and credible.
       c. A cold turkey approach that is announced, but not credible.
       d. A gradualism approach that is announced and credible.
       e. A gradualism approach that is unannounced.

17. An unanticipated increase in the money supply causes the aggregate demand curve to shift to the right along
    a. the positively sloped SRAS curve in the extended classical model in the short run, and causes the SRAS to shift up the LRAS curve in the long run.
    b. the horizontal SRAS curve in the extended classical model in the short run, and causes the SRAS to shift up the LRAS curve in the long run.
    c. the negatively sloped SRAS curve in the extended classical model in the short run, and causes the aggregate demand curve to shift back to the left in the long run.
    d. the positively sloped SRAS curve in the Keynesian model of sticky prices and real-wage rigidity in the short run, and causes the SRAS curve to shift up the LRAS curve in the long run.
    e. the horizontal SRAS curve in the Keynesian model of nominal wage rigidity in the short run, and causes the aggregate demand curve to shift back to the left in the long run.

18. An adverse supply shock will
    a. increase inflation and reduce unemployment.
    b. increase inflation and increase unemployment.
    c. decrease inflation and decrease unemployment.
    d. decrease inflation and increase unemployment.
    e. have no effect on inflation and unemployment.

19. Which of the following macroeconomic stabilization policies is most likely to be proposed by Keynesians?
    a. Increase money supply growth during a period of low unemployment and high inflation.
    b. Increase money supply growth during a period of high unemployment and hyperinflation.
    c. Increase money supply growth during a period of high unemployment and deflation.
    d. Increase money supply growth during a period of low unemployment and low inflation.
    e. Never increase money supply growth under any conditions.

20. Unemployment and inflation are sometimes referred to as the twin evils of macroeconomics, mostly because
    a. there are no economic benefits to increased unemployment and inflation.
    b. economists hope to sensationalize these socially and politically unimportant events.
    c. government policymakers who try to reduce them can then be portrayed as heroes.
    d. mankind has no earthly power to defeat them.
    e. the economic costs of high, unanticipated inflation and unemployment exceed their economic benefits.

Short-Answer Essay Questions

1. **Phillips curves and the price-adjustment process:** a) What trade-off is demonstrated by the simple Phillips curve? b) Briefly explain the expectations-augmented Phillips curve critique of the Phillips curve. c) Assuming that the natural unemployment rate is 6% and that the expected inflation rate is 5%, draw a Phillips curve diagram with an expectations-augmented Phillips curve and a long-run Phillips curve. Label the axes, curves, and equilibrium values. d) Use the diagram to compare and contrast the effects of a 3% unanticipated and anticipated increase in money supply growth rate. e) State the rational expectations theory critique and the political business cycles critique of monetary stabilization policy.

2. **Supply shocks:** a) Draw the following diagrams and use them to show the effects of the OPEC oil price increase in the mid-1970s in the United States: 1) a Phillips curve diagram; 2) an extended classical model diagram; 3) a Keynesian model diagram. b) Define stagflation and explain how an oil price shock can create stagflation. c) Why did the government use expansionary monetary policies in the late 1970s, and what was the principal negative macroeconomic effect of these policies?

3.   **Demand shocks and disinflation**: a) Draw the following diagrams and use them to show the short-run and long-run effects of an unanticipated disinflationary monetary policy: 1) a Phillips curve diagram; 2) an extended classical model diagram; and 3) a Keynesian model diagram. b) Do these diagrams show the same effect on the "misery index" (the sum of the unemployment rate and the inflation rate)? Briefly explain. c) Were wage and price controls effective in reducing inflation in the United States in the early 1970s? Briefly explain.

4.   **The costs of unemployment and inflation**: a) Compare and contrast the costs of frictional, structural, and cyclical unemployment. Briefly explain any differences. b) Does unemployment insurance reduce the unemployment rate or reduce the costs of unemployment? Briefly explain. c) Identify and briefly explain the two principal costs of anticipated inflation. d) Identify and briefly explain the two principal costs of unanticipated inflation. e) Compare and contrast the classical cold turkey approach and the Keynesian gradualism approach to reducing inflation, under conditions of moderate inflation and under conditions of hyperinflation.

5.   **Empirical evidence**: State and briefly explain whether or not the empirical evidence generally supports the following beliefs: a) There is a fixed set of (unemployment rate, inflation rate) combinations, and monetary policymakers can achieve the combination they prefer. b) Government policy attempts to improve economic conditions by exploiting an existing relationship among economic variables may change the relationship in such a way as to prevent the policies from achieving their objectives. c) A change in expected inflation or the natural unemployment rate will shift the expectations-adjusted Phillips curve. d) Government policymakers will use fiscal and monetary policies to get themselves reelected rather than to reduce business cycle fluctuations. e) Each 1% increase in cyclical unemployment reduces output by 2.5% of full-employment output.

Mathematical Problem-Solving Questions

1.   **Expectations-augmented Phillips curve**: For an economy in which the expected inflation rate = 5%, the natural unemployment rate = 6%, and the slope of the expectations-augmented Phillips curve = -h = -2, use the expectations-augmented Phillips curve equation to calculate the unemployment rate for each of the following inflation rates: a) -2%; b) 6%; c) 12%.

2.   **Unanticipated inflation**: Assume that expected inflation in the economy is 5%, so that banks pay a 5% inflation premium in addition to a 2% expected real interest rate on savings deposits, and employers increase nominal wages by 5%, as a cost-of-living adjustment, in addition to a 2% expected real wage increase. Calculate the real interest rate and the percent increase in the real wage for each of the following inflation rates: a) 2%; b) 5%, c) 10%.

Answers to Fill-In-The-Blanks Questions

1. Phillips curve	2. expectations-augmented Phillips curve	3. long-run Phillips curve
4. hysteresis	5. insider-outsider theory	6. shoe leather costs
7. hyperinflation	8. disinflation	9. cold turkey
10. gradualism		

Answers to True-False Questions

1.   F   Economists agree that the most important cause of persistent, substantial disinflation or deflation is a reduction in nominal money supply growth. Disinflation is a reduction in the inflation rate, such as when the inflation rate declines from 10% to 5%. Deflation is negative inflation, such as a 2% decline in the price level. The basic classical model contends that money is neutral; this suggests that a decline in money supply growth will not have any real economic effect, so it would not increase the unemployment rate. The Phillips curve trade-off between inflation and unemployment suggests that a tight money policy will reduce inflation at the expense of increasing unemployment, while an easy money policy reduces unemployment at the expense of higher inflation. The negative relationship between inflation and unemployment depicted by the Phillips curve is not consistent with the classical view that increases in nominal money supply growth do not have any real economic effect. However, the extended classical model based on the misperceptions theory is a recent modification of the basic classical model. The extended classical model does predict a negative relationship between unanticipated inflation and unemployment, consistent with the Phillips curve. The extended classical model still fails to explain how systematic changes in nominal money supply growth could cause the unemployment rate to change when market participants have rational expectations. Rational market participants anticipate any systematic change in money supply growth and its effect on inflation. Yet, extended classical economists believe that most monetary policy changes in the money supply are systematic and will be anticipated, so that most tight money policies will reduce inflation without increasing unemployment. The belief that most changes in inflation created by changes in monetary policy will not affect unemployment is inconsistent with the Phillips curve.

2.   F   Classical economists contend that most recessions are caused by adverse supply shocks, and most booms are created by beneficial supply shocks. Classical economists also contend that the natural unemployment rate is not fixed; it increases in recessions and declines in expansions. An adverse supply shock increases inflation and raises the natural unemployment rate to a higher rate of unemployment. A beneficial supply shock reduces inflation and reduces the natural unemployment rate to a lower rate of unemployment. While supply shocks create changes in inflation, they are not consistent with the Phillips curve view that a trade-off exists between inflation and unemployment. The simultaneous increases in inflation and unemployment created by an adverse supply or productivity shock do not fit the Phillips curve.

3.   F   The Phillips curve depicts a stable trade-off between inflation and unemployment, but the data on inflation and unemployment for the 1970s and 1980s did not support the belief that a stable trade-off between these variables exists. However, these data are consistent with the belief that the U.S. economy operated on several expectations-augmented Phillips curves during this period. Unlike the Phillips curve, whose position is fixed, the expectations-augmented Phillips curve shifts whenever there is a change in the expected inflation rate or a change in the natural unemployment rate.

4.   F   The long-run Phillips curve will shift only when there is a change in the natural unemployment rate. An increase in the natural unemployment rate will shift the long-run Phillips curve to the right. A decline in the natural unemployment rate will shift the long-run Phillips curve to the left. Any change in population demographics or change in the structure of the economy that changes the natural unemployment rate will shift the long-run Phillips curve. A change in the expected inflation rate will shift the expectations-augmented Phillips curve, but it will not shift the long-run Phillips curve. The natural unemployment rate is independent of the expected inflation rate. In the long run, general equilibrium conditions exist, all markets simultaneously clear, full-employment output is produced at the natural unemployment rate, and inflation is anticipated, so changes in the inflation rate do not create any real economic effect.

5. T   In the Keynesian sticky price model, the short-run aggregate supply curve is horizontal. Most recessions are caused by a decline in the aggregate demand for output, which is illustrated by a leftward shift of the aggregate demand curve along the horizontal SRAS curve. The decline in aggregate demand creates a decline in output, which increases unemployment. An expansionary macroeconomic stabilization policy, either fiscal policy or monetary policy, will increase aggregate demand, causing output to increase and unemployment to fall without creating inflation. The rightward shift of the aggregate demand curve along the horizontal SRAS curve largely offsets the initial leftward shift of the aggregate demand curve, so there is no intended net increase in aggregate demand. The policy goal is to stabilize the position of the aggregate demand curve at full-employment output at the initial price level.

6. T   Okun's law states that each 1% increase in cyclical unemployment will reduce output by 2.5% of full-employment output. Cyclical unemployment is the increase in unemployment above the natural unemployment rate during a recession. However, economists disagree about how much cyclical unemployment exists during recessions. Classical economists contend that most of the increase in unemployment during recessions is an increase in the natural unemployment rate, rather than an increase in cyclical unemployment. In the classical view, most recessions are caused by productivity or supply shocks, which cause the FE line, LRAS curve, and the long-run Phillips curve to shift to the left along a fixed aggregate demand curve; this causes the natural unemployment rate to decline. Keynesians contend that most of the increase in unemployment during recessions is cyclical unemployment and that the natural unemployment rate can be taken as fixed during most recessions. In the Keynesian view, most recessions are not caused by productivity or supply shocks, so the FE line, LRAS curve, and the long-run Phillips curve all remain fairly stable or fixed in most recessions, while the aggregate demand curve shifts to the left, causing cyclical unemployment to increase.

7. F   The costs of inflation and unemployment are difficult to accurately measure and can vary substantially. The costs of inflation depend in part on how high the inflation rate is, how variable it is, to what extent it is unanticipated, and how long it lasts. The costs of unemployment depend in part on how high it is, the distribution of the unemployment, the type of unemployment, and how long it lasts. In a period of high, unanticipated inflation and low unemployment, most economists and policymakers are likely to estimate the costs of inflation as being higher than the costs of unemployment. In a period of low, stable inflation and high unemployment, most economists and policymakers are likely to estimate the costs of unemployment as being higher than the costs of inflation.

8. T   Recent unemployment data suggest that gender is not an important determinant of unemployment in the United States today, since women have about the same unemployment rate as men, holding everything else constant. However, this does not mean that women have the same labor market opportunities and incentives as men. There are many characteristics of labor market conditions that could vary with gender without affecting the unemployment rate statistics. For example, gender may be a determinant of the kinds of jobs a person can easily get, the opportunities for rapid promotion, and the salary and benefit package.

9. T   Government could reduce the natural unemployment rate by reducing its regulation of labor market conditions and by cutting unemployment insurance. Government regulation of employment conditions for labor, such as the minimum wage law, increase the cost of employing labor, which causes businesses to employ fewer workers, which raises the unemployment rate, given labor supply. Unemployment insurance premiums represent a tax on labor, which increases the cost of employing labor, which causes businesses to employ fewer workers, which raises the unemployment rate, given labor supply. However, regulations that improve working conditions and provide a safety net of income for labor during temporary unemployment spells may encourage some people to work, which causes the supply of labor to increase. An increase in labor supply would dampen the increase in unemployment created by government regulation and unemployment insurance. Some recipients of unemployment insurance benefits may choose to remain

unemployed longer to search for better jobs. An increase in search time would increase frictional unemployment, but may also result in some workers finding substantially better jobs, enabling them to produce more output in the future. Although government regulation of labor markets and unemployment insurance do increase unemployment, these policies provide some benefits to at least partially offset these costs.

10. T Economists agree that the short-run economic costs of a credible disinflationary policy will be smaller than they would be for a policy that is not credible. Credible policies to reduce inflation will be anticipated, which makes them less costly in terms of increased unemployment than if they were not anticipated. The costs of an anticipated change in inflation include menu costs and shoe leather costs; these are relatively small compared to the additional costs of unanticipated inflation, which creates an arbitrary redistribution of wealth and relative price distortions. Economists disagree about what policies are credible. Classical economists believe that only cold turkey policies to reduce inflation are credible, while Keynesians believe that gradualism is credible and less costly than a cold turkey approach.

Answers to Multiple Choice Questions

1. d	8. d	15. e
2. e	9. c	16. b
3. d	10. d	17. a
4. a	11. c	18. b
5. c	12. d	19. c
6. c	13. e	20. e
7. e	14. a	

Answers to Short-Answer Essay Questions

1. **Phillips curves and the price-adjustment process:**

   a) The Phillips curve depicts various possible combinations of unemployment and inflation that could exist in the economy. The negative slope of the Phillips curve shows that these variables are negatively related. Therefore a trade-off exists between them; any decline in the unemployment rate increases the inflation rate. Any decline in the inflation rate increases the unemployment rate. The simple Phillips curve suggests that policymakers could choose the particular combination of unemployment and inflation that they prefer, and that they could use monetary policy to move the economy to that preferred point on the Phillips curve.

   b) The expectations-augmented Phillips curve critique is that the Phillips curve fails to include the expected inflation rate as a determinant of the actual inflation rate. The Phillips curve suggests that there is a stable relationship between unemployment and inflation that policymakers can exploit, but the expectations-augmented Phillips curve shows that this relationship is not stable and therefore not exploitable. Any attempt to reduce the unemployment rate below the natural unemployment rate will be effective only if unanticipated and, even then, only during the short-run period of misperceptions or wage-price rigidities. Once expectations, wages, and prices have adjusted, the Phillips curve will shift up to the right and unemployment will return to the natural unemployment rate at a higher inflation rate.

c)   A Phillips curve diagram follows, in which the natural unemployment rate = 6%.

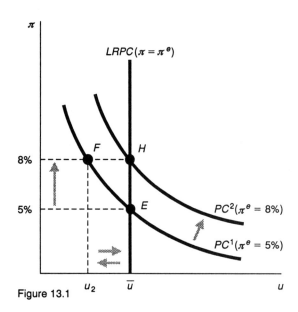

Figure 13.1

d)   The economic effects of a 3% increase in money supply growth depend on whether the increase is anticipated or unanticipated:

1)   Anticipated: If the increase in money supply growth is anticipated, then money is neutral. In the diagram, the economy moves quickly from point E to H. There is no unemployment effect or output effect. Wages, prices, and expectations quickly adjust to general equilibrium.

2)   Unanticipated: In the short run, the 3% increase in money supply growth causes the growth rate of output to increase, the unemployment rate to decline, and the inflation rate to increase as we move from point E to F in the diagram along a fixed, short-run Phillips curve with the expected inflation rate equal to 5%. In the long run, the expected inflation rate rises to 8%, causing the Phillips curve to shift up to the right. In the diagram, we move from point E to H in the long run. At point H, the inflation rate has increased to 8%, the expected inflation rate has increased to 8%, and unemployment is at the natural rate of 6%.

e)   Critiques of monetary stabilization policy:

1)   Rational expectations critique: Monetary stabilization policies are usually neutral, since most policies are systematic, systematic policies are anticipated, and anticipated monetary policies are neutral. Therefore monetary stabilization policy is completely ineffective in systematically lowering the unemployment rate, even in the short run.

2) Political business cycles critique: Monetary stabilization policies could be effective in the short run in stabilizing the economy or in destabilizing it; yet they are more likely to create business cycles than to offset them. Monetary policymakers use expansionary monetary policies before presidential elections to get the incumbent U.S. president reelected. An increase in money supply growth reduces the rate of unemployment and increases the growth rate of output before an election. After the election, monetary policymakers use contractionary monetary policy to offset the inflationary effects of the previously expansionary policy. In effect, monetary policy is inefficiently used to achieve partisan political goals rather than being used to efficiently achieve the economic goal of stabilizing the economy. The primary objective of monetary policy is not to stabilize output at the full-employment level of output.

2.   **Supply shocks:**

a)   The following diagrams show the stagflation effects of the mid-1970s oil price increase in the United States. The oil price increase is an adverse supply shock. The oil price increase causes all of the following to increase: the price level, the expected price level, the inflation rate, the expected inflation rate, the unemployment rate, and the natural unemployment rate. The oil price increase causes the following to decline: the level of employment, the level of output, the full-employment level of output, the growth rate of output, and the growth rate of full-employment output.

A Phillips curve diagram follows.

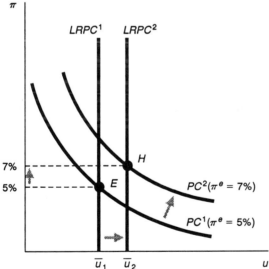

Figure 13.2

An extended classical model diagram follows.

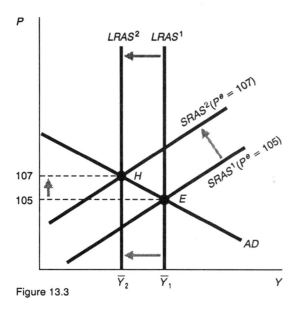

Figure 13.3

A Keynesian model diagram follows.

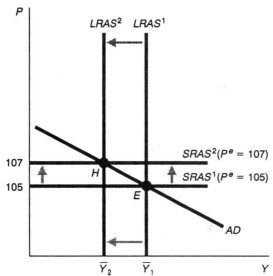

Figure 13.4

b)   Stagflation is an increase in unemployment accompanied by an increase in inflation. The increase in unemployment reduces output, creating stagnation in the growth rate of output. For a given level of aggregate demand, anything that reduces aggregate supply causes stagflation. Since oil and its close energy substitutes are important factors of production, an increase in the price of oil increases production cost, causing firms to increase prices at each possible level of aggregate output, which is a decline in aggregate supply. A decline in the short-run aggregate supply curve is consistent with an increase in the Phillips curve. A decline in long-run aggregate supply is consistent with a rightward shift of the long-run Phillips curve. Note that an increase in the unemployment rate creates a decline in the growth rate of output, and that an increase in the price level is an increase in inflation.

c)   In the late 1970s the U.S. government used expansionary monetary policies in an attempt to reduce the unemployment rate and to increase the growth rate of output. Relying on the Keynesian model to explain the slowdown in economic growth, policymakers concluded that aggregate demand had declined and that expansionary monetary stabilization policies could pull aggregate demand back to the full-employment level of output. However, aggregate demand had not declined. The recession was created by a decline in aggregate supply caused by an increase in the price of oil. Expansionary monetary policies caused aggregate demand to increase along the new aggregate supply curve, which caused inflation to increase further.

3.   **Demand shocks and disinflation:**

a)   An unanticipated disinflationary monetary policy has both short-run and long-run effects. In the diagrams, the economy moves from point E to F in the short run. The following variables decline in value: output, employment, the price level, and the inflation rate.   The unemployment rate increases. The natural unemployment rate and the full-employment level of output are unaffected. In the long run, the economy moves from point E to H. The price level declines, the inflation rate declines, and the expected rate of inflation declines, but output returns to the full-employment level of output and unemployment returns to the natural unemployment rate.

A Phillips curve diagram follows, in which the natural unemployment rate = 5%.

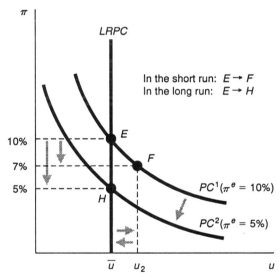

Figure 13.5

An extended classical model diagram follows.

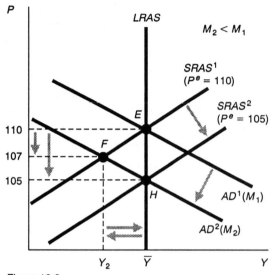

Figure 13.6

A Keynesian model diagram follows.

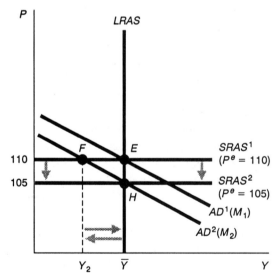

Figure 13.7

b)   In the short run, changes in the Keynesian model diagram unambiguously increase the misery index, because unemployment increases, while inflation is unchanged by the unanticipated disinflationary monetary policy. In the short run, in the extended classical model diagram and in the Phillips curve diagram, the effect on the misery index is ambiguous, because unemployment increases but inflation declines. In the long run, in all models the misery index declines, because unemployment is unchanged, while inflation has declined.

c)   In the early 1970s in the United States, the imposition of wage and price controls reduced wage increases and reduced price increases during the period of controls, but wages and prices quickly increased once controls were lifted. The 1971-1974 period of wage-price controls had no long-run effects by 1975. Wages and prices were driven up by the oil price increase, by expansionary monetary policies, and by expansionary fiscal policies in this time period.

4.   **The costs of unemployment and inflation**:

a)   The costs of unemployment include personal costs and output costs.

      1) Frictional unemployment: Frictional unemployment is temporary unemployment by people who are readily employable but are searching for better employment positions. Personal costs are expected to be small, because the duration of a typical frictional unemployment spell is short for most people. There is no output cost, since frictional unemployment enables people to find new jobs where they become more productive than they were in their previous jobs.

      2) Structural unemployment: Personal costs are the highest for structural unemployment, because structurally unemployed individuals typically suffer frequent unemployment spells of long duration. The output cost may be relatively small, because the structurally unemployed are not currently employable. Some output costs will be incurred in the form of skills training, education, or relocation costs to get these people back to work; these output costs will partially offset the increase in output produced by these people once they become employed.

      3) Cyclical unemployment: Personal costs may be moderate, particularly if the duration of individual unemployment spells is typically short, cyclically unemployed workers receive reduced paychecks from firms or unemployment insurance compensation, and workers have sufficient personal savings to use during periods of unemployment. Classical economists also argue that unemployed workers receive the personal benefit of increased leisure when they are cyclically unemployed. The output cost is the highest for cyclical unemployment, since cyclically unemployed workers could, in the aggregate, produce a lot of output if they were employed. Okun's law predicts the aggregate output cost of cyclical unemployment. Note that output produced by the employed also declines during periods of cyclical unemployment.

b)   Unemployment insurance does reduce the personal cost of unemployment by redistributing the cost to other time periods and to other people. Workers and firms pay the unemployment insurance premium all the time, not just when unemployment is high. Also, all workers and firms pay the insurance premium, while only a small percentage file for unemployment insurance income payments at any given time. Unemployment insurance increases the output cost of unemployment by prolonging the duration of unemployment spells, since those receiving the income benefits have less incentive to return to work quickly. The output cost of unemployment insurance would increase with increases in the income payments provided by the insurance, increases in the number of months over which people could collect it, and increases in the eligibility of those unemployed. Supply-side economists believe that transfer programs, like the unemployment insurance program, increase unemployment and create large output costs in the United States.

c)   Costs of anticipated inflation:

1)   Menu costs: The costs of changing prices are called menu costs. Classical economists believe these costs are small, assuming perfectly competitive market conditions. Keynesians believe these costs are large enough to create price stickiness, assuming monopolistically competitive market conditions.

2)   Shoe leather costs: The transactions costs incurred by households and firms in reducing the share of their assets they hold as money are called shoe leather costs. These costs are likely to be larger than menu costs.

d)   Costs of unanticipated inflation:

1)   Risk of redistribution of wealth cost: Unanticipated inflation creates a redistribution of wealth; what some people and firms lose, others gain. For example, creditors lose and debtors gain, because unanticipated inflation lowers the real interest rate on existing loans. Although there is no aggregate income loss from redistribution, the costs incurred by market participants trying to reduce their risk of losses may be large. For example, creditors may charge an inflation risk premium on all loans to cover their risk, even during periods when inflation is constant, thereby increasing the real interest rate in the long run.

2)   Relative price distortions cost: Unanticipated inflation causes firms to misperceive a change in the price level as changes in the relative prices of their products. This misperception causes firms to charge inefficient prices for their products, produce inefficient levels of output, and employ efficient amounts of labor at inefficient wages. These relative price distortions cause inefficiencies that are costly.

e)   With either approach, the short-run adjustment cost of reducing hyperinflation will be much higher than the cost of reducing moderate inflation.

1)   Cold turkey approach: Classical economists propose a rapid reduction in money supply growth to achieve disinflation, assuming that prices, wages, and expectations adjust quickly. Unemployment costs and inflation costs are most likely to be small if the classical assumptions about rapid market adjustments are correct, the policy is announced in advance, and the announcement is credible. Both classical economists and Keynesians agree that the inflation costs would be smaller for a cold turkey approach than for gradualism, since inflation is being reduced more quickly. However, Keynesians believe that the unemployment costs could be very high.

2)   Gradualism approach: Keynesians propose a gradualism approach of slowly reducing money supply growth over several years to achieve disinflation, assuming wages, prices, and expectations adjust slowly to changes in the inflation rate. Both classical economists and Keynesians believe that this approach would have small unemployment costs, but the inflation costs would be greater, since the inflation rate would be higher for a long period of time. Classicals contend inflation costs could be much higher than for a cold turkey approach, since an announced gradualism approach is unlikely to be credible.

5.   **Empirical evidence**:

a)   The Phillips curve suggests that there is a stable set of unemployment rate and inflation rate combinations, and that monetary policymakers could achieve the combination they prefer. The macroeconomic data for the 1950s and 1960s for many countries seemed consistent with this view, but further research using data for the 1970s and 1980s failed to show that a stable trade-off exists. The empirical evidence suggests that a stable trade-off exists only during the time period in which expected inflation and the natural unemployment rate remain unchanged. The extended classical model suggests that a nonsystematic expansionary monetary policy attempt to move up a fixed expectations-augmented Phillips curve to a lower unemployment rate and higher inflation rate will achieve its objective only for the short-run period in which the increase in inflation is not anticipated. Systematic monetary policies will be anticipated, so they cannot achieve their objective of temporarily reducing unemployment below the natural unemployment rate.

b)   The Lucas critique is that government policy attempts to improve economic conditions by exploiting an existing relationship among economic variables may change the relationship in such a way as to prevent the policies from achieving their objectives. The empirical evidence generally supports this critique. A good example of this policy problem is the U.S. government's attempts to reduce the unemployment rate by exploiting the Phillips curve trade-off between inflation and unemployment. While successful in the 1960s, it was not effective in the 1970s because the policy attempts increased expected inflation, causing the Phillips curve to shift to the right.

c)   The Friedman-Phelps theory suggests that a change in expected inflation or the natural unemployment rate will shift the expectations-augmented Phillips curve. The empirical evidence generally supports this theory. For example, structural and demographic changes in the United States after 1970 caused the natural unemployment rate to increase; the curve also shifted to the right when expected inflation increased, then shifted to the left when expected inflation declined.

d)   Nordhaus's political business cycle theory suggests that government policymakers will use fiscal and monetary policies to get themselves reelected rather than to reduce business cycle fluctuations. The empirical evidence regarding this theory is mixed, in part because it is hard to properly evaluate. To the extent that attempts to reduce business cycle fluctuations are beneficial to voters, it may be good politics as well as good economics to undertake macroeconomic stabilization policies. Critics contend that the theory wrongly assumes that policymakers are concerned only with getting reelected and are not concerned with the economic welfare of their constituents. One problem with political business cycle theory is that monetary policy is controlled by the Federal Reserve, whose members are not elected and who serve for long terms. The Federal Reserve is largely independent of elected fiscal policymakers.

e)   Okun's law contends that each 1% increase in cyclical unemployment reduces output by 2.5% of full-employment output. The empirical evidence regarding this theory is mixed, in part because it is hard to evaluate. One problem is that classical economists contend that most of the increase in unemployment in recessions is an increase in the natural unemployment rate rather than an increase in cyclical unemployment. In the classical view, there is very little cyclical unemployment in recessions and the economy continues to produce at full-employment output. The substantial loss in output suggested by Okun's law is caused not only by the increase in unemployment but by all the various ways in which labor market conditions worsen during recessions. For example, output growth declines in recessions, in part because hours worked decline and labor productivity declines. At least for very high unemployment rates, the size of the output effect suggested by Okun's law is probably exaggerated. For example, in the United States, unemployment peaked at 25% during the

Great Depression, but output fell by only about 30%, which is considerably less than the 50% decline in output predicted by Okun's law, where -50% = -2.5 x (25% - 5%), assuming that the natural rate of unemployment was 5% in 1929.

Answers to Mathematical Problem-Solving Questions

1. **Expectations-augmented Phillips curve:**   The expectations-augmented Phillips curve equation tells us that the inflation rate = the expected inflation rate -h(the unemployment rate - the natural unemployment rate). It is given that the expected inflation rate = 5, the natural unemployment rate = 6%, and h = 2. When the inflation rate is

    a)   -2%, then u = 9.5%, since -2% = 5% - 2(u - 6%).

    b)   5%, then u = 6%, since 5% = 5% - 2(u - 6%).

    c)   12%, then u = 2.5%, since 12% = 5% - 2(u - 6%).

2. **Unanticipated inflation:** The real interest rate (r) = the nominal interest rate - the inflation rate. In percentage terms, the increase in the real wage (w) = the increase in the nominal wage - the inflation rate. It is given that the expected inflation rate = 5%, the interest rate on bank savings deposits = 7%, and the increase in the nominal wage = 7%. When inflation is

    a)   2%, then r = 5% = 7% - 2%, and the increase in w = 5% = 7% - 2%.

    b)   5%, then r = 2% = 7% - 5%, and the increase in w = 2% = 7% - 5%.

    c)   10%, then r = -3% = 7% - 10%, and the increase in w = -3% = 7% - 10%.

CHAPTER 14: EXCHANGE RATES, BUSINESS CYCLES, AND MACROECONOMIC POLICY IN THE OPEN ECONOMY

A Fill-In-The-Blanks Review of Chapter Highlights: Use the following key terms to fill in the blanks. Each key term is used only once.

devaluation	exchange rate	exchange rate unions
fixed-exchange-rate system	flexible-exchange-rate system	floating-exchange-rate system
foreign exchange market	fundamental value of the exchange rate	inconvertible currency
J curve	nominal appreciation	nominal depreciation
nominal exchange rate	overvalued exchange rate	real appreciation
real depreciation	real exchange rate	revaluation
speculative run	terms of trade	undervalued exchange rate

The 1. _Nominal Exchange Rate_ is the number of units of foreign currency that exchange for one unit of domestic currency; it is the foreign currency price of the domestic currency. For example, a nominal exchange rate of 135 yen per dollar would mean that a dollar costs 135 yen or, alternatively, a dollar buys 135 yen. The nominal exchange rate is also called the 2. _Exchange Rate_. In international markets, the currency of a country is called its foreign exchange. The currencies of different countries are traded internationally in the 3. _foreign Exchange Mkt._. A currency that is not freely tradeable in the foreign exchange market is said to be an 4. _Inconvertible Currency_.

Each country prices its goods and assets in units of its own currency. Buyers of foreign goods or foreign assets must first buy the foreign currency and then use the foreign currency to buy the foreign good or foreign asset. Therefore the domestic currency price of a foreign good depends on both the exchange rate and the foreign currency price of the foreign good. For two countries that each produce one good for export, the real exchange rate is the nominal exchange rate multiplied by the domestic currency price of the domestic good divided by the foreign currency price of the foreign good ($e = e_{nom}P/P_{FOR}$). For example, 100 Japanese cameras per U.S. car = (135 yen per dollar x \$20,000 per car/27,000 yen per camera). Since a dollar buys 135 yen, an American could buy an imported Japanese camera for \$200 = (27,000 yen per camera/135 yen per dollar). For two countries that produce many goods for export, P is the domestic price level and P_{FOR} is the foreign price level. The GDP deflator and consumer price index are two alternative measures of the price level. Holding the domestic and foreign price levels constant, an increase in the nominal exchange rate is an increase in the real exchange rate. The percent increase in the real exchange rate equals the percent increase in the nominal exchange rate plus the domestic inflation rate minus the foreign inflation rate. Holding the domestic and foreign inflation rates constant, the percent increase in the nominal exchange rate equals the percent increase in the real exchange rate.

There are two principal international monetary payment systems for determining exchange rates. In a 5. _flexible Exchange Rate system_, a country's exchange rate is determined by the supply and demand for its domestic currency in the foreign exchange market. At the equilibrium exchange rate in a flexible-exchange-rate system, the quantity of domestic currency units supplied equals the quantity demanded in the foreign exchange market. At any exchange rate above the equilibrium exchange rate, the domestic currency is overvalued and the quantity supplied exceeds the quantity demanded at that exchange rate. At any exchange rate below the equilibrium exchange rate, the domestic currency is undervalued and the quantity supplied is less than the quantity demanded at that exchange rate.

In a flexible-exchange-rate system, an 6._Overvalued Exchange Rate_ will decline and an 7. _undervalued Exchange Rate_ will increase to its equilibrium value, which is the 8._Fundamental Value of Exch. Rate_. A flexible-exchange-rate system is also called a 9._Floating X-Chang Rate_. In a 10._Fixed Xchange Rate System_, a country's exchange rate is fixed at some particular rate, as determined by an international agreement among major trading countries. The central bank of a country maintains its fixed exchange rate by agreeing to buy and sell its currency at that particular exchange rate in the foreign exchange market. When a central bank prints money to sell it in the foreign exchange market in order to maintain its fixed exchange rate, it is increasing its foreign reserves and its money supply. When a central bank uses its foreign reserves to buy its own currency in the foreign exchange market, it is reducing its foreign reserves and its money supply. By forming 11._Xchange Rate Unions_, such as the European Monetary System, some countries have agreed to maintain fixed exchange rates for their currencies against the currencies of other countries in the union, while allowing their currencies to float against the currencies of nonmember countries.

The 12._Real Xchange Rate_ is the number of units of the foreign good that exchange for one unit of the domestic good; it is the foreign goods price of the domestic good. For example, a real exchange rate of 100 Japanese cameras per U.S. car would mean that it costs the Japanese 100 cameras for each American car they buy. The real exchange rate is also called the 13. _Terms of trade_.

In a flexible-exchange-rate system, a 14. _Nominal Depreciation_ is a decline in the exchange rate. For example, if the yen price of the dollar declined from 135 yen per dollar to 125, this would be a nominal depreciation of the dollar. After a nominal depreciation, it takes fewer yen to buy a dollar. A 15._Nominal Appreciation_ is an increase in the exchange rate. In a fixed-exchange-rate system, a decline in the exchange rate is called a 16. _devaluation_, whereas an increase in the exchange rate is called a 17. _revaluation_. In a fixed-exchange-rate system, if a currency is substantially overvalued, market participants may create a 18._Speculative - Run_ on the currency by suddenly selling large amounts of it in the foreign exchange market, given their expectation that it will be devalued in the near future. A speculative run increases the likelihood that the currency will be devalued soon, since the government would have to buy all the excess supply of its currency in the market to maintain the fixed exchange rate.

In a flexible-exchange-rate system, a 19. _Real Appreciation_ is an increase in the real exchange rate. For example, if the real exchange rate increased from 100 Japanese cameras per U.S. car to 110, this would be a real appreciation. A 20._Real Depreciation_ is a decline in the real exchange rate. After a real depreciation, it takes fewer units of the foreign good to buy a unit of the domestic good; alternatively, it takes more units of the domestic good to buy a unit of the foreign good.

A real depreciation makes the domestic economy's exported good cheaper, in terms of the imported good, to both domestic buyers and to foreigners, which causes people to buy more of the exported good and to buy less of the imported good. However, a real depreciation increases the value of the imported good, in terms of the exported good, such that the real value of imports may temporarily increase after a depreciation even though the volume of imports declines. The 21. _J Curve_ shows that a real exchange rate depreciation initially reduces net exports, but will increase net exports after some adjustment period. The J curve pattern of changes in the value of net exports occurs because people are slow to adjust their buying decisions to a change in the real exchange rate.

Supply and demand for a nation's currency in the foreign exchange market determine the exchange rate of one currency for another. The supply curve depicts how much domestic currency will be traded for the foreign currency at each possible exchange rate in the foreign exchange market. Market participants supply domestic currency to acquire the foreign currency needed to buy foreign goods and assets. The demand curve depicts how much foreign currency will be traded for the domestic currency at each possible exchange rate. Market participants demand domestic currency to buy domestic goods and assets. An increase in domestic demand for foreign goods and assets will increase supply, causing the supply curve to shift to the right. An increase in foreign demand for domestic goods and assets will increase demand, causing the demand curve to shift to the right. An increase in supply relative to demand will cause the exchange rate to depreciate. Holding the domestic price level and foreign price level constant, a decline in domestic currency holders' preference for domestic goods relative to foreign goods, an increase in domestic income, and an increase in the foreign real interest rate will increase supply. Holding the domestic price level and foreign price level constant, an increase in foreign currency holders' preference for domestic goods relative to foreign goods, an increase in foreign income, and an increase in the domestic real interest rate will increase demand.

IS-LM diagrams for the domestic and foreign countries are useful for analyzing the effects of changes in net exports and the exchange rate on important domestic and foreign macroeconomic variables. In an open economy, goods market equilibrium exists when $NX = S^d - I^d$. The IS curve is negatively sloped, because an increase in income reduces NX and increases $(S^d - I^d)$ at the initial real interest rate, creating an excess supply of goods; a decline in the real interest rate increases desired investment and, by creating a decline in the exchange rate, increases NX enough to restore equilibrium in the goods market. An increase in the domestic and foreign preference for domestic goods relative to foreign goods, an increase in foreign income, or an increase in the foreign real interest rate will increase net exports and cause the IS curve to shift to the right. A rightward shift of the IS curve increases domestic income and the domestic real interest rate, given incomplete price level adjustment in the short run, and causes the price level and real interest rate to increase in the long run. The effects of these changes in foreign and domestic macroeconomic variables on the foreign economy can also be determined using the IS-LM model. Similarly, the international transmission of the effects of domestic and foreign macroeconomic policies can be determined using IS-LM analysis.

The principal economic advantage of a fixed-exchange-rate system is that it encourages international trade and international financial transactions by reducing the risk that the exchange rate will change, but this system does not permit governments to use monetary policies for domestic macroeconomic stabilization. The principal advantage of a flexible-exchange-rate system is that it permits market forces to determine the exchange rate and changes in the exchange rate, but this system exposes those who engage in international trade and financial transactions to substantial foreign exchange risk created by the volatility of exchange rates.

True-False Questions: Circle T for true statements and F for false statements.

T (F) 1.   The real exchange rate increases whenever the nominal exchange rate increases.

(T) F 2.   One of the advantages of a flexible-exchange-rate system is that it permits the exchange rate to quickly adjust to changes in the fundamental value of the exchange rate.

T (F) 3.   A real depreciation will quickly eliminate a net export deficit.

(T) F 4.   In a flexible-exchange-rate system, an increase in domestic economic growth will cause the exchange rate to depreciate.

T (F) 5.   In a fixed-exchange-rate system, an increase in the domestic real interest rate will cause the exchange rate to appreciate.

(T) F 6.   Foreign shocks are principally transmitted to the domestic economy through their effects on net exports, the exchange rate, and the real exchange rate.

T (F) 7.   If money is neutral, an increase in the nominal money supply will not affect the exchange rate.

T (F) 8.   Economists agree that in an open-economy IS-LM model, an increase in net exports during a recession will cause the IS curve to shift to the right, output to rise, and unemployment to fall.

Ⓣ F 9.   In a classical IS-LM model of the world economy, a temporary increase in government purchases causes the domestic and foreign real interest rates as well as the domestic and foreign price levels to rise.

T Ⓕ 10.   In a world economy in which major trading partners face different economic shocks and are unwilling to coordinate their monetary policies, a fixed-exchange-rate system is more economically efficient than a flexible-exchange-rate system.

Multiple Choice Questions: Circle the letter corresponding to the correct answer to each question.

1.   The nominal exchange rate of the dollar is best defined as the number of units of the
   Ⓐ foreign currency that it takes to buy a dollar.
   b. foreign currency that it takes to buy a unit of U.S. goods.
   c. foreign currency that it takes to buy a unit of U.S. assets.
   d. foreign goods that it takes to buy a unit of U.S. goods.
   e. foreign asset that it takes to buy a unit of the U.S. asset.

2.   In the long run, a 5% increase in the domestic money supply will
   a. reduce both the exchange rate and the real exchange rate by 5%.
   b. reduce the real exchange rate by 5% and increase net exports.
   Ⓒ reduce the exchange rate by 5%, but have no real economic effects.
   d. increase the exchange rate by 5% and reduce net exports.
   e. increase the real exchange rate by 5%, but have no nominal effects.

3.   In the foreign exchange market,
   a. exports and imports are exchanged.
   b. domestic bonds are traded for foreign bonds.
   c. exported domestic goods are traded for imported assets.
   d. exports and imports are purchased and sold.
   Ⓔ domestic currency is traded for foreign currencies.

4.   The international monetary system in which the exchange rate is determined by the market forces of supply and demand is called
   a. a managed float.
   b. an exchange rate union.
   c. an adjustable-peg system.
   d. a fixed-exchange-rate system.
   Ⓔ a flexible-exchange-rate system.

5.   In the post-World War II period, prior to the collapse of the Bretton Woods system in the early 1970s, the exchange rate of the dollar was
   a. determined in a flexible-exchange-rate system.
   b. determined by the market forces of supply and demand.
   Ⓒ fixed at $35 per ounce of gold.
   d. determined by a managed float.
   e. fixed in terms of the Japanese yen.

6. For a given nominal exchange rate, an increase in the price of foreign goods relative to the price of domestic goods causes
    a. domestic residents to buy more foreign goods.
    b. domestic residents to buy fewer domestic goods.
    c. the real exchange rate to decline.
    d. an increase in the number of units of the foreign goods needed to buy a unit of the domestic goods.
    e. foreign residents to buy fewer domestic goods.

7. If four Saudi Arabian barrels of oil exchange for one Japanese camera, this is a measure of Japan's
    a. nominal exchange rate.
    b. terms of trade.
    c. exchange rate.
    d. price level in terms of the foreign price level.
    e. trade deficit.

8. In a flexible-exchange-rate system, a decline in the number of units of the foreign currency per unit of the domestic currency is a
    a. nominal appreciation of the domestic currency.
    b. nominal depreciation of the domestic currency.
    c. real appreciation of the domestic currency.
    d. real depreciation of the domestic currency.
    e. nominal appreciation, but a real depreciation of the domestic currency.

9. For a given real exchange rate, a nominal appreciation will result from
    a. a decline in the terms of trade.
    b. an increase in the price of the foreign good.
    c. an increase in the price of the domestic good.
    d. an increase in the domestic rate of inflation.
    e. a decline in the foreign rate of inflation.

10. In a fixed-exchange-rate system, a decline in the value of the dollar would be called
    a. a depreciation.
    b. an appreciation.
    c. a revaluation.
    d. a devaluation.
    e. a market adjustment.

11. During the period of the Bretton Woods system, the U.S. government prevented a revaluation of the dollar by
    a. offering to sell dollars at the fixed exchange rate.
    b. allowing the dollar to appreciate.
    c. liberalizing its trade policies.
    d. decreasing the money supply.
    e. decreasing government purchases.

12.   In a flexible-exchange-rate system, an increase in foreign income will
    a.   increase demand for the domestic currency, creating a real depreciation of the exchange rate.
    b.   increase demand and supply of the domestic currency, with an ambiguous effect on the exchange rate.
    c.   reduce demand and supply of the domestic currency, with an ambiguous effect on the exchange rate.
    d.   reduce demand for the domestic currency, creating a real depreciation of the exchange rate.
    e.   increase demand for the domestic currency, creating a real appreciation of the exchange rate.

13.   In a flexible-exchange-rate system, an increase in the foreign real interest rate will
    a.   increase demand for the domestic currency, creating a real depreciation of the exchange rate.
    b.   reduce demand for the domestic currency, creating a real appreciation.
    c.   reduce demand and increase supply of the domestic currency, creating a real depreciation.
    d.   increase supply of the domestic currency, creating a real appreciation.
    e.   reduce supply of the domestic currency, creating a real appreciation.

14.   In a fixed-exchange-rate system, an increase in the world demand for domestic goods will
    a.   increase net exports and create an undervalued exchange rate.
    b.   reduce net exports and create an overvalued exchange rate.
    c.   reduce net exports and create an undervalued exchange rate.
    d.   increase net exports, creating a real appreciation.
    e.   increase net exports, creating a real depreciation.

15.   The J curve illustrates that a decline in the real exchange rate of the dollar will cause net exports to
    a.   increase immediately, because prices are perfectly flexible.
    b.   increase after some adjustment period, because it takes some time for people to adjust their buying decisions to a change in the terms of trade.
    c.   decrease immediately, because prices are perfectly flexible.
    d.   decrease after some adjustment period, because it takes some time for people to adjust their buying decisions to a change in the real exchange rate.
    e.   decrease only if the domestic price level rises relative to the foreign price level.

16.   In a Keynesian IS-LM model of the world economy, an increase in net exports will
    a.   shift the FE line to the left, causing the real interest to rise and output to fall in the short run.
    b.   shift the FE line to the left, causing the real interest to fall and output to rise in the short run.
    c.   shift the FE line to the right, causing the real interest rate to fall and output to rise in the short run.
    d.   shift the IS curve to the right, causing the real interest rate and output to rise in the short run.
    e.   shift the LM curve to the right, causing the real interest rate to fall and real output to rise in the long run.

17.   A classical IS-LM model of the world economy can be used to show that in a flexible-exchange-rate system, a temporary increase in government purchases will cause
    a.   output and the real interest rate to rise, which reduces net exports but has an ambiguous effect on the real exchange rate.
    b.   output and the real interest rate to rise, which increases net exports but has an ambiguous effect on the real exchange rate.
    c.   output to rise and the real interest rate to fall, which reduces net exports and causes the exchange rate to depreciate.
    d.   the real interest rate to fall, which causes the exchange rate to rise, which reduces net exports.
    e.   the price level to fall, which causes the exchange rate to fall, which increases net exports.

18.   An important advantage of a fixed-exchange-rate system is that it
       a. prevents an exchange rate from becoming an overvalued exchange rate.
       b. prevents an exchange rate from becoming an undervalued exchange rate.
       c. protects the domestic economy from being hit by foreign shocks.
       d. permits the exchange rate to efficiently adjust to its equilibrium level in the foreign exchange market.
       e. promotes the growth of international trade and international financial transactions, by reducing the risk to market participants that exchange rates will change unexpectedly and substantially.

19.   An exchange rate union, like the European Monetary System, is
       a. unlikely to be successful when the member nations are willing to coordinate their monetary policies.
       b. unlikely to be successful when the member nations are unwilling to coordinate their monetary policies.
       c. unlikely to be successful when the economies of the member nations are so completely integrated that they experience the same business cycle fluctuations.
       d. likely to be successful when the economies do not experience the same business cycle fluctuations.
       e. likely to be successful when the member nations are very politically and economically independent from one another.

20.   If the world economy is in a recession, an increase in the money supply in the domestic economy is
       a. neutral in the Keynesian model in the short run and long run, but not in the classical model.
       b. expansionary in the Keynesian and classical models in the short run, but not in the long run.
       c. contractionary in the Keynesian and classical models in the short run, but not in the long run.
       d. contractionary in the Keynesian and classical models in both the short run and long run.
       e. expansionary in the Keynesian model in the short run, but is neutral in the long run in both the Keynesian and classical models.

Short-Answer Essay Questions

1.   **Exchange rates and net exports:** a) Define the nominal exchange rate. b) Define the real exchange rate. c) State the real exchange rate equation and use it to develop an equation for the nominal exchange rate in terms of the real exchange rate. d) Use the equation for the percent change in the nominal exchange rate to identify the conditions under which a percent increase in the nominal exchange rate represents an equal percent increase in the real exchange rate. e) Briefly explain the difference between a nominal revaluation and a real depreciation of the exchange rate.

2.   **Supply and demand in the foreign exchange market:** a) Draw a diagram showing how the supply and demand for U.S. dollars in the foreign exchange market determine the yen/dollar exchange rate in a flexible-exchange-rate system. Label the axes, curves, and equilibrium values. b) Briefly explain the slopes of the supply and demand curves. c) Identify changes in two variables that would cause the supply curve to shift to the right. d) Identify changes in two variables that would cause the demand curve to shift to the right. e) Draw a supply and demand diagram that illustrates an overvalued exchange rate in a fixed-exchange-rate system. Label the axes, curves, the fundamental value of the exchange rate, and the fixed exchange rate.

3.   **The IS-LM model of an open economy:** a) Use a saving-investment diagram to construct an open-economy IS curve. b) Compare and contrast the shift variables for a closed-economy IS curve and an open-economy IS curve. c) Why is the IS curve negatively sloped? d) Briefly explain how a change in the domestic economy is transmitted to the foreign country in a two-country model of the world. e) In the world economy, compare and contrast the Keynesian and classical output effects of an increase in domestic aggregate demand.

4.   **Domestic fiscal policy in the world economy**: a) Define the term expansionary fiscal policy. b) Briefly explain why Keynesians propose using expansionary fiscal policy during a recession, and explain why the classical economists disagree with this proposal. c) Draw a domestic IS-LM diagram and a foreign IS-LM diagram in a two-economy model of the world economy. Label the axes, curves, and equilibrium values. d) Use the diagrams to show a Keynesian analysis of the short-run effects on the world economy of a decline in investment. e) In the Keynesian model, could an expansionary fiscal policy offset these short-run effects? Briefly explain.

5.   **Domestic monetary policy in the world economy**: a) Define the term expansionary monetary policy. b) Briefly explain why Keynesians propose using an expansionary monetary policy in a recession, and why the classical economists disagree with this proposal. c) Draw a domestic IS-LM diagram and a foreign IS-LM diagram for a two-economy model of the world economy. Label the axes, curves, and equilibrium values. d) Use the diagrams to show a Keynesian analysis of the short-run effects on the world economy of a decline in foreign demand for domestic goods. e) In the Keynesian model, could an expansionary monetary policy offset these short-run effects? Briefly explain.

Mathematical Problem-Solving Questions

1.   **Real and nominal exchange rates**: Given that the United States produces only cars at a domestic price of $15,000 per car, Japan produces only computers at a price of 312,500 yen per computer, and the nominal exchange rate is 125 yen per dollar, calculate: a) the real exchange rate; b) the percent change in the real exchange rate when the price of U.S. cars increases by 4%, the price of Japanese computers increases by 2%, and the nominal exchange rate declines by 5%.

2.   **Net exports**: Given goods market equilibrium in an open economy with Y = $7000 billion, calculate: a) S^d and NX, when C^d = 60% of output, I^d = 15% of output, and G = 20% of output; b) NX, when S^d = 25% of output and I^d = 10% of output.

Answers to Fill-In-The-Blanks Questions

1. nominal exchange rate
2. exchange rate
3. foreign exchange market
4. inconvertible currency
5. flexible-exchange-rate system
6. overvalued exchange rate
7. undervalued exchange rate
8. fundamental value of the exchange rate
9. floating-exchange-rate system
10. fixed-exchange-rate system
11. exchange rate unions
12. real exchange rate
13. terms of trade
14. nominal depreciation
15. nominal appreciation
16. devaluation
17. revaluation
18. speculative run
19. real appreciation
20. real depreciation
21. J curve

Answers to True-False Questions

1. F   The nominal exchange rate is $e_{nom} = eP_{FOR}/P$, so the nominal exchange rate would increase while the real exchange rate declined if the increase in the foreign price level exceeded the decline in the real exchange rate. For example, a 1% increase in the nominal exchange rate could be created by a 2% decline in the real exchange rate and a 3% increase in the foreign price level.

2. T   In a flexible-exchange-rate system, the exchange rate is a market price whose value is determined by the market forces of supply and demand. Because the foreign exchange market is active and competitive, adjustments should take place quickly.

3. F   The J curve shows that a real depreciation temporarily increases a net export deficit before reducing it. The J curve relationship occurs because a real depreciation increases the price of imports in terms of exported goods, and this effect is initially greater than the increase in the volume of net exports. A real depreciation initially increases the net exports by increasing the value of imports more than it increases the value of exports. After some adjustment period that could take several years, the effect of a real depreciation is to reduce a net export deficit.

4. T   In a flexible-exchange-rate system, supply and demand for domestic currency in the foreign exchange market determine the exchange rate. An increase in economic growth is an increase in the percent growth rate of output, which is also called income. An increase in domestic income increases domestic spending on imports, which shifts the supply curve for domestic currency to the right and reduces net exports and the exchange rate. In a flexible-exchange-rate system, a decline in the exchange rate is a nominal depreciation; it is also a real depreciation when the domestic price level and foreign price level remain constant.

5. F   In a fixed-exchange-rate system, supply and demand for domestic currency in the foreign exchange market determine the fundamental value of the exchange rate, but the government sets the exchange rate and keeps it fixed at some official value despite fluctuations in its fundamental value. An increase in the domestic real interest rate is an increase in the expected rate of return on domestic assets relative to foreign assets; this causes supply of the currency to decline and demand for the currency to increase in the foreign exchange market, which causes the fundamental value of the exchange rate to increase. If the fixed exchange rate initially equaled its fundamental value, an increase in the fundamental value creates an undervalued exchange rate. To maintain its fixed nominal exchange rate, the government must reduce its fundamental value, which it can do by increasing the money supply of the domestic currency. An increase in the nominal money supply increases the supply of domestic currency in the foreign exchange market, which causes the supply curve to shift to the right, which reduces the fundamental value of the exchange rate to the value of the fixed exchange rate.

6. T   If a foreign shock does not affect net exports, the exchange rate, or the real exchange rate, it will not be transmitted to the domestic economy. However, most macroeconomic foreign shocks, including changes in foreign income, the foreign real interest rate, and foreign macroeconomic policies, will affect net exports, the nominal exchange rate, or the real exchange rate, so they will be transmitted to the domestic economy.

7. F   If money is neutral, an increase in the nominal money supply will not affect the real exchange rate, which is also called the terms of trade, but it will reduce the exchange rate, which is also called the nominal exchange rate. When money is neutral, an increase in the nominal money supply creates a proportional increase in the price level. In a flexible-exchange-rate system, an increase in the domestic price level causes the nominal exchange rate to decline for a given real exchange rate. In a fixed-exchange-rate system, an increase in the nominal money supply does not change the nominal exchange rate, but it reduces the fundamental value of the exchange rate. In a fixed-exchange-rate system, if the fixed exchange rate initially is set at its fundamental value, the government cannot increase the money supply and maintain its fixed exchange rate as an overvalued exchange rate. In a fixed-exchange-rate system, there is only one money supply level at which the fixed exchange rate equals the fundamental value of the exchange rate. In a fixed-exchange-rate system, too much money creates an overvalued exchange rate, while too little money creates an undervalued exchange rate.

8. F   Economists agree that in an open-economy IS-LM model, an increase in net exports during a recession will cause the IS curve to shift to the right, but they disagree about the real economic effects of this shift in the IS curve. Keynesians contend that output will increase and unemployment will fall in the short run, given that wages and prices adjust slowly. Classicals contend that output and unemployment will not be affected, because wages and prices adjust quickly. While an increase in net exports increases the aggregate demand for domestic goods, output and unemployment are independent of the level of aggregate demand in the classical model.

9. T   In a classical IS-LM model of the world economy, a temporary increase in domestic government purchases causes the IS curve to shift to the right, the FE line to shift to the right, and the LM curve to shift to the left, assuming that the rightward shift in the IS curve exceeds the rightward shift in the FE line in the domestic economy. As a result, output, the real interest rate and the price level rise in the domestic economy. The increase in domestic output increases domestic spending on foreign goods, causing imports to rise and net exports to fall. The increase in the domestic real interest rate causes the exchange rate to appreciate in a flexible-exchange-rate system, which also reduces net exports. A decline in the net exports of the domestic economy is an increase in the net exports of the foreign economy. An increase in foreign net exports causes the foreign IS curve to shift to the right, creating an excess demand for foreign goods, which causes the foreign price level to rise and the foreign real interest rate to rise.

10. F   In a world economy in which major trading partners face different economic shocks, their economies will not follow the same business cycle pattern. Consequently, monetary policymakers in some countries may want to undertake expansionary monetary policies, while those in other countries want to undertake contractionary monetary policies. When independent countries are subject to different economic shocks, they are usually less willing to coordinate their monetary policies for the primary purpose of maintaining fixed exchange rates. Under these economic conditions it is tempting to sacrifice external balance in order to maintain internal balance. If monetary policymakers are unwilling to coordinate their domestic monetary policies under these economic conditions, they will be unable to maintain a fixed-exchange-rate system. Under these conditions a flexible-exchange-rate system would be more economically efficient, because it would permit exchange rates to adjust to the different shocks and the different macroeconomic policies of the different countries in the world economy.

Answers to Multiple Choice Questions

1. a   8. b   15. b
2. c   9. b   16. d
3. e   10. d   17. a
4. e   11. a   18. e
5. c   12. e   19. b
6. c   13. c   20. e
7. b   14. a

Answers to Short-Answer Essay Questions

1. **Exchange rates and net exports:**

    a)   The nominal exchange rate is the number of units of the foreign currency that exchange for one unit of the domestic currency. For example, 135 yen per dollar.

b)   The real exchange rate is the number of units of a foreign good that exchange for one unit of a domestic good. For example, in a two-good model, 100 Japanese cameras per U.S. car.

c)   The real exchange rate equation is $e = e_{nom}P/P_{FOR}$. Therefore the nominal exchange rate is $e_{nom} = eP_{FOR}/P$. In a two-good model, the price of the domestic good is the macroeconomic price level; the price of the foreign good is the foreign macroeconomic price level. In a multigood model, the macroeconomic price level of a country is a weighted average of the prices of products sold in that country. Given the price level in each country, the equilibrium nominal exchange rate provides for purchasing power parity between the two countries. In a two-good model with purchasing power parity, the dollar price of a camera is the same in the United States and Japan, and the yen price of a car is the same in Japan and the United States. In a multigood model with purchasing power parity, the price of a standard basket of products denominated in one currency is the same in both countries.

d)   The percent change in the nominal exchange rate = the percent change in the real exchange rate + the foreign inflation rate - the domestic inflation rate. When the difference between the foreign inflation rate and the domestic inflation rate remains constant, the percent increase in the nominal exchange rate creates an equal percent increase in the real exchange rate. One case in which the difference between the foreign and domestic inflation rates remains constant is when the domestic and foreign price levels remain constant.

e)   A nominal revaluation is an increase in the exchange rate in a fixed-exchange-rate system. A real depreciation is a decline in the terms of trade.

2.   **Supply and demand in the foreign exchange market:**

a)   A supply and demand diagram for U.S. dollars follows. The diagram illustrates that the market forces of supply and demand in the foreign exchange market determine the yen/dollar exchange rate in a flexible-exchange-rate system.

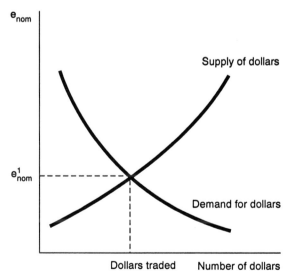

Figure 14.1

b)   The positively sloped supply curve for dollars illustrates that at a higher exchange rate, more dollars will be supplied in the foreign exchange market. The supply curve for dollars can also be viewed as a demand curve for yen, in that it depicts the number of dollars that market participants are willing and able to trade for yen at each possible nominal exchange rate. Market participants supply dollars and demand yen in order to use the yen to buy Japanese goods and assets. Holding the domestic and foreign price levels constant, an increase in the yen/dollar exchange rate is an increase in the cost of U.S. goods and assets relative to the cost of Japanese goods and assets, so that holders of dollars will offer to sell more of them in order to buy more yen in order to buy more Japanese goods and assets while buying fewer U.S. goods and assets. The demand curve for dollars can be viewed as a supply curve for yen. Market participants demand dollars to use them to buy U.S. goods and assets. The negatively sloped demand curve illustrates that at a higher exchange rate, fewer dollars will be demanded by holders of yen because fewer U.S. goods and assets will be demanded.

c)   An increase in U.S. output or an increase in Japan's real interest rate will cause the supply curve for dollars to shift to the right. A rightward shift in the supply curve causes the exchange rate to depreciate in a flexible-exchange-rate system.

d)   An increase in Japan's output or an increase in the U.S. real interest rate will cause the demand curve for dollars to shift to the right. A rightward shift in the demand curve causes the exchange rate to appreciate in a flexible-exchange-rate system.

e)   A supply and demand diagram follows. This diagram illustrates an overvalued exchange rate in a fixed-exchange-rate system.

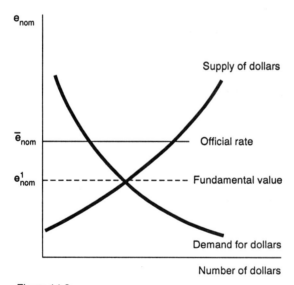

Figure 14.2

3.   **The IS-LM model of an open economy:**

a)   A saving-investment diagram and a corresponding IS curve for an open economy follow.

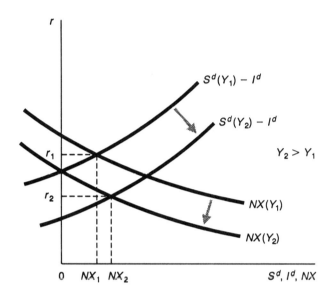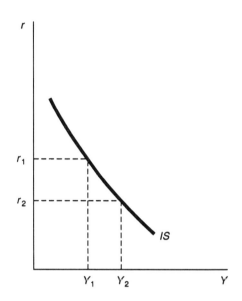

Figure 14.3

b)   The shift variables (i.e., factors) for the IS curve in a closed economy also shift the open-economy IS curve. In addition, the open-economy IS curve shifts if net exports change at a given income level and a given real interest rate.

c)   The negative slope of the open-economy IS curve shows that real output and the real interest rate are negatively related variables. Each point on the IS curve is an equilibrium (Y, r) point at which $S^d - I^d$ = NX. An increase in output increases ($S^d - I^d$) while reducing NX. Now at the initial interest rate, $S^d - I^d$ > NX. Therefore the interest rate must decline enough to achieve a new equilibrium in the goods market at the higher output level. A fall in the interest rate restores equilibrium by lowering S^d, raising I^d, and (because it leads to a real depreciation of the exchange rate) raising NX.

d)   Domestic economy changes are transmitted to the foreign economy through changes in the exchange rate and through changes in net exports. An economic change in the domestic economy that changes net exports shifts the IS curve in the foreign country. In a two-country model, the exports of one country are the imports of the other; an increase in domestic net exports is also a decline in foreign net exports.

e)   In the classical model, there is no real output effect of an increase in aggregate demand assuming government purchases are held constant, since the price level fully adjusts immediately. Likewise, in the Keynesian model in the long run, there is no real output effect of an increase in aggregate demand. However, in the short run in the open-economy Keynesian model, an increase in aggregate demand increases domestic output, which causes domestic economy imports to increase, which causes foreign output to increase.

4. **Domestic fiscal policy in the world economy:**

a) An expansionary fiscal policy is an increase in government purchases or a reduction in taxes that causes the IS curve to shift up to the right.

b) Keynesians believe that most recessions are caused by a decline in aggregate demand, which causes output to decline and unemployment to increase in the short run. Keynesians propose expansionary fiscal policy to quickly raise the level of aggregate demand back to the full-employment level of output. In the Keynesian view, expansionary fiscal policy can reduce the duration and severity of a recession. In contrast, classical economists believe that most recessions are caused by a decline in aggregate supply. From a classical viewpoint, business cycle fluctuations in output are the economy's best response to these small fluctuations in aggregate supply. Expansionary fiscal policy would not efficiently offset an adverse supply shock.

c) IS-LM diagrams of the domestic and foreign economies follow.

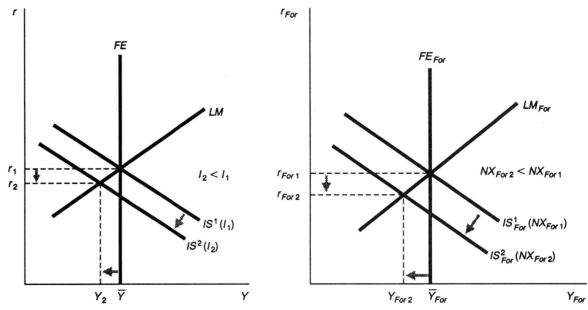

Figure 14.4

d) In the Keynesian model, the short-run effects of a decline in domestic investment are as follows: The IS curve shifts down to the left, causing Y to decline and r to decline. The decline in Y causes imports to decline and NX to increase. The effect on the exchange rate is ambiguous, because the increase in NX causes the exchange rate to rise, while the decline in r causes it to fall. The increase in NX causes NX_{FOR} to decline, which causes the foreign IS curve to shift to the left, causing Y_{FOR} and r_{FOR} to decline.

e) An expansionary fiscal policy could offset these short-run effects by offsetting the initial shift to the left in the domestic IS curve. Countercyclical expansionary fiscal policy attempts to stabilize the IS curve at full-employment output.

5.   **Domestic monetary policy in the world economy**:

a)   An expansionary monetary policy is an increase in the money supply that shifts the LM curve down to the right.

b)   Keynesians believe that most recessions are caused by a decline in aggregate demand, which causes output to decline and the unemployment rate to increase. Expansionary monetary policy can reduce or offset the decline in aggregate demand, thereby reducing the duration and severity of a recession. During a recession, expansionary monetary policy can be used to stabilize aggregate demand at the full-employment level of output. In contrast, classical economists believe that most business cycles are caused by adverse supply shocks that cannot be efficiently offset by an expansionary monetary policy. In the classical model of perfectly flexible price adjustments, money is neutral; therefore an expansionary monetary policy has no real output effect.

c)   IS-LM diagrams of the domestic and foreign economies follow.

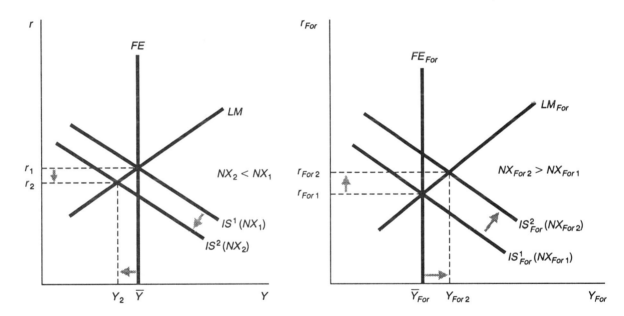

Figure 14.5

d)   In the Keynesian model, the short-run effects of a decline in the foreign demand for domestic goods are as follows. The decline in foreign imports causes NX_{FOR} to increase, causing the foreign IS curve to shift up to the right, causing Y_{FOR} and r_{FOR} to increase. An increase in NX_{FOR} is a decline in NX. The decline in NX and the increase in r_{FOR} cause the exchange rate to depreciate. The decline in NX causes the domestic IS curve to shift to the left, causing Y and r to decline.

e)   In the Keynesian model, an expansionary monetary policy could reduce or offset the short-run decline in output, but it would cause the real interest rate to decline further in the short run. The increase in domestic output would increase imports, causing net exports to decline further.

The decline in NX and r would cause the exchange rate to depreciate further. The increase in domestic imports would increase NX_{FOR}, causing the foreign IS curve to shift further to the right.

Although some of the effects of an expansionary monetary policy may be undesirable, Keynesians would argue that, most importantly, it could quickly pull the domestic economy out of the recession by quickly returning the level of aggregate demand in the domestic economy to the full-employment level of output.

Answers to Mathematical Problem-Solving Questions

1.   **Real and nominal exchange rates:**

a)   The real exchange rate equation is $e = e_{nom}P/P_{FOR}$. When $e_{nom} = 125$ yen per dollar, $P = \$15,000$ per car, and $P_{FOR} = 312,500$ yen per computer, $e = 6$ computers per car = (125 yen per dollar x $15,000 per car)/ 312,500 yen per computer. A Japanese computer sells for 312,500 yen per computer/125 yen per dollar = $2500 in the United States. $2500 per computer = $15,000 per car/6 computers per car.

b)   The percent change in the real exchange rate = the percent change in the nominal exchange rate + the percent change in the domestic price level - the percent change in the foreign price level. When the nominal exchange rate declines by 5%, the price of U.S. cars increases by 4%, and the price of Japanese computers increases by 2%, the percent change in the real exchange rate = -3% = -5% + 4% - 2%.

2.   **Net exports:** The goods market equilibrium equation for an open economy is $NX = S^d - I^d$. Since $S^d = Y - C^d - G$, an alternative equation for goods market equilibrium is $NX = Y - C^d - I^d - G$. Given that $Y = \$7000$ billion:

a) $C^d = .60$ x $7000 billion = $4200 billion.
$I^d = .15$ x $7000 billion = $1050 billion.
$G = .20$ x $7000 billion = $1400 billion.
$S^d = \$7000$ billion - $4200 billion - $1400 billion = $1400 billion.
$NX = \$1400$ billion - $1050 billion = $350 billion.

b) $S^d = .25$ x $7000 billion = $1750 billion.
$I^d = .10$ x $7000 billion = $700 billion.
$NX = \$1750$ billion - $700 billion = $1050 billion.

CHAPTER 15: MONETARY POLICY AND THE
FEDERAL RESERVE SYSTEM

A Fill-In-The-Blanks Review of Chapter Highlights: Use the following key terms to fill in the blanks. Each key term is used only once.

bank reserves
#3 Board of Governors of the Federal Reserve System
credibility
depository institutions
discount window lending
#2 Federal Open Market Committee (FOMC)
fractional reserve banking
high-powered money
intermediate targets
monetary base
#1 multiple expansion of loans and deposits
open-market purchase
reserve-deposit ratio
vault cash

bank run
central bank
currency-deposit ratio
discount rate
discretion
Fed funds rate
game theory
instruments
monetarism
money multiplier
100% reserve banking
open-market sale
rules

In most countries, monetary policy is conducted by a 1. *Central Bank* . The central bank of the United States is the Federal Reserve System. The Federal Reserve (i.e., the Fed) is one of the principal regulators of the banking industry. Private banks and thrifts, called 2. *Depository Institutions* , are assisted by the central bank in providing banking services.

The Fed issues currency in the form of coins and paper money (i.e., Federal Reserve notes) based on the U.S. dollar monetary standard; this currency is legal tender in the United States. As legal tender, dollars are widely accepted in exchange for resources, products, and assets in the United States.

The Federal Reserve controls the money supply principally through its control over the 3. *Monetary Base* , which is also called 4. *High-Powered Money* . The monetary base equals 5. *Bank Reserves* plus currency in circulation. In a 6. *100% Reserve Banking* system, banks would hold all deposits on reserve, and they would charge fees to cover the cost of banking services. The 7. *Reserve-Deposit Ratio* in a 8. *Fractional Reserve Banking* system is less than 100%, and banks cover a large share of their operating costs with the interest earned on loans made with bank deposits.

In accepting deposits and using these funds to make loans, banks and thrifts create money with a 9. *#1* . The money supply includes currency in circulation plus deposits at these depository institutions. The public's demand for currency relative to deposits determines the 10. *Currency Deposit Ratio* . An increase in the currency-deposit ratio reduces the amount of deposits created by a given amount of bank lending, which also reduces the 11. *Money Multiplier* . The money multiplier is the increase in the money supply created by each dollar increase in the monetary base. In a fractional reserve banking system with currency in circulation, the money multiplier = $[(cu + 1)/(cu + res)]$, where cu is the currency-deposit ratio and res is the ratio of bank reserves to deposits.

The Federal Reserve controls the money supply indirectly through its control over the monetary base. Its principal monetary policy instrument for changing the size of the monetary base is open-market operations. An 12._Open Market Purchase_ of government securities (e.g., U.S. Treasury bonds) by the Fed increases the monetary base. An 13._Open-Market Sale_ of government securities by the Fed reduces the monetary base.

The seven members of the 14. _#2_ are nominated by the president of the United States and confirmed by the U.S. Senate for staggered terms of fourteen years. The Board of Governors proposes regulations and deregulations for the banking industry, sets reserve requirement ratios, and sets the discount rate. The Board of Governors, the president of the Federal Reserve Bank of New York, and the presidents of four other Federal Reserve regional banks make up the 15._#3_, which controls monetary policy.

Private banks use 16._Vault Cash_, made up partly of daily deposits, to meet the daily withdrawal demands of depositors. On occasions for which a bank does not have enough vault cash to satisfy withdrawal demands, the bank can draw down its deposits at the Fed or it can borrow the amount it needs from the Fed. The inability of a bank to meet depositors' withdrawal demands could precipitate a 17._Bank Run_, which could quickly spread to a banking panic and broader financial crisis. To help prevent bank runs and banking panics, the Fed serves as a lender of last resort in its 18._Discount Window lending to_ private banks. The Fed charges banks an interest rate, called the 19._Discount Rate_, on these discount window loans. Banks also borrow and lend to each other at the 20. _Fed Funds Rate_. Unlike open-market operations and the discount rate, the Fed funds rate is not one of the policy 21. _Instruments_ of the Fed, but it is one of the Fed's 22._Intermediate Targets_. Although the Fed does not directly set the Fed funds rate, it can use its policy instruments to cause the Fed funds rate to rise or fall to some target rate.

There are two opposing approaches to conducting monetary policy; 23. _Rules_ versus 24._Discretion_. Keynesians propose that the Fed adopt a discretionary approach, while monetarists and classical economists propose that the Fed adopt a rules-based approach. Discretionary monetary policy requires that policymakers continuously monitor the performance of the economy and actively use monetary policy to respond to economic events to achieve monetary policy goals.

Monetarism is an important school of macroeconomic thought. Monetarism and classical economic theory both provided a foundation for the development of the extended classical model. 25. _Monetarism_ suggests that Keynesians underestimate the real economic effects of changes in the money supply, but overestimate the usefulness of discretionary monetary policy. Monetarists contend that discretionary monetary policy attempts to stabilize the economy are likely to destabilize it. From a monetarist viewpoint, the economy would be reasonably stable if the Fed would just stop destabilizing it.

A recently developed theoretical argument against discretionary monetary policy is the credibility argument. Some economists contend that discretionary policies lack 26. _Credibility_, which causes them to create different real economic effects than the effects intended by policymakers. From this viewpoint, only policy rules are credible, and only credible policies are economically efficient. 27. _Game Theory_ provides one way of analyzing how the effectiveness of monetary policy may depend on its credibility.

True-False Questions: Circle T for true statements and F for false statements.

T (F) 1.   The central bank of the United States completely controls the money supply.

T (F) 2.   The only monetary policy instrument that the Fed can use to change the money supply is open-market operations.

T (F) 3.   In part because they are democratically elected, members of the Board of Governors of the Fed are likely to favor monetary policies that best serve the interests of the general public.

(T) F 4.   Political decision-making power within the Fed is highly centralized.

T (F) 5.   An increase in the reserve-deposit ratio or the currency-deposit ratio will increase the size of the money multiplier.

(T) F 6.   Keynesians contend that the instability of money demand is an important problem for monetary policy and for the economy.

T (F) 7.   In targeting short-term interest rates, the Fed can keep the nominal interest rate and real interest rate at very low rates in the long run.

T (F) 8.   Monetarists recommend that the Fed adopt a constant money growth rule to best achieve its goal of reducing business cycle fluctuations in output and unemployment.

T (F) 9.   When the central banks of the United States, Germany, and Japan pursued predetermined money supply growth targets in the 1970s and 1980s, they were able to substantially reduce inflation without increasing unemployment in the short run.

T (F) 10.   Game theory suggests that the only credible policy statement by the Fed is that it is fully committed to maintaining price level stability.

Multiple Choice Questions: Circle the letter corresponding to the correct answer to each question.

1.   Monetary policy in the United States is principally controlled by
     a. the president of the United States.
     b. the U.S. Senate.
     c. the U.S. Congress.
     d. fiscal policymakers.
     (e.) the central bank.

2.   Which of the following are depository institutions?
     a. The Federal Reserve Banks of New York and Chicago
     b. The U.S. Treasury and the IRS
     (c.) Banks and thrifts
     d. Investment banks and finance companies
     e. Banks and insurance companies

3.   If a currency is legal tender in a country, then
     a. the government will readily exchange it for gold.
     b. the government will not accept it in payment of taxes.
     c. it is the only legal form of wealth.
     (d.) it is widely accepted as a means of payment, and creditors are required to accept it in settlement of debts.
     e. it could not be used for illegal activities.

4.   The monetary base (BASE) equals
        a. CU + RES.
        b. RES.
        c. CU + DEP.
        d. M - CU.
        e. M - RES.

5.   Banks hold some deposits on reserve at the Fed because
        a. the Fed pays a higher interest rate than banks can get in the private market.
        b. the Fed will insure those deposits, but will not insure regular bank deposits.
        c. these are membership dues for being a member bank.
        d. these deposits meet the reserve requirements of the Fed.
        e. the Fed will not allow them to hold all bank deposits at the Fed; banks have to make some loans.

6.   In a fractional reserve banking system
        a. most deposits are used to make bank loans.
        b. 100% of deposits are held as reserves.
        c. the money supply = high-powered money.
        d. the money multiplier is less than one.
        e. there has to be more than one bank, because one bank is allowed to hold only a fraction of all deposits.

7.   In a fractional reserve banking system with no currency, the money multiplier is
        a. $[(cu + 1)/(cu + res)]$.
        b. $1/(cu + res)$.
        c. $1/res$.
        d. BASE/M.
        e. res.

8.   If the public's demand for currency increased relative to its demand for deposits, the
        a. monetary base would decrease.
        b. reserve requirement ratio would decrease.
        c. currency-deposit ratio would decrease.
        d. reserve-deposit ratio would increase.
        e. money multiplier would decrease.

9.   If the Fed makes a large open-market sale of bonds to the public, the
        a. money supply will increase.
        b. money multiplier will increase.
        c. Fed funds rate will decrease.
        d. unemployment rate will decrease.
        e. money supply will decrease.

10.   Members of the Board of Governors are
        a. democratically elected by popular vote every four years.
        b. appointed by the U.S. president and confirmed by the U.S. Senate, as relatively independent policymakers.
        c. appointed by the U.S. president and serve as part of the executive branch of the federal government.
        d. appointed by the U.S. Congress and serve as part of the legislative branch of the federal government.
        e. appointed by the Supreme Court and serve as part of the judicial branch of the federal government.

11.   Within the Fed, the FOMC
a. sets the discount rate.
b. controls monetary policy.
c. regulates securities markets.
d. sets reserve requirement ratios.
e. handles check clearance and settlement of bank balances.

12.   By lending at the discount window, the Fed
a. prevents banks from going bankrupt.
b. ensures that banks will make healthy profits.
c. eliminates the need for banks to pay market interest rates to attract deposits.
d. acts as a lender of last resort to enable banks to meet unexpectedly high withdrawal demands.
e. insures bank deposits.

13.   The Fed funds rate is
a. the interest rate on federal government bonds.
b. the interest rate banks charge other banks for short-term loans.
c. the growth rate of the federal debt.
d. the interest rate penalty on late federal tax payments.
e. an intermediate monetary aggregate target of the Fed.

14.   The dominant policy instrument typically used to change the money supply is
a. deregulation.
b. fiscal policy.
c. monetary policy announcements.
d. the discount rate.
e. open-market operations.

15.   If the principal source of instability in the economy is instability in money demand, the best intermediate target of monetary policy is
a. the discount rate.
b. a monetary aggregate.
c. the short-term interest rate.
d. the monetary base.
e. government bonds.

16.   A monetary policy rule proposed by monetarists is to
a. follow political business cycles.
b. use long and variable policy lags.
c. reduce money supply growth quickly.
d. stabilize the domestic economy before stabilizing the exchange rate.
e. increase the money supply at a low, constant rate of growth every year.

17.   The basic Keynesian argument for discretionary monetary policy is that
a. monetary policy is the principal cause of business cycles.
b. monetary policy is much more effective than fiscal policy.
c. aggregate demand is unstable and monetary policy can help to stabilize it.
d. reducing unemployment is much more important than reducing inflation.
e. policy rules are likely to be destabilizing.

18.   Money is neutral in the long run; this is the view of
       a. classical economists, Keynesians, and monetarists.
       b. only classical economists.
       c. only monetarists.
       d. Keynesians and classical economists, but not monetarists.
       e. Keynesians and monetarists, but not classical economists.

19.   In response to the credibility argument against discretionary monetary policies, Keynesians contend that
       a. policies do not need to be credible for money to be neutral.
       b. discretionary monetary policies caused the Great Depression.
       c. cold turkey policies are more credible and efficient than gradualism.
       d. policymakers need flexibility, even if it reduces their credibility.
       e. discretionary policies should be replaced by a rules-based approach.

20.   According to game theory analysis of the game between firms and the Fed,
       a. the firms cannot determine the Fed's most preferred outcome.
       b. the Fed cannot determine the firms' least preferred outcome.
       c. the Fed and firms negotiate to reach a cooperative solution.
       d. the Fed and the firms act independently in their own rational self-interest.
       e. monetary policy has real effects in the short run, even when the firms anticipate the Fed's next move.

Short-Answer Essay Questions

1.   **Federal Reserve control over the money supply**: a) Use the money supply and monetary base equations to develop an equation for the money supply in terms of the monetary base. b) Identify the market actors who control each of the following variables, and state whether the money supply is positively related or negatively related to each variable: the monetary base, the reserve-deposit ratio, and the currency-deposit ratio. c) Was the money multiplier stable during the Great Depression, and why would an unstable money multiplier pose a problem for monetary policy? d) Why does the United States use a fractional reserve banking system? e) Why does the Fed impose a minimum reserve requirement ratio on bank deposits?

2.   **Monetary policy instruments of the Fed**: a) Identify the most commonly used policy instrument for changing the money supply, and explain how the Fed can use this policy instrument to increase and decrease the money supply. b) What policy-making body within the Fed controls monetary policy and how are its members chosen? c) Identify two other monetary policy instruments, and explain how each can be used to increase the money supply. d) Explain why the Fed typically does not use all its instruments together to change the money supply. e) Given an economy with no currency and a reserve-deposit ratio of 10%, explain how the banking system creates money when the Fed buys a $1000 bond from a bank.

3.   **Monetary policy targets of the Fed**: a) Identify the two principal intermediate targets of monetary policy, and explain why they are efficient targets. b) Why does the Fed set a target range for its intermediate target? c) Why do monetarists object to the Fed's use of multiple intermediate targets? d) What is the optimal intermediate target of monetary policy when nominal shocks are the principal cause of instability in the macroeconomy? e) What is the intermediate target recommended by monetarists, and why do they propose this target?

4.   **Ultimate targets and monetary policy approaches**: a) Identify the principal short-run ultimate target of monetary policy in the Keynesian model, and explain why it is not a long-run target. b) Identify the principal long-run ultimate target of monetary policy in the Keynesian model, and explain why it is not a short-run target. c) Compare and contrast the classical and monetarist reasons for opposing monetary stabilization policy. d) Explain why monetarists believe their monetary policy rule will best achieve price level stability. e) From a Keynesian viewpoint, what is wrong with the monetarist argument against an activist monetary policy?

5.   **Game theory, credibility, and monetary policy effects**: a) Use game theory to explain why the Fed may not be able to achieve its stabilization policy goal. b) Use game theory to explain why the Fed may be able to best achieve its goal under a rules-based approach. c) State the Keynesian critique of the credibility argument against discretionary monetary policy. d) State the empirical effects on unemployment and inflation of using a policy rule in West Germany, Japan, and the United States during the late 1970s and early 1980s. e) Evaluate the empirical evidence to determine whether it supports the credibility argument and the monetarist argument for using a policy rule.

Mathematical Problem-Solving Questions

1.   **Money multiplier**:   Calculate the money multiplier for: a) cu = .40 and res = .07; b) cu = .40 and res = .08; c) cu = .45 and res = .07.

2.   **Money supply**: Calculate the money supply for : a) money multiplier = 3.0 and BASE = $350 billion; b) money multiplier = 3.5 and BASE = $350 billion; c) money multiplier = 3.0 and BASE = $400 billion.

Answers to Fill-In-The-Blanks Questions

1. central bank	2. depository institutions
3. monetary base	4. high-powered money
5. bank reserves	6. 100% reserve banking
7. reserve-deposit ratio	8. fractional reserve banking
9. multiple expansion of loans and deposits	10. currency-deposit ratio
11. money multiplier	12. open-market purchase
13. open-market sale	14. Board of Governors of the Federal Reserve System
15. Federal Open Market Committee (FOMC)	16. vault cash
17. bank run	18. discount window lending
19. discount rate	20. Fed funds rate
21. instruments	22. intermediate targets
23. rules	24. discretion
25. monetarism	26. credibility
27. game theory	

Answers to True-False Questions

1.   F   The central bank of the United States is the Federal Reserve System, which is also called the Fed. The Fed is the government agency primarily responsible for monetary policy. In conducting monetary policy, the Fed does not always try to control the money supply. In the post-World War II period, the Fed has pursued a short-term interest rate as its principal intermediate target more frequently than a money supply target. The

money supply is jointly determined by the actions of the Fed, banks, and the general public. By increasing or decreasing their excess reserves, banks can change the reserve-deposit ratio. By increasing or decreasing their use of currency, the general public can change the currency-deposit ratio. Changes in reserve-deposit ratio and currency-deposit ratio create changes in the money multiplier, which cause the money supply to change for a given money base. The Fed controls the size of the monetary base; it can increase or decrease the size of the monetary base to offset the effects on the money supply of undesirable changes in the money multiplier. In order to hit a money supply target, the Fed must accurately estimate the size of the money multiplier, which may be difficult to do during short periods of time (e.g., six months or less) when the reserve-deposit ratio or currency-deposit ratio is unstable.

2. F The Fed can change the money supply by using open-market operations, by changing the reserve requirement ratio, or by changing the discount rate. To increase the money supply, the Fed could execute an open-market purchase, reduce the reserve requirement ratio, or reduce the discount rate.

3. F The Board of Governors of the Fed are not democratically elected. They are nominated by the U.S. president and confirmed by the U.S. Senate. Since the U.S. president and members of the U.S. Senate are democratically elected public officials, they are likely to select and confirm individuals who they expect will best serve the interests of the general public. However, political leaders may not agree on what monetary policies best serve the public interest. Some political leaders agree with Keynesian proposals for discretionary policies to smooth business cycles, while others agree with monetarist and classical proposals for adopting policy rules.

4. T While the Federal Reserve System is a large organization, with twelve regional Federal Reserve banks spread throughout the United States, most of the important policy decisions are made by twelve members of the Federal Open Market Committee, which is dominated by the seven members of the Board of Governors, which is in turn dominated by the Chairman of the Board of Governors.

5. F The money multiplier = $[(cu + 1)/(cu + res)]$, where cu is the currency-deposit ratio and res is the reserve-deposit ratio. An increase in cu or res will reduce the size of the money multiplier.

6. T If we interpret unstable to mean unpredictably volatile, then money demand has been unstable in the United States since the early 1970s. Keynesians contend that nominal shocks, including changes in money demand, will shift the LM curve in the short run, because wages and prices adjust slowly. For a given money supply, an increase in money demand will shift the LM curve to the left, causing the interest rate to rise, output to fall, and unemployment to rise in the Keynesian model. An increase in the interest rate also reduces desired consumption, desired investment, and net exports. According to the Keynesians, money demand instability is an important cause of business cycle fluctuations. Keynesians propose that monetary policymakers target short-term interest rates to reduce business cycle fluctuations caused by the instability of money demand. To hit a short-term interest rate target, the Fed must prevent the LM curve from shifting; it tries to achieve this by changing the money supply in the opposite direction to changes in money demand. In contrast, classical economists and monetarists do not believe that money demand is unpredictably volatile. In the classical model, nominal shocks do not have any real economic effects; there is no short-run period in which money is nonneutral.

7. F In the long run, money is neutral. Therefore monetary policy changes in the money supply have no effect on the real interest rate in the long run. In the long run, the real interest rate is independent of the money supply. Short-run expansionary monetary policies increase the nominal interest rate in the long run by increasing inflation. In the classical model, there is no short-run period in which money is nonneutral; increases in the money supply do not reduce the nominal or real interest rate in the short run. In the Keynesian view, expansionary monetary policy can reduce the nominal and real interest rates in the short-run,

which may last for several years. Keynesians agree with the classical view that expansionary monetary policies will increase the nominal interest rate in the long run by increasing inflation.

8. F   Monetarists recommend that the Fed adopt a constant money growth rule to best achieve its long-run policy goal of maintaining price level stability. Monetarists do not believe that monetary policies should attempt to reduce business cycle fluctuations. Monetarists contend that monetary policy attempts to stabilize the macroeconomy are very likely to inadvertently destabilize it.

9. F   When the central banks of the United States, Germany, and Japan pursued predetermined money supply growth targets in the 1970s and 1980s, they were able to reduce inflation, but unemployment rose substantially in the United States and Germany. This empirical evidence suggests that even when monetary policymakers adopt a credible, rules-based approach to conducting monetary policy, they still face a short-run Phillips curve trade-off between inflation and unemployment.

10. F   Monetarists and classical economists oppose the use of short-run discretionary monetary policies, but they are concerned that the Fed continues to engage in these economically inefficient policy attempts to smooth business cycles, rather than credibly, fully commit itself to its efficient long-run policy goal of maintaining price level stability. Game theory suggests that failure of the Fed to credibly commit itself to maintaining price level stability causes the equilibrium outcome of the game to make the Fed and businesses worse off than they would be if the Fed were to credibly commit to a fixed policy rule to maintain price level stability.

Answers to Multiple Choice Questions

1. e	8. e	15. c
2. c	9. e	16. e
3. d	10. b	17. c
4. a	11. b	18. a
5. d	12. d	19. d
6. a	13. b	20. d
7. c	14. e	

Answers to Short-Answer Essay Questions

1. **Federal Reserve control over the money supply:**

    a)   Using the money supply and monetary base equations to develop the money supply equation in terms of the monetary base:
    1) M = CU + DEP
    2) BASE = CU + RES
    3) res = RES/DEP
    4) cu = CU/DEP
    5) BASE = cu x DEP + res x DEP = (cu + res) x DEP
    6) DEP = [1/(cu + res)] x BASE
    7) M = CU + DEP = cu x DEP + DEP
    8) M = (cu + 1) x DEP
    9) M = [(cu + 1)/(cu + res)] x BASE
    The money multiplier is [(cu + 1)/(cu + res)] = M/BASE.

b)   Determinants of the money supply:

      1) The monetary base (BASE) is positively related to the money supply; an increase in the base increases the money supply. The Fed controls the monetary base.

      2) The reserve-deposit ratio (res) is negatively related to the money supply; an increase in the reserve-deposit ratio reduces the money multiplier and thus reduces the money supply. The Fed sets the minimum reserve requirement ratio on bank deposits, but the private banks can change the reserve-deposit ratio by changing their holdings of excess reserves (i.e., reserves in excess of required reserves).

      3) The currency-deposit ratio (cu) is negatively related to the money supply; an increase in the currency-deposit ratio reduces the money multiplier and thus reduces the money supply. The public (i.e., everyone except banks, thrifts, and the Fed) controls the currency-deposit ratio by deciding how much of their money they want to retain as currency, rather than as deposits in banks and thrift institutions.

c)   No. The money multiplier was not stable during the Great Depression. In the 1931 to early 1933 period, the money multiplier declined sharply, because the currency-deposit ratio and the reserve-deposit ratio both rose dramatically. Market actors increased their demand for currency, and banks increased their demand for excess reserves. Instability in the money multiplier creates instability in the money supply for a given monetary base. The Fed could offset any undesirable effect of a change in the money multiplier on the money supply by changing the monetary base. However, the Fed did not sufficiently compensate for the change in the money multiplier, so the money supply declined by 35% in this period. More than one-third of the banks in the country failed or were acquired by other banks in the 1930-1933 period. This financial crisis was stopped in 1933, when President Roosevelt temporarily shut down the banking system by declaring a "bank holiday."

d)   The United States uses a fractional reserve banking system to enable banks to act as financial intermediaries between depositors and borrowers. By bringing depositors and borrowers together at a low transactions cost, banks greatly facilitate the flow of money to its highest valued uses. An efficient banking system is therefore an important institutional arrangement for promoting economic growth. Under a 100% reserve banking system, banks could still provide a low-cost checking account system for making payments, but they would have to charge fees for these checking account services, because banks could not make loans to help cover these expenses.

e)   The reserve requirement ratio is a monetary policy instrument (i.e., tool) of the Fed. The Fed uses the reserve requirement ratio and the reserves that it creates to control the money supply. In a monetary system with no currency, the money multiplier is (1/res) and the monetary base is RES. If banks keep the reserve-deposit ratio constant (e.g., by holding only required reserves), the Fed can use open-market operations to increase the money supply [M = DEP = (1/res) x RES = (1/res) x BASE] by (1/res) for every dollar increase in the monetary base. The Fed could also increase the money supply by reducing the reserve requirement ratio or reducing the discount rate. Lowering the discount rate encourages banks to borrow reserves from the Fed, so reserves (RES) increase.

2.   **Monetary policy instruments of the Fed**:

a)   Open-market operations are the most commonly used policy instrument for changing the money supply. The Fed can increase the money supply by making an open-market purchase of government securities (i.e., bonds) from the public or banks. An open-market purchase increases currency in circulation and bank reserves, which is an increase in the monetary base. An increase in the monetary base increases the money supply by the amount of the money multiplier times the increase in the money base. Alternatively, the Fed can reduce the monetary base and the money supply by making an open-market sale of government securities.

b)   The Federal Open Market Committee (FOMC) controls monetary policy. There are twelve members of the FOMC, including the seven members of the Board of Governors, the president of the Federal Reserve Bank of New York, and the presidents of four other Federal Reserve regional (i.e., district) banks. The members of the Board of Governors are nominated by the U.S. president and confirmed by the U.S. Senate. The presidents of the Federal Reserve district banks are appointed by the nine-member directorate of each district bank.

c)   Two other monetary policy instruments (i.e., tools):

1)   Reserve requirement ratio: The Fed could increase the money supply by reducing the reserve requirement ratio. If banks maintain a fixed ratio of excess reserves to deposits, a decline in required reserves will reduce the reserve-deposit ratio, which increases the money multiplier, which increases the money supply for a given monetary base.

2)   Discount rate: The Fed could increase the money supply by reducing the discount rate. A lower discount rate encourages banks to borrow more reserves from the Fed, causing bank reserves and the monetary base to increase. An increase in the monetary base increases the money supply.

d)   For several reasons, the Fed predominantly uses open-market operations (OMO) to change the money supply. First, OMO is the best instrument for making small, controllable changes in the money supply, in part because there is a large, well-developed market for these securities. Second, the Fed does not change the reserve requirement ratio frequently, in part because a stable reserve requirement ratio helps to stabilize the money multiplier, through which open-market operations work. Even small changes in the reserve requirement ratio create large changes in the money supply that are hard to control; this suggests that the reserve requirement is a powerful but blunt instrument, rather than a precision instrument. Third, the Fed may announce changes in the discount rate when it is changing the money supply, but this is a relatively "weak instrument" in itself for changing the money supply. The principal effect of lowering the discount rate is to give the public and banks a clear, credible announcement that monetary policy is becoming tighter or easier.

e)   For an economy with no currency and a reserve-deposit ratio of 10%, a $1000 open-market purchase from a bank increases the bank's excess reserves by $1000. The bank can make loans up to the limit of its excess reserves, so it makes a $1000 loan to some borrower. The borrower deposits the amount of the loan in his bank account. The bank retains 10% of the $1000 deposit as reserves and now makes a $900 loan, using its excess reserves. The amount of the $900 loan is deposited in a second bank, which retains 10% as reserves and makes a loan for the $810 balance. The borrower deposits the amount of the $810 loan in a third bank, which retains 10% as reserves and lends out the balance. When all possible loans have been made by the banking system, this multiple expansion of loans and deposits will increase the money supply by $10,000 = (1/.10) x $1000.

3.   **Monetary policy targets of the Fed:**

a)   The two principal intermediate targets of the Fed are a monetary aggregate (e.g., M2) and a short-run interest rate (e.g., the Fed funds rate). These intermediate targets are efficient in the sense that the Fed can use its policy instruments to create predictable changes in the values of intermediate targets, and changes in the values of intermediate target variables create predictable changes in the values of the ultimate targets of monetary policy. In trying to hit an ultimate policy target, the Fed can gauge how well it is doing by observing changes in its intermediate targets. Changes in the values of intermediate targets are reported more frequently than changes in the values of ultimate target variables. In brief, an intermediate target is easier for the Fed to hit than an ultimate target; also, the Fed gets earlier feedback on its effectiveness (i.e., how close it came to hitting the target), so intermediate targeting increases the overall effectiveness of monetary policy in achieving its policy goals.

b)   The Fed sets a target range rather than a target point for its intermediate targets because generally, it cannot hit a target point (e.g., the center of the target range), and because it generally does not have to hit a target point to achieve its ultimate target range. For example, a change in the monetary base would not increase the money supply as much as the Fed planned if the Fed has overestimated the size of the money multiplier.

c)   The Fed has often set multiple intermediate targets. For example, it may set an interest rate target and targets for M1, M2, and M3 in one policy period. The monetarists object to multiple intermediate targets because the Fed can, at best, hit only one target. With multiple targets, we don't know which one the Fed is committed to hit. For example, if the Fed plans to reduce the interest rate and the money supply, its plans cannot be achieved. It could reduce the interest rate by increasing the money supply. It could reduce the money supply, but the interest rate would increase. It cannot achieve both of these targets simultaneously, but we don't know which one is the real target. Therefore a monetary policy directed at multiple intermediate targets is not credible.

d)   When nominal shocks (e.g., changes in money demand) are the principal cause of economic instability, the optimal intermediate target of monetary policy is the short-run interest rate (e.g., the Fed funds rate). Changes in money demand primarily affect macroeconomic variables by directly changing the market interest rate. Instability in money demand creates instability in the interest rate, which causes other undesirable macroeconomic effects. By trying to stabilize the Fed funds rate, monetary policy can help to stabilize the market interest rate, which can help to stabilize the macroeconomy.

e)   The monetarists recommend that the Fed choose a monetary aggregate as an intermediate target, such as M2. They propose a monetary aggregate target for several reasons. First, they do not believe that nominal shocks are an important source of instability in the economy. In the monetarist view, money demand is reasonably stable. Second, they believe that the macroeconomy is reasonably stable and self-regulating, and normally operates at full-employment output, consistent with the natural unemployment rate. Third, they believe that the money supply largely determines the level of aggregate demand, and that aggregate demand determines the price level; therefore the money supply determines the price level. Fourth, in a stable economy operating at full employment, the ultimate target of monetary policy should be to maintain price level stability (i.e., zero inflation). Fifth, to hit the price level target, we need to achieve a constant rate of money supply growth (i.e., a constant rate of growth in some monetary aggregate).

4.   **Ultimate targets and monetary policy approaches:**

a)   Keynesians recommend that monetary policymakers attempt to maintain a low, stable market interest rate as its ultimate policy target in the short run. Keynesians believe that nominal shocks are a major source of economic stability, and that monetary policy can help to reduce the economic effects of nominal shocks. However, the real interest rate cannot be a long-run target, because money is neutral in the long run. In the long run, money has no real economic effects. In the long run, monetary policy cannot lower the real interest rate, and has only nominal effects.

b)   All economists agree that the ultimate long-run target of monetary policy is price level stability, which means a zero rate of inflation. Some economists believe that the best we can achieve is a very low rate of inflation (e.g., 3%). In the Keynesian model, the price level is fixed (i.e., perfectly stable) in the short run; therefore monetary policy does not have to stabilize it.

c)   According to the basic classical model, money is neutral; this means that changes in the money supply have no real economic effects. In the basic classical model, the only goal, and therefore best goal, that monetary policy can achieve is to maintain price level stability. In the extended classical model, only unanticipated monetary policies could have short-run real economic effects. Although these real economic effects are relatively small and short-lived in the extended classical model, they are undesirable effects. Therefore the extended classical model supports the basic classical model conclusion that monetary stabilization policy cannot produce significant, desirable economic effects even in the short run. The monetarists, however, conclude that monetary stabilization policies can have very large real economic effects in the short run; money is nonneutral in the short run. The monetarists reject the use of short-run monetary stabilization policies, because they believe that attempts to stabilize the economy have been and will be mostly destabilizing. For example, monetarists believe that monetary policy caused the Great Depression. Monetarists and classicals agree that the economy is stable and self-regulating. They also agree that monetary policy is not likely to have any significant stabilizing effect. Unlike the classicals, however, monetarists believe that monetary policy attempts to stabilize are very destabilizing. Monetarists conclude that the best way to reduce business cycle fluctuations is to prohibit the use of monetary stabilization policies.

d)   Monetarists believe that business cycle fluctuations will be small in the absence of the destabilizing effects of monetary stabilization policies. Monetarists propose that the money supply be increased at 3% per year without variation. If monetary policymakers adopted this constant money growth rule (CMGR), output would grow along the potential output growth path at about 3% per year. According to the quantity theory of money, the inflation rate will be zero when the money supply grows at the same rate as money demand grows. Since money demand grows by a fixed percentage of output, money demand growth is constant when output growth is constant. At zero inflation, the price level is stable.

e)   Keynesians do not believe that the economy is stable and self-regulating. Consequently, the economy does not quickly recover from recessions. In the Keynesian view, recessions may be severe and persistent, as was the Great Depression. Keynesians do not accept the monetarist view that only a decline in the money supply could reduce aggregate demand and thereby create a recession. Keynesians emphasize that a decline in any type of spending (i.e., C, I, G, or NX) will reduce aggregate demand and thereby create a recession. In the Keynesian view, the Great Depression was initially caused by a decline in investment spending. Unlike the monetarists, Keynesians believe that the Fed is reasonably efficient and can use monetary stabilization policy efficiently to stabilize aggregate demand at the full-employment level of output. Keynesians contend that using monetary policy to greatly reduce the duration and severity of recessions is very economically beneficial.

5. **Game theory, credibility, and monetary policy effects:**

a) In a game theory analysis of the game between firms and the Fed, the self-interest of the firms conflicts with the self-interest of the Fed. Firms believe that the Fed will choose the outcome that it prefers, and firms know the preferences of the Fed. If the Fed pursues monetary stabilization policy, it may promise to choose a monetary policy that maximizes the interest of firms, but such a policy is not credible. Firms will choose the set of possible outcomes that provide them with the best outcome when the Fed acts in its own self-interest. In brief, firms prevent the Fed from achieving its announced stabilization policy goal (i.e., outcome), because they don't believe the Fed will act against its own self-interest to do what it has promised to do.

b) Under a rules-based approach, the Fed does not adjust monetary policy in response to the decisions made by market actors. Under a policy rule, an announced policy is the actual policy that the Fed will execute, no matter what. If the Fed announces that it will increase the money supply only at a rate consistent with zero inflation (e.g., 3% per year), firms know that the Fed is totally committed to do exactly that. In effect, the Fed's policy is credible, so firms believe the Fed's policy announcement. Under a policy rule, the firms must respond to the Fed's policy, because the Fed decides first; whereas under discretionary stabilization policy, the Fed responds to the firms' decision, since the firms effectively choose first.

c) Keynesians contend that in general, monetary stabilization policy does not depend on the Fed making hollow threats. In the Keynesian analysis, firms unintentionally create recessions by individually deciding to reduce their investment spending. By their individual, profit-maximizing actions, they do not intend to create a recession, but that is the aggregate effect of a decline in investment spending by many individual firms. Contrary to the credibility argument, the interests of the Fed and the firms are not in conflict. The Fed can use expansionary monetary stabilization policy to reduce the real interest rate, which lowers firms' cost of financing investments, which causes firms to increase investment spending, which increases aggregate spending, which helps return the economy to full-employment output. Keynesians emphasize that monetary stabilization is needed at times, and generally is efficient in reducing the severity and persistence of recessions. Thus monetary policy should be flexible rather than fixed. Skilled, educated, informed policymakers should be able to use their discretion in implementing the monetary policies that they believe are best for the economy under various economic conditions.

d) At various times during the late 1970s and early 1980s, the central banks of West Germany, Japan, and the United States effectively followed a monetary policy rule of slow money supply growth per year for several years. In all cases, reducing money supply growth reduced the rate of inflation but, with the exception of Japan, unemployment increased significantly and remained high for several years.

e) The monetarists believe that wages and prices quickly adjust to economic shocks, but expectations are slow to adjust to unanticipated shocks. This suggests that an anticipated reduction in money supply growth would simply move the economy down the vertical long-run Phillips curve, as both inflation and expected inflation decline. To reduce expected inflation quickly, however, monetary policy must be credible. Game theory suggests that a rules-based approach will be credible. The empirical evidence cited here does not strongly support the monetarist argument for a policy rule, nor does it strongly support the credibility argument. The increase in unemployment that accompanied the decline in inflation suggests that the West German and U.S. economies were moving down fixed, short-run Phillips curves for sustained periods of time, because wages, prices, and expectations adjust slowly to changes in monetary policy. Following a credible policy rule therefore did not prevent the short-run real economic costs of a disinflationary monetary policy. In Japan, however, the decline in inflation did not produce any significant increase in unemployment; the empirical evidence for Japan supports the monetarist views and supports the credibility argument. Although the failure of unemployment to rise in Japan may be explained by other institutional conditions (e.g., long-term employer-employee relationship commitments), the overall empirical evidence is mixed. It is noteworthy that worsening economic conditions (e.g., trade deficits) caused each country to abandon their policy rules. This suggests that none of these monetary policymakers were willing to follow a policy rule once economic conditions worsened. They all acted as if they believed that using discretionary monetary stabilization policies would improve the performance of their respective economies. Keynesians contend that only a discretionary approach to monetary policy is sustainable, and that an unsustainable policy rule is not credible.

Answers to Mathematical Problem-Solving Questions

1. **Money multiplier:** The money multiplier = $(cu + 1)/(cu + rcs)$.

    a) For cu = .40 and res = .07, the money multiplier = $1.40/0.47 = 2.98$.

    b) For cu = .40 and res = .08, the money multiplier = $1.40/0.48 = 2.92$.

    c) For cu = .45 and res = .07, the money multiplier = $1.45/0.52 = 2.79$.

2. **Money supply:** The money supply, M = money multiplier x BASE.

    a) For money multiplier = 3.0 and BASE = $350 billion, M = $1050 billion.

    b) For money multiplier = 3.5 and BASE = $350 billion, M = $1225 billion.

    c) For money multiplier = 3.0 and BASE = $400 billion, M = $1200 billion.

CHAPTER 16: GOVERNMENT SPENDING AND ITS FINANCING

A Fill-In-The-Blanks Review of Chapter Highlights: Use the following key terms to fill in the blanks. Each key term is used only once.

automatic stabilizers
full-employment deficit
inflation tax
seignorage

average tax rate
government capital
marginal tax rate
supply-side economics

distortions
government debt
primary budget deficit
tax rate smoothing

For a given fiscal year, the 1. _Primary Budget deficit_ is the amount by which current government spending (i.e., outlays) on current programs exceeds current tax revenue. The primary budget deficit equation is [(G + TR) - T]. The budget deficit [i.e., (G + TR + INT) - T] is the primary budget deficit plus net interest payments on outstanding government debt. If the government has outstanding debt and the primary budget is balanced, interest payments on the debt create a budget deficit.

In a recession, 2. _automatic stabilizers_ increase the budget deficit and the primary budget deficit. Two examples of automatic stabilizers are a progressive income tax system and transfer programs. Automatic stabilizers are fiscal policy stabilizers, but they are not discretionary fiscal policy stabilizers. The 3. _Full-Employment deficit_ is calculated by subtracting the deficit created by automatic stabilizers from the budget deficit. A full-employment deficit measures the amount of a budget deficit created by expansionary fiscal policy. The economic costs and benefits of a deficit-financed increase in government spending depends in part on what government buys. Some economists have proposed dividing the federal budget into two budgets: a 4. _Govt. Capital_ budget and a current budget. They contend that budget deficits in the capital budget may be economically efficient, in the same way that it is efficient for businesses to borrow to finance their capital investments.

One instrument of discretionary fiscal policy is the tax rate. During a recession, Keynesians may propose that fiscal policymakers reduce the tax rate to help the economy quickly return to the full-employment level of output. During inflationary periods, at the full-employment level of output, Keynesians may propose that fiscal policymakers increase the tax rate to reduce the rate of inflation. Since there are many different kinds of taxes (e.g., the personal income tax, sales tax, and corporate profits tax), policymakers must decide whose taxes are going to be cut or raised by how much.

A tax on any economic activity reduces the after-tax rate of return to that activity. A tax increase creates both a substitution effect and an income effect. A tax increase has a substitution effect, because it reduces the return on the activity taxed relative to the return on alternative activities; the substitution effect causes people to do less of any activity whose after-tax return has declined. A tax increase has an income effect, because it reduces the wealth of those who pay the tax; the income effect causes people to do more of any activity whose after-tax return has declined in order to recover from their loss of wealth. An increase in the 5. _Marginal Tax Rate_, holding the average tax rate constant, has a pure substitution effect. An increase in the 6. _Avg. Tax Rate_, holding the marginal tax rate constant, has a pure income effect. Proponents of 7. _Supply Side Economics_ strongly favored the substantial marginal tax rate cuts in U.S. federal personal income tax rates enacted in 1981 and 1986; they expected these marginal tax rate cuts would substantially increase labor supply. Tax-induced changes in the behavior of market actors are called 8. _distortions_. Critics of tax-based changes in fiscal stabilization policy argue that the economic costs of the distortions created by fiscal stabilization policies are high. These critics favor annually balanced budgets, but annually balanced budgets do not allow for 9. _Tax Rate Smoothing_ when government spending fluctuates. Frequent changes in tax rates required to finance changes in government spending also may create high economic costs.

10. _Govt. debt_ is the sum of all unpaid government budget deficits plus unpaid accrued interest on these deficits. The debt-GDP ratio is one useful measure of the relative size of the government debt. Over the decade of the 1980s, the debt-GDP ratio for the federal debt of the U.S. government increased substantially. The significant increase in the debt-GDP ratio during the 1980s highlights the effect on the ratio of rolling over the debt, which means issuing new debt to pay off maturing debt. Other factors that caused the debt-GDP ratio to increase in the 1980s included ongoing budget deficits, a high real interest rate, and a low output growth rate.

In addition to selling government securities to the public to finance its deficits and debt, a government could also finance its deficits and debt by selling some of its securities to the central bank, which prints money to buy them. The government revenue raised by printing money is called 11. _Seignorage_. Assuming that output remains unchanged, printing money to finance excess government spending is purely inflationary. Inflation is a (hidden) tax on money, because it reduces the real purchasing power of money. In calculating the real seignorage revenue from printing money, the inflation rate is the tax rate and the real money supply is the tax base. The real seignorage revenue collected by government equals the inflation rate times the real money supply. Using unanticipated increases in inflation to finance excess government spending is an inefficient financing method, in part because the 12. _Inflation tax_ is hidden. However, economic analysis shows that governments can raise revenue by this method, and history shows that on occasion they have done so.

True-False Questions: Circle T for true statements and F for false statements

T (F) 1.   An increase in net interest payments will increase the primary budget deficit, the budget deficit, the government debt, and the amount of government bonds outstanding.

(T) F 2.   Since World War II, government spending on transfer payments by all levels of government in the United States has grown faster than any other type of government spending.

T (F) 3.   In 1990 the government spent about 35% of GDP in the United States, which was considerably higher than the percentage of GDP spent by the governments of Canada and Germany.

(T) F 4.   In a severe recession of long duration, automatic stabilizers would create a government budget deficit in a budget that would be balanced at full-employment output.; under these circumstances, Keynesians would probably propose a tax cut.

T (F) 5.   The size of the budget deficit is an accurate measure of the extent to which discretionary fiscal policy is expansionary.

T (F) 6.   From a classical viewpoint it is irresponsible of government policymakers to spend more than they can finance with current tax revenue.

T (F) 7.   Whether the government sells its bonds to the public or to the central bank, taxes must be increased in the future to pay off these government bonds.

T   (F) 8.   Regardless of borrowing constraints, the Ricardian equivalence proposition accurately predicts that a temporary tax cut will have no real economic effects.

(T) F   9.   Supply-side economists overestimated the incentive effects on labor supply of the U.S. federal personal income tax cuts introduced in 1981 and 1986.

(T) F   10.   The U.S. debt-GDP ratio increased in the 1980s, because primary budget deficits were high and the nominal interest rate usually exceeded nominal GDP growth.

Multiple Choice Questions: Circle the letter corresponding to the correct answer to each question.

1.   The budget deficit will exceed the primary budget deficit in a given fiscal year if
      a. government spending exceeds tax revenue.
      b. the economy is in a recession.
      c. the rate of inflation exceeds zero.
      d. net interest payments on outstanding debt exceed zero.
      e. fiscal policy is expansionary.

2.   An example of an automatic stabilizer is
      a. consumer spending.
      b. inflation.
      c. unemployment insurance.
      d. discretionary fiscal policy.
      e. investment spending.

3.   During a recession, discretionary fiscal policy is expansionary if
      a. tax revenue falls.
      b. government spending increases.
      c. money supply growth increases.
      d. there is a full-employment deficit.
      e. transfer payments increase.

4.   Assuming that market prices are efficient, imposing taxes on various economic activities creates
      a. inflation.
      b. a budget surplus.
      c. an efficient tax system.
      d. tax rate smoothing.
      e. distortions.

5.   If a government is highly committed to tax rate smoothing, it will
      a. require annually balanced fiscal budgets.
      b. reduce tax rates during a temporary recession.
      c. tax every activity and every source of income at the same tax rate.
      d. balance the budget over the business cycle.
      e. not change tax rates frequently to finance fluctuations in government spending.

6.   According to the Ricardian equivalence proposition, a government budget deficit created by a temporary tax cut
      a. does not affect desired national saving.
      b. does not affect expected future taxes.
      c. reduces desired investment spending.
      d. increases the real interest rate.
      e. increases aggregate demand.

7.   Since the end of the Great Depression, the United States had the highest debt-GDP ratios in the
      a. 1940s.
      b. 1950s.
      c. 1960s.
      d. 1970s.
      e. 1980s.

8.   In the United States, which of the following is the least involved in the federal budget process?
      a. The U.S. president
      b. The U.S. Senate
      c. The U.S. House of Representatives
      d. The Federal Open Market Committee of the Federal Reserve System
      e. The Council of Economic Advisers

9.   Assuming that output is fixed, the real revenue raised by government from printing money in an all-currency economy is
      a. M/P.
      b. the inflation rate times the real money supply.
      c. the real interest rate times the real money supply.
      d. the tax rate times the increase in the growth rate of output.
      e. always zero, because money is neutral.

10.   The inflation tax is primarily a tax on
      a. government bonds.
      b. Social Security recipients.
      c. money.
      d. real income.
      e. foreigners.

11.   If the government budget is initially balanced and the economy is operating at the full-employment level of output, a temporary tax cut will most likely
      a. reduce labor supply.
      b. reduce investment spending.
      c. reduce government purchases.
      d. create a nominal deficit.
      e. create tax rate smoothing.

12. The equation for calculating the growth rate of the debt-GDP ratio shows that the growth rate of this ratio will increase when the
     a. nominal GDP growth increases.
     b. real GDP growth increases.
     c. nominal money supply growth decreases.
     d. inflation rate decreases.
     e. nominal interest rate increases.

13. If government outlays exceed current tax revenue, the government could best finance its deficit by
     a. eliminating student loan guarantees.
     b. reducing its spending on human capital investments.
     c. privatizing its infrastructure investments.
     d. using "smoke and mirrors."
     e. selling government securities.

14. Real seignorage revenue is most likely to be a significant source of revenue for
     a. international development organizations.
     b. developing countries during times of war.
     c. developed countries during periods of slow output growth.
     d. periods of disinflation.
     e. state and local governments in the United States.

15. In the 1985-1990 period, after the Gramm-Rudman-Hollings bill was signed into law in the United States
     a. federal budget deficits and debt increased.
     b. the debt-GDP ratio declined.
     c. the federal budget was balanced and the government debt was paid off.
     d. the government significantly increased tax rates.
     e. the government increased its seignorage revenue.

16. Holding the average tax rate on income constant, an increase in the marginal tax rate on income will
     a. increase income.
     b. increase tax revenue.
     c. increase the labor force participation rate.
     d. increase labor supply.
     e. reduce labor supply.

17. A tax cut that reduces the marginal tax rate and the average tax rate on income will
     a. substantially increase income.
     b. substantially increase tax revenue.
     c. have an ambiguous effect on the labor force participation rate.
     d. substantially increase labor supply.
     e. substantially reduce labor supply.

18. Which of the following policies are supply-siders most likely to propose?
     a. Increase government regulation of business.
     b. Increase corporate taxes.
     c. Expand welfare and social security programs.
     d. Develop a managed health care program with government as the single payer.
     e. Reduce tax rates and reduce government spending.

19. Which of the following expenditures does not represent government capital formation?
    a. Government spending to improve public education services
    b. Government spending to improve access to public health care services
    c. Government spending to improve the national transportation system
    d. Government spending to improve the national communications system
    e. Government spending on welfare and Social Security programs

20. Even if a temporary tax cut does not cause tax rates to be increased until the next generation of taxpayers has arrived, this long delay in increasing future taxes would not in itself cause the Ricardian equivalence proposition to fail to accurately predict the effects of the tax cut, unless the
    a. parents failed to leave bequests.
    b. parents saved the tax cut.
    c. parents invested the tax cut.
    d. parents were far-sighted in their expectations of future tax increases.
    e. next generation was poorer than their parents.

Short-Answer Essay Questions

1. **Government budgets:** a) Identify the two largest sources of tax revenue and the two largest outlays in the U.S. federal government budget. b) Identify the two largest sources of tax revenue and the two largest outlays in the combined state and local government budget. c) State the primary budget deficit equation, the actual budget deficit equation, and the difference between them. d) In comparing federal government budget deficits of various years, how do nominal deficit comparisons differ from real deficit comparisons? e) Identify and briefly explain one argument for and one argument against removing the Social Security surplus from the federal government budget deficit calculations.

2. **Fiscal policy:** a) Compare and contrast automatic stabilizers and discretionary fiscal stabilization policy in terms of flexibility and policy lags. b) Compare and contrast the effects of automatic stabilizers during recessions on the budget deficit and the full-employment deficit. c) Compare and contrast the Keynesian and classical models in terms of the incentive effects of a marginal tax rate cut on labor supply and output. d) Why do economists endorse tax rate smoothing?   e) Why are some government budget deficits more inflationary than others?

3. **Government budget deficits and debt:** a) Define the terms deficit and debt, and explain how they are related. b) State the growth rate of debt-GDP ratio equation and define the variables. c) Use the growth rate of the debt-GDP ratio to explain why the debt-GDP ratio grew in the 1980s in the United States. d) Identify and briefly explain two reasons why a large government debt may not be a major burden on the future generation asked to pay it off. e) State one argument in favor of a balanced budget amendment to the U.S. Constitution, and state one argument against a balanced budget amendment.

4. **Ricardian equivalence proposition:** a) State the Ricardian equivalence proposition. b) Does Barro's theoretical research support the Ricardian equivalence proposition? Briefly explain. c) Identify two conditions under which the Ricardian equivalence proposition may not hold. d) Does the empirical evidence strongly support the Ricardian equivalence proposition? Briefly explain. e) Compare and contrast the short-run effects of a tax cut on unemployment and output in the classical and Keynesian models.

5.   **Deficits and inflation**: a) Define seignorage. b) State the nominal and real seignorage equations for an all-currency economy, and explain why they are equivalent. c) Use AD-AS analysis to explain what causes inflation. d) Explain how governments could use seignorage to finance deficits or debt. e) Draw a real seignorage revenue diagram in terms of inflation, and use the diagram to show why government policymakers might prefer an intermediate rate of inflation over a high rate of inflation.

Mathematical Problem-Solving Questions

1.   **Growth rate of debt-GDP ratio**: Calculate the growth rate of debt-GDP ratio for each of the following, given that outstanding government debt = $5000 billion and primary budget deficit = $250 billion: a) nominal interest rate = 8% and nominal GDP growth = 2%; b) nominal interest rate = 5% and nominal GDP growth = 2%; c) nominal interest rate = 15% and nominal GDP growth = 4%.

2.   **Real seignorage revenue**: Calculate the real seignorage revenue in an all-currency economy, given each of the following conditions: a) inflation rate = 3% and M/P = $1000 billion; b) inflation rate = 6% and M/P = $700 billion; c) inflation rate = 12% and M/P = $400 billion.

Answers to Fill-In-The-Blanks Questions

1.   primary budget deficit
4.   government capital
7.   supply-side economics
10. government debt

2.   automatic stabilizers
5.   marginal tax rate
8.   distortions
11. seignorage

3.   full-employment deficit
6.   average tax rate
9.   tax rate smoothing
12. inflation tax

Answers to True-False Questions

1.   F   An increase in net interest payments will not increase the primary budget deficit, although it will increase the budget deficit, the government debt, and the amount of bonds outstanding. The primary deficit does not include that part of the budget deficit created by net interest payments. An increase in the budget deficit is financed by the sale of government bonds, which increases the amount of bonds outstanding. Whenever the government borrows money by selling government bonds, its debt increases.

2.   T   Figure 16.1 in the textbook shows that government spending on transfer payments by federal, state, and local levels of government combined increased in dollar amounts and as a share of GDP more than any other type of government spending in the 1939-1992 period.

3.   F   Table 16.1 in the textbook shows that the government spent about 35% of the GDP of the United States in 1990, which was significantly less than the 44% and 43% of their national incomes spent respectively by the governments of Canada and Germany.

4.   T   Without any discretionary change in tax rates or spending programs, automatic stabilizers cause tax revenue to decline and government spending to increase in a recession. If the government budget is balanced at full employment, a decline in tax revenue or increase in government spending will create a budget deficit. Keynesian analysis suggests that most recessions are caused by a decline in aggregate spending on the output produced, and that a tax cut would increase aggregate spending, which would help to pull the economy out of a severe, protracted recession. In a severe recession of long duration, Keynesians would probably propose a

tax cut to increase aggregate demand, which would cause output to rise to full-employment output. In the Keynesian view, it is more economically efficient to use budget deficits during recessions and budget surpluses during booms to smooth business cycles than to maintain an annually balanced government budget at the expense of permitting large, costly business cycle fluctuations in macroeconomic variables.

5. F   A government budget deficit could be caused by high net interest payments or by automatic stabilizers in a recession, without any expansionary fiscal policy. A primary budget deficit could be created by automatic stabilizers, without any expansionary fiscal policy. The size of the full-employment budget deficit is an accurate measure of the extent to which discretionary fiscal policy is expansionary. If the full-employment budget is balanced at full-employment output, then discretionary fiscal policy is neither expansionary nor contractionary. If there is a budget surplus in the full-employment budget, then discretionary fiscal policy is contractionary.

6. F   While classical economists generally oppose discretionary fiscal policy attempts to smooth business cycles, they would generally support a budget deficit program that clearly created net economic benefits for the economy. For example, classical economists would generally support a substantial increase in government spending on national defense during a war that greatly threatened national security, even if it created a temporary budget deficit, such as occurred in the United States during World War II. For another example, classical economists would generally support some increases in spending for government capital formation, even if it created a temporary budget deficit, such as government spending on public infrastructure investments in transportation facilities, communication facilities, education services, and health care services.

7. F   If the government sells its bonds to the central bank, the central bank prints money to buy them, which causes the money supply to increase, which causes inflation. Inflation is called a hidden tax, because it reduces the real purchasing power of each dollar in the economy. When a budget deficit is financed by inflation, market participants' real income falls without any increase in tax rates. If the government sells its bonds to the public, taxes must be increased in the future to pay off these government bonds unless government spending rises less than tax revenue in the future. Given tax rates, tax revenue normally increases when output increases; some of this tax revenue increase can be used to reduce the government debt unless government spending increases as much or more than tax revenue.

8. F   The Ricardian equivalence proposition contends that a temporary tax cut will have no real economic effects, because it will not change desired consumption or desired saving. If a substantial share of households face borrowing constraints that limit their current consumption spending, the Ricardian equivalence proposition may fail to accurately predict the real economic effects of a tax cut. Shortsighted consumers, the absence of bequests, or tax cuts that are not lump-sum could also cause the Ricardian equivalence proposition to fail to accurately predict the real economic effects of a temporary tax cut.

9. T   Supply-side economists and other proponents of supply-side theory overestimated the incentive effect on labor supply of the U.S. federal personal income tax cuts introduced in 1981 and 1986. Supply-siders contended that substantially reducing marginal tax rates would increase after-tax wages, which would substantially increase the quantity of labor supplied, which would increase output enough to increase tax revenue at the lower tax rate. Standard economic theory suggests that reducing the marginal tax rate on income for a given average tax rate will increase labor supply, while reducing the average tax rate on income for a given marginal tax rate will reduce labor supply. Consequently, reducing both the marginal and average tax rate has an ambiguous effect on labor supply. In 1981 both the marginal tax rate and average tax rate were reduced; this had no significant effect on labor supply, contrary to supply-side predictions but consistent with standard economic theory. In 1986 the marginal tax rate was reduced and the average tax rate increased slightly; this increased labor supply slightly, contrary to supply-side predictions but consistent with standard economic theory.

10. T U.S. primary budget deficits were high in the 1980s, and the nominal interest rate usually exceeded nominal GDP growth. The growth rate of the debt-GDP ratio equation shows that these events caused the U.S. debt-GDP ratio to increase during the 1980s.

Answers to Multiple Choice Questions

1. d	8. d	15. a
2. c	9. b	16. e
3. d	10. c	17. c
4. e	11. d	18. e
5. e	12. e	19. e
6. a	13. e	20. a
7. a	14. b	

Answers to Short-Answer Essay Questions

1.   **Government budgets**:

a)   Table 16.2 in the textbook shows that the two largest sources of tax revenue in the U.S. federal government budget for 1992 were personal taxes (i.e., federal personal income taxes) and contributions for social insurance (i.e., FICA taxes). The two largest outlays were transfer payments and federal government purchases of goods and services (e.g., national defense).

b)   In the combined state and local government budget for 1992, the two largest sources of tax revenue were indirect business taxes (e.g., sales and excise taxes) and grants in aid received from the federal government. The two largest outlays were purchases of goods and services (e.g., education and highways) and transfer payments (e.g., welfare assistance).

c)   The primary budget deficit = [(G + TR) - T)]. The budget deficit = [(G + TR + INT) - T]. The budget deficit exceeds the primary budget deficit by the value of net interest payments on government debt. Note that budget deficits may be positive, negative, or zero; a negative budget deficit is a budget surplus.

d)   Nominal deficits are government budget deficits measured in current dollars at the time they are incurred. Real deficits are government budget deficits measured in constant dollars, which means for a given value of the dollar. Nominal deficit figures can be converted to real deficit figures by using a price level index to deflate the nominal values. Comparisons of nominal deficits are distorted by changes in the price level over time (i.e., by inflation). For example, budget deficits under the Reagan Administration were higher in nominal terms than budget deficits under the Carter Administration, because the price level rose each year over the 1977-1988 period. Unlike comparisons of nominal deficits, comparisons of the real deficits in 1982 dollars are not distorted by inflation.

e)   In recent years and for the next couple of decades, the financial managers of the Social Security program must accumulate a surplus in order to finance the increased Social Security payments out of a declining tax base when the baby boomers retire. The current Social Security surplus is now considered to be part of general tax revenue, which is all spent on general government outlays. One argument against including the surplus in the government budget is that all the surplus is now being spent, leaving no money for future retirees. An argument in favor of leaving the Social Security surplus in the government budget is that the Social Security fund is receiving an equivalent value of government bonds that can be cashed in the future to pay future retirees. However, to cash these bonds in the future, the government will either have to achieve a primary budget surplus or roll over this huge amount of debt, thereby substantially increasing the amount of outstanding debt.

2.   **Fiscal policy**:

a)   Automatic stabilizers have virtually no policy lags, and they are very flexible in creating changes in government spending and taxes, because these adjustments are automatic. In contrast, discretionary fiscal stabilization policy changes in government spending and taxes have long policy lags (e.g., eighteen months) and are not very flexible.

b)   During a recession, automatic stabilizers increase government spending in the form of transfer payments and reduced taxes, thereby creating a budget deficit. In contrast, automatic stabilizers do not create a full-employment deficit, because automatic stabilizers do not create a deficit at the full-employment level of output. The full-employment deficit is the amount of the budget deficit created by discretionary fiscal stabilization policy. The difference between the budget deficit and the full-employment deficit is the deficit created by automatic stabilizers.

c)   In economic analysis, the real after-tax wage provides an income incentive to supply labor in the market economy. A temporary decline in the marginal tax rate increases the after-tax real wage return on the last unit of labor supplied. The increase in the return that could be obtained by supplying more labor causes labor supply to increase in both the classical and Keynesian models; this is the substitution effect of a tax cut. Usually, a decline in the marginal tax rate would also cause the average tax rate to decline, which increases labor's wealth, which causes workers to supply less labor; this is the income effect of a tax cut. If a temporary tax cut causes both the marginal tax rate and average tax rate to decline, labor supply will increase when the substitution effect exceeds the income effect. If a temporary tax cut reduces the marginal tax rate without changing the average tax rate, it has a pure substitution effect on labor supply, so labor supply unambiguously increases. In the classical model, an increase in labor supply increases employment and output. In the Keynesian efficiency-wage model, an increase in labor supply does not affect employment or output; an increase in labor supply simply increases the excess supply of labor that exists at the efficiency wage.

d)   Tax rate smoothing reduces the output cost of raising a given amount of tax revenue over a number of years. Imposing a tax on the return to some factor of production, output, or asset typically creates a distortion in its market price and rate of return. The tax increases the market price to buyers and reduces the after-tax rate of return to sellers both in absolute and relative terms. The increase in the market price to buyers causes them to buy less; the decline in the rate of return to sellers causes them to produce and sell less. Consequently, the imposition of a tax or an increase in a tax creates a decline in the equilibrium amount bought and sold. For example, a tax on labor income causes workers to substitute toward leisure and away from work, so that less labor is supplied. It also causes firms to substitute away from labor and toward capital, so that less labor is demanded. The net effect is that employment declines, and the decline in employment causes output to decline. This reduction in output is the output cost of a tax distortion. The degree of distortion and the consequent output cost increases with increases in the tax rate; a high tax rate creates a greater tax distortion and output cost than a low tax rate. A government can reduce the output cost of an income tax distortion by maintaining a fixed income tax rate over a number of years, even though business cycle fluctuations in output would cause that tax rate to create budget deficits in some years financed by budget surpluses in other years. Because of the potentially high output costs of high tax rate distortions, it may not be efficient to maintain an annually balanced government budget over the business cycle if this requires raising the income tax rate in recessions when income declines and reducing the income tax rates in booms when income rises. Procyclical income tax rate changes could increase business cycle fluctuations in output, employment, and related macroeconomic variables.

e)   If the government budget is initially balanced, an increase in outlays and/or a reduction in tax revenue will create a budget deficit. The government budget deficit equation shows that all deficits are financed by the sale of government bonds to the public or to the central bank. A deficit financed by selling bonds to the central bank is more inflationary than a deficit financed by selling bonds to the public. The central bank prints money to pay for the bond purchase. Printing money increases the money supply. If output and money demand remain unchanged, an increase in the money supply is purely inflationary; the money supply increase causes the price level to increase proportionally. In terms of aggregate supply and aggregate demand analysis, the increase in the money supply causes the aggregate demand curve to shift up to the right along the vertical aggregate supply curve in the long run, causing the price level to rise. In this case the deficit is financed by the inflation tax created by printing money. By selling (i.e., issuing) bonds to the public, the government is creating a liability for taxpayers and an asset for those who buy the bonds; there is no net change in real wealth for the macroeconomy, and there is no change in the money supply. Taxpayers expect that taxes will be increased in the future to pay off the government debt created by the sale of bonds to the public. If the budget deficit is created by a temporary tax cut, the Ricardian equivalence proposition suggests that it will have no inflationary effect; it will not affect the position of the aggregate demand curve nor the position of the aggregate supply curve, so the price level will not change. If the budget deficit is created by a temporary increase in government purchases, aggregate supply and aggregate demand will both increase; the effect on the price level and inflation is ambiguous. If aggregate demand increases relative to aggregate supply, the price level will rise slightly.

3.   **Government budget deficits and debt:**

a)   A budget deficit is the amount by which government spending (i.e., G + TR + INT) exceeds tax revenue in some fiscal year. In the absence of inflation, budget deficits are financed by borrowing from the public. As a result of borrowing from the public to finance a budget deficit, the government now owes debt. Each deficit adds to the outstanding (i.e., unpaid) debt. The government debt is the sum of accumulated, unpaid budget deficits.

b)   The growth rate of debt-GDP ratio = primary deficit/B + i - growth rate of nominal GDP. The primary deficit (for the current fiscal year) = (G + TR) - T. B = outstanding debt at the beginning of the fiscal year. i = nominal interest rate. The growth rate of nominal GDP = the growth rate of the value output measured at the current price level.

c)   The debt-GDP ratio for the United States grew in the 1980s, because primary deficits were high and the nominal interest rate usually exceeded the growth rate of nominal GDP.

d)   Two reasons why a large government debt might not be a large burden on the future generation asked to pay it are:

1)   This generation might have received bequests to cover the debt payments from the generation that incurred the debt.

2) If the debt is "internal debt," then the future generation owes the debt to itself. Although some people are harmed by having to pay it off, others gain by receiving the debt payments.

e) A balanced budget amendment to the U.S. Constitution would force fiscal policymakers to balance the government budget each fiscal year. One potentially positive effect cited by proponents of the amendment is that it would prevent the government from incurring huge deficits. One potentially negative effect cited by opponents of the amendment is that the government would have to stop using discretionary fiscal stabilization policy and would have to eliminate its automatic stabilizers.

4. **Ricardian equivalence proposition:**

a) The Ricardian equivalence proposition states that a tax cut financed by the sale of bonds is not expansionary, because the effect of bond financing on the present value of lifetime resources of the public is equivalent to tax financing. The Ricardian equivalence proposition assumes that the public does not face binding borrowing constraints and that future taxes will increase enough to pay off the bonds and the interest earned on the bonds.

b) Yes, Robert Barro's theoretical research fully supports the Ricardian equivalence theory. David Ricardo and Robert Barro reach the same conclusion, which is that reducing current taxes and selling bonds to offset the decline in tax revenue is not expansionary. One theoretical argument made against the Ricardian equivalence proposition is that the current taxpayers may not incur higher taxes in the future as a result of the deficit if the government continues to roll over the debt forever. Robert Barro answered this objection by showing that the current generation will save all the income they receive from any temporary tax cut and bequeath this accumulated tax savings plus interest to the future generation that is asked to pay off the debt. Barro recognizes that the current generation could burden the future generation by borrowing against its future income, but he contends that the current generation does not choose to do that, since it values the well-being of its offspring. Since the current generation prefers to transfer income and wealth to the future generation, it will not take the opportunity provided by a budget deficit to reverse this transfer. A budget deficit will not change the preferences of the current generation.

c) The Ricardian equivalence proposition may not hold when either of its two principal assumptions is violated. If a significant percentage of taxpayers face binding borrowing constraints, they will spend some of the extra after-tax income they receive from the tax cut. Likewise, if people are shortsighted and consequently do not believe that their future taxes or their children's future taxes will be increased by enough to pay off the government debt, they will spend some of the extra after-tax income they receive from the tax cut. If the Ricardian equivalence proposition fails to hold, a temporary tax cut will increase aggregate spending, which is expansionary.

d) The empirical evidence is mixed. For example, the decline in aggregate saving that followed the Reagan tax cuts in the United States in the early 1980s does not support the Ricardian equivalence proposition. However, temporary tax cuts in some foreign countries in recent years did not significantly reduce aggregate saving; this empirical evidence is consistent with the Ricardian equivalence proposition.

e) The Ricardian equivalence proposition holds in the classical model, but not in the Keynesian model. Given the Ricardian equivalence proposition, a temporary tax cut does not change saving in the classical model; because it does not change saving, it has no output or employment effect. In the Keynesian model, a temporary tax cut reduces saving, which causes aggregate demand to increase, which causes output to increase, which causes unemployment to decline.

5.   **Deficits and inflation**

a)   Seignorage is the government revenue raised by printing money.

b)   The nominal value of seignorage revenue equation is (change in M) = inflation rate x M.

The real revenue value of seignorage equation is R = (change in M)/P = inflation rate x M/P.

In converting the nominal equation to real terms, we simply divide both sides of the equation by the price level, which does not change the equality. Therefore the equations are equivalent, meaning that they express the same relationship. At a given price level the nominal value of seignorage revenue equals the real value of seignorage revenue.

c)   In terms of aggregate demand and aggregate supply (AD-AS) analysis, any economic event (e.g., an increase in the money supply) that causes AD to increase relative to AS causes inflation. Since inflation is the percent increase in the price level, anything that causes the price level to increase creates inflation. For example, an increase in AD shifts the AD curve up to the right along a given AS curve, which increases the price level, which creates inflation.

d)   Excess money supply growth creates inflation, which reduces the real value of outstanding government nominal debt, thereby reducing the amount of real tax revenue needed to pay off a fixed amount of nominal debt. More importantly, and more directly, the government uses newly printed money to pay for some of its expenditures.

e)   The real seignorage revenue diagram follows. This diagram shows that government policymakers might prefer an intermediate rate of inflation (e.g., 8%), because it raises more seignorage revenue than would be raised by a high rate of inflation (e.g., 20%).

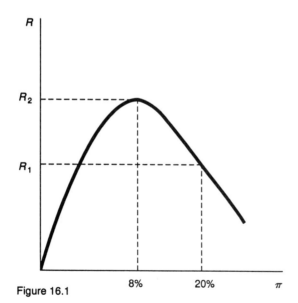

Figure 16.1

Answers to Mathematical Problem-Solving Questions

1. **Growth rate of debt-GDP ratio:** The growth rate of debt-GDP ratio = (primary deficit)/B + i - growth rate of nominal GDP, where B = outstanding government debt and i = nominal interest rate.   It is given that the primary deficit = $250 billion and B = $5000 billion, so (primary deficit)/B = $250 billion/$5000 billion = 5%.

    a) For i = 8%, and the growth rate of nominal GDP = 2%, the growth rate of debt-GDP ratio = 5% + 8% - 2% = 11%.

    b) For i = 5%, and the growth rate of nominal GDP = 2%, the growth rate of debt-GDP ratio = 5% + 5% - 2% = 8%.

    c) For i = 15%, and the growth rate of nominal GDP = 4%, the growth rate of debt-GDP ratio = 5% + 15% - 4% = 16%.

2. **Real seignorage revenue:**   For an all-currency economy, real seignorage revenue, R = (inflation rate) x M/P, where M/P is the real money supply.

    a) For an inflation rate = 3%, and M/P = $1000 billion, R = 3% x $1000 billion = $30 billion.

    b) For an inflation rate = 6%, and M/P = $700 billion, R = 6% x $700 billion = $42 billion.

    c) For an inflation rate = 12%, and M/P = $300 billion, R = 12% x $300 billion = $36 billion.